Advance Praise for *Overcoming Fake Talk*

"*Overcoming Fake Talk* is not only a terrific book title, but it also should be the mantra of anyone who's determined to get consistently great results. Many well-intended people dance around the issues that beg for open and candid discussion. Trouble is, when the topic is risky, they simply don't have the skills to carry on a real conversation. So they engage in fake talk. Then, when the tough issues don't get resolved, they engage in more fake talk and the cycle starts to resemble a scene from *Groundhog Day*. John Stoker's book is a breakthrough because it so clearly identifies a common problem that few have really talked about, and it offers principles, practices, and skills so necessary for honest, trust-building conversation. If you're truly interested in respect, relationships, and results, this book is for you."
—Stephen M. R. Covey, bestselling author of *The Speed of Trust* and *Smart Trust*

"John R. Stoker's book *Overcoming Fake Talk* offers the principles, paradigms, and processes for holding REAL conversations to enhance results while other authors only focus on the process for holding conversations that really matter. Not only does the author deal effectively with the psychology for holding any difficult conversation, but he also offers practical tools and techniques that can be applied in the toughest business and personal situations. I would recommend this book to anyone who wants to hold REAL conversations and build better relationships in their personal and professional lives."
—Ricardo Lillo, president and CEO, DOOR Training International

"Nothing about authentic leadership is fake—and that includes all forms of talk and walk. So, if you are now a leader—or if you aspire to be a leader—you need to learn how to have REAL conversations. John Stoker's enlightening and entertaining book, *Overcoming Fake Talk*, will help you to gain and maintain influence with key stakeholders by holding REAL conversations that get results."
—Marshall Goldsmith, *New York Times* bestselling author of *MOJO* and *What Got You Here Won't Get You There*

"REAL conversations help you find your competitive edge. In John Stoker's book, *Overcoming Fake Talk*, he provides us with simple and profound skills for cultivating the ideas and energy that drive organizational change and innovation through people. Truly, the types of conversations we hold create respect, build relationships, and uncover opportunities for growth by tuning in to what people say in entirely new ways."
—Andrea Kates, author of the bestselling business strategy book *Find Your Next*

"John Stoker's book *Overcoming Fake Talk* provides a very balanced approach to the art and science of conversation that engages your head, heart, and hands—all essential elements to connect with people at a deeper, more meaningful level. This book gives you clear theory and the practical skills you need to achieve desired results, earn respect, and develop effective relationships, personally and professionally. I highly recommend it!"

—Dennis S. Reina, PhD, coauthor of the award-winning, bestselling business books *Trust and Betrayal in the Workplace* and *Rebuilding Trust in the Workplace*, www.ReinaTrustBuilding.com

"Now more than ever healthcare leaders are challenged with providing exceptional and compassionate service for our patients and families. As costs continue to increase and reimbursement declines, physicians, healthcare executives, and associates must work together to reduce costs and increase efficiency. We must also improve our relationship with our community to strengthen its confidence that we will consistently deliver on our brand promise to provide an excellent patient and family experience. John Stoker's book *Overcoming Fake Talk* teaches the skills and process for holding REAL conversations that increase engagement and get results."

—Kenneth R. Buser, president and CEO, Wheaton Franciscan Healthcare–All Saints, www.mywheaton.org

"There is more in John Stoker's *Overcoming Fake Talk* than a bookshelf of self-help books about communication, relationship building, and career advancement can hope to provide. In plain language—backed by hard scientific data—John lays out everything anyone needs to know about authentic connectedness with others. In a world gone mad with pseudo-intimacy and hypocrisy, *Overcoming Fake Talk* just might save us from the phony tweets, Facebook 'likes,' and all other manner of ersatz self-expression that threaten to erode the fabric of our society."

—Dr. Steven Berglas, former faculty member, Harvard Medical School Department of Psychiatry; world-renowned expert and lecturer (USC, UCLA) on the Psychology of the Entrepreneurial Spirit; and author of *Reclaiming the Fire: How Successful People Can Overcome Burnout* as well as numerous other books and articles

"So many leaders have failed themselves, their families, their shareholders, and their neighbors on the most important of leadership behaviors: honesty, integrity, and ethical decision making. Given the resultant state of the economy, geopolitical instability, and competitive leadership challenges, I cannot imagine a strategy more necessary than REAL conversation. *Overcoming Fake Talk* by John R. Stoker provides sound principles, effective tools, and compelling stories

to encourage the practice of more authentic, transparent, and impactful human interactions. A great storyteller, Mr. Stoker uses interesting and relevant stories to provide the rationale for the effectiveness of each tool and method. With proper application, one can use REAL conversations to achieve extraordinary results. In sum, it is a good primer to expand self-awareness and improve performance."
—Michael G. Winston, past EVP and Global Head—Leadership and
Organization Strategy at five *Fortune* 100 companies

"It is about time that someone had the guts and the intelligence to expose our phony and empty conversations. In *Overcoming Fake Talk*, John Stoker not only provides many examples of how we distort and play one-upmanship ego games, but he also prescribes eight principles to cure once and for all our conversational lameness, lapses, and lies. Take the cure!"
—Irving H. Buchan, PhD, Capella University

"John Stoker is right on target with his message of *Overcoming Fake Talk*; as I've learned over 30 years of coaching leaders, the only way to **Lead NOW** is to engage in REAL conversation with team members about what matters most. John zeros in on the keys behind developing vital results-driven relationships through genuine and focused communication. All leaders need to study and apply his timely prescription!"
—John Parker Stewart, Leadership Coach, Executive
Development Specialist, and author of several books including *LEAD NOW!*;
president and founder, Stewart Systems, Inc.; www.johnparkerstewart.com

"John Stoker scores early and often with his groundbreaking book *Overcoming Fake Talk*. He begins with the premise that much of what passes for meaningful conversation is counterfeit because the participants either tiptoe around the real issues or ignore them altogether. Then he offers a wealth of easy-to-understand principles and practices that help you engage in the REAL conversations that produce deeper respect, better relationships, and stronger results. I like this book so much I wish I'd written it myself."
—Rodger Dean Duncan, bestselling author of *Change-Friendly Leadership*

"For 30 years, I've tried to help people see the difference between fake (counterfeit) and real (authentic) leadership. John Stoker not only reveals fake talk, but he also delivers spot-on advice for holding REAL conversations that cultivate relationships, respect, and results. Read it and reap. You'll be a better, more effective leader."
—Ken Shelton, editor, *Leadership Excellence*
magazine, and author of *Beyond Counterfeit Leadership*

"John has written an engaging book filled with interesting stories that guide the reader through the land mines of having difficult conversations. I can attest personally to the consequences of having bad results come from poorly managed conversations. I have had many. John gives me and others like me multiple ways to redeem myself in future conversations. John provides a step-by-step process to help us prepare to have REAL conversations that lead to positive results. We all know that tough conversations are not easy to have and can often spiral in a negative direction because we lack the skill and confidence to manage the process. John provides a step-by-step approach that gives the reader the skills and confidence to have these conversations. This book balances the latest theory with real-world practical advice. The result: happier, more productive relationships with others. As John promises, this is the last book on having tough conversations that you need."

—Norm Smallwood, cofounder, The RBL Group, and
coauthor with Dave Ulrich of *Leadership Sustainability*

"*Overcoming Fake Talk* is both profound and refreshing. Profound in its insights about how we converse with one another and how this impacts our personal and corporate success. Refreshing in that it is easy to read, uses many real-life examples, and offers the reader some real guidance. John Stoker becomes your coach, whose practical frameworks and case examples will prepare you for more productive discussions and then enable you to review them afterward to keep progressing."

—David Hanna, principal, The RBL Group

"At the core of every change effort, conflict, feedback session, and dialogue is a one-to-one conversation. It is an essential yet often overlooked ingredient for success. *Overcoming Fake Talk* provides a comprehensive and practical approach to a topic all of us can improve."

—Ralph Jacobson, principal, The Leader's Toolbox, and author of *Leading for a Change: How to Master the Five Challenges Faced by Every Leader*

"Thank you, John Stoker! *Overcoming Fake Talk* is a refreshing look at how to hold REAL conversations that get results. As an executive coach working with senior leaders around the globe, I know that conversation is the engine of how so much work gets done, and that far too much time and energy is wasted in unproductive communication (fake talk). I heartily endorse this book as a road map and handbook for tough conversations, written in an engaging and entertaining style."

—Patricia Wheeler, PhD, contributor, Coaching for Leadership; publisher, Leading News; managing partner, The Levin Group

"John gets to the heart of effective communication and leadership "Fake Talk." The serious student of leadership will have multiple copies of this book on the shelf."

—Dr. Bruce H. Jackson, CEO, The Institute of Applied
Human Excellence, and author of *Finding Your Flow*

"John R. Stoker's book *Overcoming Fake Talk* is a natural extension of the training and leadership development he has provided within our company. His concepts are clear, his explanations down-to-earth, and in my experience, what he teaches really works. Our organization places great emphasis on the quality of our people and on creating a healthcare and work environment where we treat each other with compassion, dignity, and respect—this book is a primer for developing precisely those characteristics."

—Ed Oxford, EdD, SVP, Human Resources and
Chief Talent Officer, Banner Health

"*Overcoming Fake Talk* is a must-read book for all who want to improve the effectiveness of their verbal communication. This insightful book is full of concise suggestions on how to dramatically improve interpersonal communications. It helps individuals get their heads right so they can have practical conversations that will get better results. It is easy to read and full of great illustrations that help the reader to remember the skills being taught."

—Roice N. Krueger, author and senior consultant

"John Stoker has been a white-water rafter, an attorney, a speaker, and now a thoughtful writer. His book *Overcoming Fake Talk* is a thorough compendium of ideas, frameworks, examples, and actions to improve conversations. His four REAL conversation skills and eight principles give the novice and master insights and guidelines for improving conversation. His book will help get people talking in ways that create respect, build relationships, and get results."

—Dave Ulrich, professor, Ross School of Business, University of Michigan;
partner, The RBL Group; and author of *The Why of Work*; www.rbl.net

"Not only does *Overcoming Fake Talk* uncover the key principles to REAL conversations, but it offers a true road map to mastering the skills necessary for building lasting relationships. Adhering to and implementing these principles will dramatically increase your ability to communicate and improve your relationships in your professional and personal life."

—Hyrum W. Smith, cofounder, FranklinCovey

"As Peter Drucker wisely observed, nearly all leadership and management challenges come back to breakdowns in communication. This book is an insightful blend of rock-solid theory accompanied by compelling examples of the huge distinction between real and fake communication. It would be hard to read it and not gain valuable tips."

—John H. Zenger, CEO, Zenger Folkman, and
coauthor of *How to Be Exceptional*, www.zengerfolkman.com

"Wow! I just finished reading *Overcoming Fake Talk*. I have taught communication skills for over 40 years; I wish this book had been available 40 years ago. The book provides the most needed and helpful communication tools in a very effective manner. Stoker teaches true principles for getting Results, Respect, and great Relationships using REAL conversation."

—Brent D. Peterson, PhD, coauthor of *Fake Work: Why People Are Working Harder Than Ever but Accomplishing Less, and How to Fix the Problem*

"I love the title of this book! How often do we get the sense that another person is not speaking his or her truth? How often do we wear our own political or social masks in the workplace? What a great book to help us stop both of these disingenuous conversations and turn around the opportunities in front of us. This conversation book is truly worth adding to your shelf . . . and maybe even replacing others. The author knows his material and takes a straightforward, practical look at the subject. He reframes old notions and applies the principles to anyone, anywhere, in any position. Great questions, great suggestions . . . that is, if you want to change. Bravo! I will put his ideas to use in my own practice."

—Beverly Kaye, founder and co-CEO, Career Systems
International, and coauthor of *Help Them Grow or
Watch Them Go: Career Conversations Employees Want*

OVERCOMING
FAKE
TALK

OVERCOMING
FAKE
TALK

How to Hold **REAL** Conversations
That Create Respect, Build
Relationships, and Get Results

JOHN R. STOKER

New York   Chicago   San Francisco   Lisbon   London   Madrid   Mexico City
Milan   New Delhi   San Juan   Seoul   Singapore   Sydney   Toronto

1 2 3 4 5 6 7 8 9 0   QFR/QFR   1 9 8 7 6 5 4 3

ISBN 978-0-07-181579-6
MHID 0-07-181579-1

e-ISBN 978-0-07-181580-2
e-MHID 0-07-181580-5

Library of Congress Cataloging-in-Publication Data
Stoker, John R.
 Overcoming fake talk : how to hold real conversations that create respect, build relationships, and get results / by John R. Stoker.
     pages cm
 Includes bibliographical references.
 ISBN 978-0-07-181579-6 (alk. paper)—ISBN 0-07-181579-1 (alk. paper)
 1. Interpersonal communication. 2. Conversation analysis. 3. Communication—Psychological aspects. I. Title.
 HM1166.S76 2013
 302—dc23
                                                                                      2013002313

McGraw-Hill Education books are available at special quantity discounts to use as premiums and sales promotions or for use in corporate training programs. To contact a representative, please e-mail us at bulksales@mcgraw-hill.com.

This book is printed on acid-free paper.

I dedicate this book to my parents
Don and Jeanne—
whose conversations touched the hearts of many and
drew others to them, and to my wife and children,
Stephanie, Bryson, Zachary, Matthew, Brianna, and Livya,
whose patience and support are never-ending.
They continue to teach me more about REAL
conversation than I could ever have learned on my own.

CONTENTS

FOREWORD

Leaders of Influence

They engage in real conversations.

Nothing about *authentic leadership* is *fake*—and that includes all forms of *talk* and *walk*. So, if you are now a leader—or if you aspire to be a leader—you need to learn how to have *REAL conversations* (as John Stoker calls them in his entertaining and enlightening book, *Overcoming Fake Talk*) to gain and maintain influence with key stakeholders.

As an executive coach who helps leaders who are already very good at what they do become even better, *as judged by the people they work with*, I have learned that how you are perceived and regarded by the people you work with is largely determined by *how you relate and converse with them*.

I find that most aspiring leaders, especially knowledge workers, know more about what they are doing than their senior managers do; however, *few know how to effectively influence their bosses and converse with other key people*. In fact, the item "Knows how to influence up in a constructive way" scores *last* on evaluations. I am not surprised. This is the norm, not the exception. Most aspiring leaders simply do not effectively *influence up*. They are guilty of *fake talk*; or *failed talk*. They don't engage in *real conversations*. As a result, their good, if not brilliant, ideas are rarely converted into meaningful action; and, they struggle to gain the recognition and rewards they seek.

Many smart people blame their bosses for not buying their ideas. I remind them: When presenting your ideas, realize that *it is your responsibility to sell—not their responsibility to buy.* Influencing up is similar to selling to customers. They don't have to buy—you have to sell and take responsibility for results. You can't blame your customers for not buying your product. You *disempower* yourself when you focus on what others have done to make things wrong and not what you can do to make things right.

So, as Stoker suggests, you need to develop your ability to present yourself favorably and converse intelligently to sell your ideas. Stop blaming management and start focusing on contributing to a larger good—beyond achieving your objectives. Effective salespeople would never say to a customer, "You need to buy this product, because if you don't, I won't achieve my goals!" They relate to the needs of the buyers and to larger organizational needs, not just to the needs of their unit or team. Focus on the impact of the decision. Don't assume that executives can automatically "make the connection" between the benefit to your unit and the benefit to the larger corporation.

Like Stoker, I see many smart and able people wasting their time, energy, and *psychological capital* on trivial points instead of striving to win the big battles. So, in your *REAL conversations,* be willing to *lose* on small points and trivial arguments. People become more annoyed with you for having to *win* and be *right* all the time, even when it doesn't matter. Focus less on winning and more on making a difference—the more *other* people can *be right* or *win* with your idea, the more likely your idea will be accepted. Also, focus on the future and let go of the past. Avoid *whining* about the past. When you whine, you inhibit your chances to positively affect the future. Your managers tend to view you as annoying and your direct reports as inept.

By learning to hold *REAL conversations,* you gain more influence, improve your relationships, and get better results! Yes, you want better results. But as Stoker says, your relationships impact your results. REAL conversations get real results.

One of Stoker's key points—*Ask questions to increase your understanding*—correlates with one of my executive coaching tenets: **Have the courage to ask.** As a leader, start asking key coworkers for their ideas on what needs to be done. Thank them for their input, listen to them, learn as much as you can, incorporate the ideas that make the most sense, and follow up. As Peter Drucker said, "The leader of the past knew how to tell; the leader of the future will know how to ask."

I've reviewed feedback on thousands of leaders. If the item "Asks people what he or she can do to improve" is included in the leadership inventory, it is always near the bottom. As a rule, leaders don't ask! One reason is an inflated ego. When I ask leaders to rate themselves relative to their peers, about *85 percent of them rank themselves in the top 20 percent*! And performance has little to do with their assessment!

When we succeed, we tend to attribute good results to our own motivation and ability and attribute poor results to environmental factors, bad luck, or random chance. When we overrate our own performance and knowledge, we easily justify not asking others for their input.

As a coach, I encourage my clients to *ask, listen, and learn* from everyone around them. Improving your interpersonal relationships need not take a lot of your time. It does require having the courage to ask for people's opinions and the discipline to follow up and do something about what you learn. That's the essence of *REAL conversations.*

—Marshall Goldsmith

Marshall Goldsmith is the New York Times *bestselling author of* MOJO *and* What Got You Here Won't Get You There.

ACKNOWLEDGMENTS

I am grateful to the many people whose words and lives have contributed to this work.

My mentors and teachers: Truman G. Madsen, who moved me beyond myself and would never let me give up; Rex E. Lee, whose boundless optimism was inspiring and reassuring; Bonner Ritchie, who continually challenged my thinking; Warner Woodworth, whose concern for others brings a balance of perspective; Paul Thompson, who let me graduate in spite of myself; Brent Peterson, whose love for training and unleashing human potential is contagious; and Al Switzler and Kerry Patterson, who talked me out of my law practice and set me on this path.

My colleagues: John Vitale, with whom I have a creative synergy that has helped me to create solutions that really work; Kathy Birch, for her refinement of my ideas and unsurpassed creativity in placing those ideas on paper; Roice Krueger, for his expertise in nurturing organizations and people so they can succeed; Ken Shelton of Leadership Excellence, whose precision and power with words is unparalleled; Rebecca Bradley, whose coaching has assisted me to cut through the interference of my own life; and Debra Lund and Diane Lefrandt, whose belief in dreams made this work possible.

My learning partners, all of whom have helped me to move this work forward and are committed to talking about what matters most: Laura Roccaforte, Rodger Dean Duncan, Jack Skalican, Kathie Orlay, Mike Adair, Karen Ramsey, Frantz Belot, Melanie Olm, Jim Bell, Mauni Krueger Nielsen, Stephanie Empey, Deborah Exner, Kirk Duncan, Wayne Whiting, Jim Hunt, Barbara S.

Ford, Mark Atkinson, Annie Oswald, Nikia Green, Dianne Davenport, Rich Hill, Ron Thurman, Todd Cook, Carolyn Moore, David Mayne, Maggie Long, Stephanie Terry Stewart, and Tom and Mimi Hanks.

The talented staff at Quantum Media: Terry, Robin, and Reni Wardle; Sean Leavitt; and Tiffany De Sousa.

My agent, Shannon Marven and her assistant, Nicki Miser, for their hard work and diligence in "living the dream." My publisher, Donya Dickerson, and all the people at McGraw-Hill who supported this endeavor.

Our clients, who are committed to organizational excellence through people, and who in and of themselves struggle, learn, and create results.

Finally, to everyone I may have forgotten, and to all those I have encountered who have demonstrated the impact of fake talk and the necessity of engaging in REAL conversation: Thank you for sharing the gift of yourselves.

INTRODUCTION:
HOW DO YOU BEGIN?

Obviously, you must begin any journey right where you find yourself. But you have to be willing to admit where you really are! If you can objectively assess the effectiveness of your current results, the amount of respect you are currently receiving, and/or the quality of your current relationships, you will begin with a truer sense of where you currently stand. And you will gain a clearer sense of where you want—or need—to go in communicating and interacting with others. You are the only one who can manage the challenge to change and improve your results.

The Reason: Why Do We Need Another Conversation Book?

A flurry of conversation books over the past 10 years describe difficult, fierce, crucial, productive, courageous, challenging, and trusted conversations. Obviously dealing with the topic of improved conversation is an issue that many people feel they need to address. After all individual and organizational effectiveness is dependent upon everyone being able to talk about what matters most. The existing literature seems to lack something, or there wouldn't be so many attempts to readdress the topic. Something about the content simply is not working.

Some books are too theoretical—they provide wonderful explanations of models or constructs, but offer little by way of practical application or feeling. You might say that they use lots of "head" stuff, but not enough heart or hands. Other works are too mechanical—they provide helpful instruction on how to choose just the right words and offer scripted sentences for use in a variety of situations. These books focus on application (the hands) but are devoid of head and heart. Finally, the rest of the conversation books out there are primarily metaphysical in nature, describing abstract elements, or the "feeling" for a conversation, without presenting enough practical explanations and useful skills. These works focus on the heart and ignore the head and the hands.

REAL conversation is a more balanced and complete approach to the art of communication; the head, the heart, and the hands are all necessary in order to accomplish what we really want in our conversations with others. This book will likely be the last conversation-related book you will ever read. Why? Because it offers clear explanations of the theoretical aspects of conversation along with the practical application of real skills that will help you to connect with others in a deep and meaningful way.

The Adventure:
Where Are We Going?

While I was in college and graduate school, I had the opportunity to work as a whitewater guide on the Colorado River in the Grand Canyon. In all, I spent 13 summers running the rapids with adventure-seeking tourists between Lee's Ferry, Arizona, and Pierce Ferry on Lake Mead—covering about 288 miles of wilderness area. I learned many things while working with widely diverse groups of people in nature, much of which gave me great insights into human nature and the ways in which we human beings communicate and interact with one another.

Every river trip, every new group of people, every rapid, and even every new and unexpected danger presented new challenges and adventures—some exhilarating and some more "instructive." In much the same way, every conversation we hold is an opportunity for discovery, growth, and learning—if not adventure.

I often had people ask me every morning of their river trip, "Where are we going today?" I would simply reply, "Downstream." I wasn't merely being facetious—in all actuality, I never really knew exactly what would happen during the day's journey, what we would see, or what hidden secrets Mother Nature would reveal to us. All I could say with any degree of surety was that we had to be willing to get in the boat and then go more or less wherever the current would take us.

Naturally, I learned over time to manage many of the dynamics of our daily adventures. Likewise, you too will learn to manage the dynamics of your conversations so that they result in maximum value, but you will have to be willing to go with the flow and enjoy the ride while you learn to manage those dynamics. I hope you will enjoy some of the analogies I will make between river-running and conversation skills during our adventure.

The Orientation: What Do You Need to Know?

Every river trip began with an orientation because my passengers really did not know what they had gotten themselves into. One of the activities on everyone's bucket list seems to be an adventure running the rapids through the Grand Canyon. But most people do not realize that they are embarking on a journey that, in every sense of the word, will become a matter of life or death. Most of my passengers booked their trip, and then showed up with an expectation of a prolonged version of the Jungle Cruise ride at Disneyland, but in the setting of one of the seven wonders of the world. However, by the time I had finished my orientation for the trip, I often heard people mutter to their companions, "What have we gotten ourselves into?"

I always explained to my passengers that it was vital for their own safety and survival that they follow five principles:

1. Follow my directions.
2. Know before you go.
3. Hold on!
4. Drink plenty of fluids.
5. Protect yourself from the sun.

Invariably, on every trip, something like the following story would happen sometime during the week. This is, by the way, a true story.

TOO MUCH BIKINI

One afternoon after we had made camp, Lee approached me, still wearing her swimsuit. She asked whether she could climb to the top of a nearby hill to take some photos of the beautiful flowers in the cactus beds.

"Sure thing," I replied. "But before you go, take off your flip-flops and put on your tennis shoes. And throw on a pair of jeans and a t-shirt too."

She said that she would. Thirty minutes later, her husband came barreling into camp, calling for me frantically. Lee had not followed my instructions, but had gone up the hill to photograph the cactus beds still wearing only her sandals and swimsuit. She had slipped in the loose gravel and fallen face-first into the cactus.

I ran with him back to their tent, where we found Lee crying in agony. I spent the next two hours painstakingly removing cactus spines one at a time from her neck, arms, chest, and stomach. Lee was in so much pain that her husband simply couldn't bring himself to do it.

She broke the first rule: Follow my directions! Why didn't she follow my directions? Lee, like most people, thought she knew better. She probably did not even hear what I said about shoes and pants—or at least she did not listen past what she thought she knew. She did not ask any questions to clarify or increase her understanding of my instructions, nor did she express any disagreement with what I told her. Her actions, however, did express her disregard for my expertise over her opinion. Lee was on autopilot in this instance, and she made no intentional or deliberate attempt to understand, express her views, or challenge her or my thinking.

Whether you are a leader, a manager, a supervisor, an employee, a spouse or partner, a parent, or someone's child, your conversations are a matter of life or death. Of course you will probably not die physically, but if your conversations don't work, then your results may leave you dead on arrival. Worst-case scenario: the state of your results, respect, and relationships may make you wish you were dead when you inevitably have to face them.

Isn't it time to take action and make your conversations work?

The Destination:
What Will You Learn?

To overcome fake talk, you need to hold REAL conversations. REAL conversations include eight principles that govern every conversation, as well as a number of skills that will breathe life into every principle.

The first four chapters of this book will help you identify what conversations need your immediate attention. You will become more aware of the dynamics that influence a conversation's success, and learn how to identify when a conversation is going awry. Next you will learn the skills and process for holding any particularly difficult or sensitive conversation with anyone, anytime, and anywhere. You also will learn about the different styles of communication that people have—styles that sometimes unintentionally cause offense or friction between individuals. If you are able to identify different styles, you will be able to manage your own style in a way that will increase engagement and make personal connections with others.

The middle of the book is comprised of five chapters that dive deeper into four specific skills you will need in order to hold

REAL conversations: Perception, Expression, Discovery, and Connection. Finally, a chapter on Preparation will help you put all the skills together. Each chapter includes numerous examples and applications to your own challenging conversations.

To round out your experience, the final chapter contains several concrete suggestions you can adapt and apply to immediately and measurably improve the quality of your conversations.

The Promise:
What's in It for You?

I have been teaching, practicing, and applying the principles and skills taught in this book for more than 20 years. My colleagues and I have seen them work time and time again, and we know that they are both effective and comprehensive. I also know that they will work for you if you internalize the principles and practice the skills, and that improving the quality of your communication will also improve the quality of your professional and personal life. You can achieve amazing results, increased respect, and more satisfying relationships!

Isn't that what we all want? Results, respect, and relationships! Achieving these goals really is a matter of life and death. Become a REAL conversationalist, and choose life.

Let's begin . . .

CHAPTER 1

What Keeps You Up at Night?

Picture yourself on a warm summer's day, pulling into Lee's Ferry, Arizona, on a rickety old yellow school bus— your transportation from Page, Arizona. You unpack your belongings, stuff them into a dry bag, and begin the orientation for the eight-day river trip through the Grand Canyon. During your plane ride and bus ride to the middle of nowhere, your cares have melted away. Your only frustration is that you didn't bring enough sunblock. As your adventure down the Colorado River begins, your attention for the next eight days turns to nothing more than the whitewater and red rock. Not surprisingly, when you crawl into your sleeping bag at night, the only thing keeping you awake is the panorama of the Milky Way.

Then, almost as quickly as it began, you're in that small plane once again, heading toward your connecting flight in Las Vegas— and the life you left behind. You return home tired and sunburned, but totally refreshed. After you unpack and unwind a bit, you climb into bed and suddenly your normal life reasserts itself.

Whether it's sick and crying children, flu pandemics, an ornery boss, higher taxes, a nagging recession, an angry ex-spouse, the prospect of losing your job, not being able to retire, or troubled and puzzling relationships, a myriad of frustrations play out on the stage of your mind as you lie in bed at night. Your river trip has quickly become a distant memory.

What Do You Really Want?

If you ask yourself, "What's keeping me awake at night?" your answer may be different from the answer of the person you're sleeping next to, but almost everyone's answers center on one fundamental concern:

I am not getting the results I want!

Your concern may be with a surly teenager who seems incapable of turning in a homework assignment. You and he have been fighting about results—short term (as in making it through the term with passing grades) and long term (as in his not looking back 40 years down the road and wishing he had that high school diploma).

Your concern may be with a 401(k) that is still in the toilet and seems incapable of climbing out. Again, you're talking about results, like being able to retire before you're 80.

Your concern may be work-related—a difficult boss who won't listen to reason, an impossible task with an even more impossible deadline, that coworker in the office next door whose voice is like fingernails on a chalkboard and who seems to spend all day on the phone with her sick (and apparently emotionally unstable) mother.

Most challenges are tied to the results that we want and the expectation we have of others to provide them. Have any of the following situations ever held you back from results you want?

Difficulties at Work

Sometimes we engage in "work-arounds" to get our work done, whether we're dealing with coworkers, family members, or other associates. We may also find ourselves working around certain people, processes, or policies that end up dictating what we do. It's just easier to avoid everything we think is "difficult" and just do it in a way that works for us.

"Problem Children"

Problem children fall into two categories: the ones we work with and the ones we gave birth to. At home, how much time have you spent arguing with a child over taking out the trash, doing homework, or meeting curfews, only to have the same argument the next day or week?

At work, you likely deal with people who are unreliable, uncooperative, or unskilled—and who consume enormous amounts of time and energy. Perhaps you have spent hours talking with such people, but little if anything changes. So, rather than continuing to engage with them, you give their work to someone you know will perform. Or you do it yourself. Either way, work isn't getting done and frustrations, on all sides, continue to mount.

Groundhog Day Repeats

You won't get results if you hold a meeting or have a conversation—and then repeat it over and over again. If you can't come to an agreement, you have a problem. If you come to an agreement and then have to come to the same agreement again, you have a bigger problem.

Deference to Authority

It's one thing to be respectful, or to expect employees, children, and the like to show deference. But if we're continually deferring to those we answer to or expecting complete compliance from those who answer to us, we'll never deal with issues effectively. Worse, such behavior leads to wasted energy and frustration because nothing ever changes and even less gets achieved. And no one ever feels comfortable enough to tell you what's really going on or to disagree, so little in the way of learning ever occurs. It's just easier to go along to get along.

Abuse of Authority

Parents have authority. Employers have authority. When it's used judiciously, good things happen. When it's abused—through micromanagement, intimidation, or verbal or nonverbal threats—people shut down and productivity ceases.

"Lip-Service" Change Initiatives

How many times have you watched a leader make a pronouncement or implement a change plan that is then left to wither on the vine? Lots of talk and no action. Unfortunately, even though the person with the plan may have forgotten his or her empty challenges or promises, those on the receiving end have long memories. The outcome is that the next time around, people will say "yes" with their lips while their heads, hearts, and hands say "NO!"

Fear of the Unknown

For whatever reason, be they real or imagined, people fear speaking up because of what might happen to them. "Better to be safe than sorry," they believe, so candor and openness are what you read about in leadership books.

No Accountability

When people aren't held accountable, deadlines are missed, commitments are broken, skepticism and cynicism abound, and everyone blames someone else. Then, the lack of accountability seems to become the norm rather than the exception.

Lack of Respect

Unwarranted blame, harsh criticism, and other aggressive behaviors lead to disrespect and mistrust. Then, the resulting lack of respect leads to disengagement, disloyalty, and an absence of initiative.

Lack of Feedback

Whether in our personal or our professional lives, most of us avoid talking about poor performance, personal hygiene, inappropriate behavior, weight, relationships, money, sex, laziness, or appearance. The results are the continued violation of our expectations and an absence of results.

These frustrations are some of the more common ones. You could certainly add to the list! But what all our frustrations have in common is that they all deal with US and our interactions with others. These frustrations do not happen in a vacuum—you contribute to your own frustration.

And, we all want results! We all want to achieve our goals and meet the expectations of those for whom we work. We all want to surprise and delight our clients or customers. We all want to have and keep a good job or to be wildly successful in our chosen field or profession. We all want a life partner, family members, and children with whom we have loving, positive relationships rather than just "tolerating" each other. We also want to have positive relationships with our friends, neighbors, and those around us. And we all want the respect of those with whom we associate.

We may not always couch the complexities of what we want in life in a single word, but we really are—at the end of the day— looking for results. And when we lie down at night feeling we've come up short in achieving the results we want, sleep can be incredibly elusive.

Why Don't We Get the Results We Want?

What we often fail to recognize is that we are dependent upon others in achieving results, and we can't talk about improving results without considering the impact that respect and our relationships have on results.

Notice in the diagram in Figure 1.1 that "results" both affect and are affected by "relationships," which is also true for "respect." Establishing a precise hierarchy among the three is a little like trying to definitively answer the old conundrum about which came first, the chicken or the egg. But what we know with certainty is that when respect is strengthened, the quality of our relationships improves, and our results follow suit. In other words, enhance one and you will improve the other two. On the other hand, if you neglect or abuse any one of these three elements, the other two will suffer.

The next time you can't sleep, look at the results you have, the relationships you are in, and the respect you bring to or receive in any conversation. You can't improve results without addressing respect and relationship. Results, respect, and relationship are a part of every conversation you hold.

In my first job after graduate school, I had a manager who exemplified all of these values. On my first day on the job, I was beset with the usual fears and anxieties that set in when you are hit with the reality that the real world of work is not like college.

FIGURE 1.1   The Effectiveness Model

Terry came into my office and politely introduced himself. He then asked a million questions about me, what I wanted to learn, how I saw myself developing in this position, and how I thought he could help me. He developed some ground rules for working together, and he left me with some questions to think about and clarify as a starting point to building a solid working relationship. He was clearly more interested in me than in himself. In fact, I actually had to stop him from leaving my office and make him sit back down to answer my questions about him and his professional experience.

Even after all these years I remember how he eased my fears and made me feel like I mattered to him and to the organization. In the following months, we worked hard and talked regularly, and I benefited tremendously as he mentored and managed my daily work and career. Even when he had some harsh criticism to give, he was respectful of our relationship as I worked to achieve our intended results. From that first conversation, I never doubted that he had my best interests at heart. He exemplified the power that building relationships, creating respect, and achieving results can have.

How Do Your Conversations Affect Your Results?

Every conversation that you hold creates the results, respect, and relationship that you experience. Indeed, your *result* is the conversation; the *respect* you experience is the conversation; and your *relationship* with everyone you interact with is the conversation. Finally, you are at the core of every conversation you hold—you are responsible for what you get.

Because *you* are the only one who has control over *you*, your relationships, the respect you bring to those relationships, and the results you achieve, this book is about *you* and what you really want. If you're not realizing the results you want, it's up to you to fix what isn't working. So, before you close this book and explain to the cosmos that you're reasonable, rational, and respectful; that you know how to hold the difficult conversation; and that the problems you're having are someone else's fault—know that while you may be right, *you're also dead wrong.*

You see, if you're part of a relationship—whether at work or home or on the golf course or in the boardroom—you're part of the conversation. And if the relationship isn't working, you can *likely* change the way you're engaging in the conversations to positive effect. (I say *likely* because I know there actually are some circumstances that are beyond your control. But those exceptions are far fewer than you realize.) However, what you do or don't do contributes to every conversation that you hold. You just can't let yourself off the hook.

Now, let's explore what kind of conversations we hold, what kind of conversations we should hold, and the principles that will help us successfully navigate any difficult conversation.

Why Don't Your Conversations Work?

Have you ever been in a prickly situation where you just don't know how to talk about what really matters, so you don't bring up the tough issue? Or how about those times when everyone nods in agreement during a conversation that seems to go great, but then the expected outcome never materializes? Then you have those times when you try your best, but somehow you (or the person you're talking with) make a mess of it. Such scenarios are what we call *counterfeit conversations* or "fake talk." Such conversations can be about any topic: changing, improving, requesting, or correcting something. The conversation seems to go well, but then nothing happens! Simply put, a *counterfeit conversation* never produces desired results.

At work or home, we have all held these conversations and then ended up mystified when performance or behavior remained the same, accountability or responsibility never improved, problems

8

weren't solved effectively, customers weren't satisfied, quality and safety continued to be at risk, and change challenges went unaddressed. We thought we shared our message, but found out later, after not getting the expected results, that the conversation went awry.

Sometimes *fake talk* occurs because we expect people to read our minds. Consequently, our listeners keep on doing what they have always done, even though we think our intentions should be obvious. People who engage in fake talk may beat around the bush or are so vague that even a mind reader would misinterpret what is being said, let alone have any idea of performing up to expectations or being accountable.

Fake talk is also marked by a rise in the frustration level by one or all of the participants. Such conversations can be so filled with emotion, aggression, and disrespect that people are too busy "fighting or flighting" to understand what is really being said. Fake talk is vague, manipulative, covert, shortsighted, problematic, disrespectful, accusatory, noncomplimentary, or an outright lie. Such conversation can be passive, aggressive, or both.

Here's an example of a *counterfeit conversation* that begins with a lack of respect that undermines whatever relationships may have existed, and leads to a complete lack of results:

DUCK AND COVER

Henry stormed into his staff meeting. He started shouting and yelling and demanded to know who had borrowed his thumb drive.

"I know one of you took my thumb drive to make a copy of the proposal we outlined in our last meeting!" he ranted.

Staring everyone down, he continued, "Why don't you fess up and just admit that you lost your copy and borrowed my thumb drive? Don't play dumb with me! Who has it?"

Everyone just looked at the floor and said nothing. Finally, in a rage, Henry shouted "Meeting over, until I find my thumb drive!"

After berating and blaming his staff, the manager stormed out of the con-ference room—with the thumb drive hanging around his neck! When asked why no one said anything, one of the attendees replied, "No one wanted to make our boss look more ridiculous than he already looked! Let alone be the one to incur his wrath!"

Note that the way the manager treated and related to his people affected their willingness to share their thinking, influenced how they performed in the moment, and created lost energy and wasted resources to resolve key work issues. In other words, no results! Not to mention the perpetuation of continued mistrust and this man's reputation as an ineffective manager.

What Kind of Conversations Should We Hold?

Instead of counterfeit conversations, we should be holding *REAL* conversation. REAL conversations get results. REAL conversations change things. The parties to REAL conversations not only understand, they come away feeling valued and respected. The behavior and the relationship of the parties are changed for the positive, and something actually gets done. Such conversation leads to the opportunity for transformation.

These types of conversations are specific, direct, open, insightful, solution-oriented, respectful, accountability-based, and encouraging or complimentary. If you want to check up on the quality of your conversations, answer these three simple questions:

- How do my conversations impact the quality of my results?
- How would I describe the quality of the relationships that I have?
- Is respect one of the hallmarks of how I treat others or how they treat me?

If you answered any of these questions with a degree of negativity, you are probably engaging in fake talk. After all, some of the greatest opportunities for holding REAL conversations come when no one agrees with our view, we don't get what we want, or others are repeatedly violating our expectations. The quality of all we receive reflects the quality of the conversations that we hold. Unfortunately, when we engage in fake talk not only do we not get results, but we also put respect and our relationships in jeopardy.

What Are REAL Conversations?

The *REAL* in *REAL conversations* is an acronym for the conversational skills that are used in all effective conversation. These four skills include the following:

- **R**ecognizing and suspending your thinking or judgments
- **E**xpressing your thoughts, feelings, experience, or opinions without creating resistance in others
- **A**sking questions to increase your understanding
- **L**istening and attending to the messages that others are expressing verbally and nonverbally

We'll learn more about these skills and how they contribute to the eight principles for conducting REAL conversations. These skills and principles apply to every conversation that you hold and their application will ensure your success.

Principles for Creating REAL Conversations

The *eight principles* for holding REAL conversations are the basis for holding any conversation. You've either observed them in others or experienced them firsthand. We have spent the past

20 years identifying these principles and putting them to the test. Now it's time for you to put them into practice for yourselves. Let's review each one briefly.

The Awareness Principle—Choose to Be Conscious

Awareness is the first principle of effective conversation. It is essential that we see and understand the dynamics of the conversation in which we are involved. Such awareness requires that we expand our "conscious" awareness of what is happening in the conversation. We must learn to be "consciously conscious" in the moment. If you can't see the dynamics of the conversation, then you can't manage them. You will learn to be both a participant and an observer in the conversation.

The Knowledge Principle—Do to Know

Knowledge requires that we not only understand the skills and the process or framework for holding any difficult conversation, but that we also can use or apply what we know. We really don't know what we know, until we use it. It is in doing that we come to know what we know or don't know. We each are responsible to know and use what we know if we really want to improve our results. You will learn to deliberately increase your knowing by doing.

The Reflection Principle—Reflect Reflections

Reflection occurs as individuals constantly reflect messages to us about who they are, what they think, and what they want. Likewise, we reflect distinct messages to others as well. We are usually quite oblivious to the messages being sent our way and that we are sending. Reflection increases respect and the personal engagement of your listener. You will learn to reflect the reflection of others in everything you do and say.

The Perception Principle—Recognize and Suspend to Uncover

What we think drives everything we say and do. Our *perception* then impacts the creation of a personal reality that either helps or hinders how we communicate with others. Learning to see outside what we think we know will help us broaden our perspective and deal more effectively with others. Learning to recognize and suspend your thinking demands that you broaden your perspective by challenging reality. You will learn to see outside yourself.

The Preparation Principle—Prepare or Beware

Preparation allows anyone to talk about what matters most instead of being sideswiped by the brain's programming. Understanding how to identify assumptions, clarify intent, and focus the attention of one's listener is essential for beginning any conversation. Using a simple framework for holding a potentially difficult conversation also increases success. You will learn to hold a conversation with confidence that will increase accountability and yield results, but you must learn to think before you speak.

The Expression Principle—Express Your Intention

Expression is a reflection of our intention that influences the entire delivery of any message. How we express our views either helps others to receive and think through the issues or creates defensiveness that leads to rejection and irrationality. Effective expression increases the likelihood of achieving results. You will learn to create cooperation and contribution rather than using manipulation and compulsion to achieve results.

The Discovery Principle—Ask to Reveal

The key to increased *discovery* is asking questions. Whether you ask to explore, clarify, or learn, you will increase your capacity to discover new perspectives and solidify what you think you know,

13

and discover what you don't. As we ask questions, we also increase respect and engagement with others. You will learn how to ask questions that create safety and respect for your listener while diving to deeper levels of understanding as you seek answers.

The Connection Principle—Listen and Attend to Connect

Connection is created as we listen and attend to others while being present. Understanding how to effectively and actively listen creates connection because we are focused, nonjudgmental, specific, and empathetic in listening to others. Listening and attending is also the key to resolving conflict by defusing defensiveness and uncovering the meaning behind other's "hot" emotion. You will learn to defuse emotional reactions and increase your understanding of what matters most.

Because these principles overlap, dealing with one principle impacts the others—thereby increasing the effectiveness of all your conversations. REAL conversations increase respect, build relationships, and achieve results. Whether you are living, leading, loving, teaching, mentoring, or associating with others, you are always in conversation.

Is there any aspect of your personal or professional life that isn't affected by your conversations—the way you deal and speak to others? If you want to achieve the results that you seek, stop engaging in fake talk; instead, hold REAL conversations. Learn how to talk about what matters most. Engage in conversations that express what you truly think, feel, or want—and give people what they need to succeed.

Holding REAL conversations requires having courage, being honest with yourself, looking at your thinking, learning the principles, and then applying them to your most challenging conversations. In this book, you will learn many practical skills that you can use and apply immediately. My wish is to provide hope to all whose heads, hearts, and hands hang down. You can then talk about what matters most. And I promise you this: the results—and the accompanying good night's sleep—will be worth it.

In Summary

We are confronted with any number of difficult or frustrating situations that we usually avoid. We don't often recognize how our results are affected by the respect and the quality of the relationships that we have. Understanding the REAL skills and the principles for holding any difficult conversation will help us to be successful.

Get REAL: Identify the source of your frustration or what keeps you up at night. This realization will be your first clue to the types of situations or individuals that may need your attention. Once you are clear on your challenges, look to learn a number of skills in the following chapters that will help you hold REAL conversations and avoid fake talk.

Gentle Reminders

- Recognize your distress to achieve success.
- The quality of your respect, relationships, or results is a measure of your responsibility—you get exactly what you create.

You can find more information about this topic at
www.overcomingfaketalk.com/gentlereminders.

CHAPTER 2

Why Can't You See What's Happening?

The Awareness Principle— Choose to Be Conscious

When I first started working as a river guide in the Grand Canyon, I had to learn to "read" the river. Ripples on the surface, rolling waves, and frothing foam are all reflections of what lies beneath the river's surface. For example, smooth, dark green water indicates that the river is deep and probably has a sandy bottom; whereas, foaming waves tell you the water is shallow with rocks not far below. When you're running a rapid, being aware of what lies beneath the surface is crucial to continuing your trip without mishap. In conversation, the same is true: what you see on the surface can tell you a lot about what is going on underneath. And what is happening beneath the surface is often where you need to be focusing your attention. People's outside expression is a reflection of what's going on inside.

Where do we start in conversation? Awareness is the first principle in creating REAL conversations. Awareness is about improving your social intelligence. If you don't know what is going on in a conversation or interaction, if you can't see, hear, or feel the dynamics, then you can't manage them. And you've got to see the dynamics to manage them and use them to your advantage. Knowing where a conversation is and where it is headed is the first principle for holding REAL conversations.

Taking Responsibility

To hold REAL conversations, you must take responsibility for how you speak and interact with others. You can't go around blaming everyone and everything else for your lack of results in creating REAL conversations that work!

Sometimes we just aren't *consciously conscious*—or perhaps we have never been conscious about "people" dynamics. Usually we're on autopilot, so when things don't go according to plan, we find it convenient to blame everyone and everything else for our outcomes. After all, when others are to blame, we can avoid responsibility. Avoiding responsibility keeps us from looking at ourselves and our contribution. Unfortunately, you may never look at yourself until someone you respect candidly tells you that your behavior is inappropriate or offensive. We should be so lucky. Until we receive such feedback, we just keep doing what we've always done and never recognize how our behavior contributed to or created what we receive.

Let's suppose you just finished attending an expensive, two-day "conversations" class in connection with your work. Or maybe you just finished reading the latest book on becoming a more effective communicator as a leader. You are revved up, ready to go, and can't wait for the next opportunity to practice your newfound skills to talk about the things that really matter. And sure enough, you soon have the opportunity to provide feedback to a coworker.

For reasons that escape you, the conversation doesn't go so well. Instead of engaging with you and working toward a solution, your coworker ends up proclaiming that you are a real jerk. A few days later, you try again . . . and bomb again. Badly! Now the situation is even worse because the rumor mill is churning. No one in your department will even talk to you.

You feel hoodwinked. Frustrated, you proclaim, "This fuzzy stuff never works! The class (or book) was worthless, not to mention the coworker!" So you return to your old habits, you achieve the same poor results, and your relationship with the difficult coworker remains mired in disrespect, only now your reputation is in question.

Notice that the problem is the "soft" stuff or class or book or other person—never *you*. That's where you're wrong! We are responsible for the conversations we create. Unfortunately, if we don't take responsibility for what we create, we miss the opportunity to create a REAL conversation every time. What is difficult about awareness is that it's hard to see how we come across to others—to see ourselves as we are seen. We allow our lack of self-awareness to affect our sense of personal responsibility and our ability to recognize the dynamics in conversation. We miss the signals that the conversation is hurling toward a train wreck until it's too late.

Developing Self-Awareness

Being self-aware is not easy. It's not a good idea to walk around with a mirror so we can check our reflection and our reactions. And if we did, we might not be ready for what we see. Nor do we go around asking everyone to give us feedback all the time. That leaves us to take particular notice of what others tell us, how they react to us, or whether we stop to notice what our results tell us about us.

YOU GOT A "B" IN MATH?

I had been helping my son Bryson with his math all semester. He was receiving an A– up until the final exam. After the semester, he delivered his report card to his mother and me. We opened the envelope and . . . he had received a B.

I was shocked and I said, "You only got a B in math? What happened?"

Bryson rolled his eyes, looked away, threw his head back, and said, "Thanks a lot, Dad!" He then flounced out of the room like a typical 14-year-old.

My wife looked at me with that stare that could melt plate metal and said, "You know, your intent is probably pure, but your delivery sucks!"

"What do you mean by that?" I demanded.

"He already feels bad enough, and then you basically accuse him of being stupid or lazy. You are so insensitive, sometimes I can hardly believe it," she retorted.

"Come on! I wasn't thinking anything of the kind. I was disappointed that he didn't get a good grade after he worked so hard. That's what I was thinking!" I pleaded.

"Well that's not how you came across. Your tone suggested you thought he was stupid or something. And notice, he read it the same way that I did."

That stung. And it made me think about how I had come across to my son for a long time.

Recognizing the quality of results, respect, and relationships that we find ourselves receiving can help us to start to build some degree of self-awareness. Let's be more specific.

How Do We Become More Self-Aware?

Most of us lack an objective perspective of how we come across to others. So it helps to realize that other people usually reflect back to us what we reflect to them. The disrespect my son reflected to me was a reflection of the disrespect that I reflected to him with my comment, "You got a B in math?" along with the tone and nonverbal behavior that I displayed to him.

Reflecting on the previous interaction forced me to examine what I was really thinking at that moment. As I sorted through my own thoughts and feelings, I had to admit I was frustrated and irritated that I had spent so much time helping him and that he had not measured up to my expectations. Those thoughts and feelings were reflected to him in the way I spoke and the tone I took. His reaction simply reflected what he had received from me.

If you step back and look at what you bring to a conversation, you may see yourself through the reflections of others. And if you think you can hide your thoughts and feelings from those you are speaking with, you are mistaken—your thoughts and feelings are reflected to others in everything you say and do.

Developing an Awareness of Dynamics

In addition to our lack of personal awareness, we often lack an awareness of the dynamics at play in conversation, so we don't manage what we don't see. We are like my four-year-old daughter when I give her feedback about her misbehavior. Her general reaction is to hide her head under a blanket, or to pull her tee shirt or blouse up over her head. She believes that if she can't see me then I don't exist—and will soon go away.

We may not be as intentional as my daughter, but we often turn a blind eye to the situation because we either can't see or choose not to see what is happening in the moment. Here's one example of how a lack of awareness can manifest itself.

TURNING RED

During his staff meeting, a CEO started to put a member of his team on the spot. He peppered her with questions he wouldn't let her answer, cranked up his volume, used some expletives, and whipped out his index finger to accentuate his accusations. All the while, the poor woman, who sat across from him, turned redder and redder.

Finally, I leaned over and said, "Jack, look at Samantha's face. What color is it?"

"Why, red," Jack exclaimed.

"What do you think that means?" I asked.

"That I'm offending her?" he queried.

"Why don't you ask her?" I suggested.

"Am I offending you?" asked Jack.

Samantha then erupted in tears. To his credit, this CEO then turned to the rest of his team and asked if he had behaved similarly with any of them. Not surprisingly, each of them replied in the affirmative. He promptly apologized to everyone.

Jack isn't a bad person but, like many of us, he was caught up in the passion of the moment and just was not aware of what he was doing and how he was coming across to others. He was unconsciously unconscious of his behavior.

Why Don't We See What's Right Under Our Noses?

Most of us are so focused on what we are thinking, what *we* should say next, what *we* didn't get, what expectations of *ours* were violated, or what we want others to do that we miss most of what goes on in our conversations. We "participate" in the conversation, but we don't observe the conversation, so we are solely preoccupied with ourselves—it's one-sided at best. As a result, we miss what is happening in "the process" of the conversation. We need to learn to be both a participant in and an observer of what is happening in our conversations.

For example, if Jack had been observing Samantha instead of being so focused on forcibly making his point, maybe he would have seen that Samantha was turning red, clamming up, and shutting down. Then he could have stopped the conversation and checked out her reaction and what she was thinking. Fortunately, I had received permission to coach Jack in front of his team, so I was able to stop his confrontation and help him make a different choice in the moment. Given that no one is monitoring you, *you* need to observe you and what is happening when you engage in conversation. Remember, you can learn to manage, explore, and understand what you see.

At other times we may be aware that a conversation is "going south," but we don't know what to do to turn it in a different direction. Sometimes our conversations are fueled by too much emotion. When we are hit with emotion we didn't see coming, we unconsciously react. Then our reaction fuels a reaction in the other person, and the conversation spirals out of control. To increase your awareness of conversation dynamics, you must recognize *downward spirals*.

Recognizing Downward Spirals

A *downward spiral* is a conversation that is about to go over a cliff. Downward spirals occur in a fairly predictable manner or pattern: Steve says or does something that Jim interprets negatively, which leads Jim to assume the worst about Steve or his intentions. Jim's interpretation then leads him to react. Steve observes Jim's negative reaction and interprets Jim's behavior negatively. So then Steve reacts. Jim, in turn, interprets Steve's reaction in the worst possible way and he, again, reacts. And the spiral continues downward.

Such conversations are easy to spot. They are characterized by negative interpretations, blame, raised voices, expletives, sarcastic tone, creative nonverbals, hand gestures, and indecision. These offensive exchanges are exercises in futility and do more harm than good to results. These behaviors "signpost" or signal fake talk.

Here's an example of how the downward spiral conversation shows up:

TALL, BLACK, AND HANDSOME
Beth, a middle-aged African American woman, believes that most people have disparaging views of her ethnic origin. Brian, her teammate, has just

23

returned from a two-week vacation in the Caribbean. While exiting a meeting, Beth overhears a conversation between Brian and another colleague.

"Well you sure are the tan man, aren't you?" the colleague observes.

Brian gleefully replies, "Yep, that's me—tall, black, and handsome!"

Beth interrupts and says, "I'm offended by your reference to my race as 'black,'" he declares.

"Oh, give it a rest, will you? This is ridiculous!" Brian replies.

"If you had any sensitivity to others, you might not be so CLUELESS. I want to talk about this now!" demands Beth.

"Well, I'm not talking about it NOW or ever, so forget it!" Brian declares, as he turns his back and walks off, leaving Beth standing by herself in the hall.

Here's another situation a little closer to home.

OFF TO THE RACES

I return from a difficult day in the office and just want to sit down for some quiet time reading the paper. My wife, however, wants to talk about when I am going to paint the dining room. She brings up the subject, and away we go!

"Can we talk about this later?" I ask in as nice a tone as I can muster.

"When!? You never want to talk about this! I bought the paint a month ago, my parents are coming for a visit in two weeks, and you haven't done a single thing!" she replies.

"Oh, yeah. You decide to invite your parents here for a visit without even talking to me about it. And now you want me to clean this and paint that?" I retort.

She blasts back, "You know, I ask you to do one simple thing, and you refuse. You really don't do anything around here!"

"Oh, give it a rest, will you?" I say as I throw my paper to the ground and storm out to the garage.

Unfortunately, this is how many of us deal with challenging conversations—avoidance, blame, accusation, sarcasm, misplaced interpretations, and judgments. Notice that the first conversation began to spiral downward when Brian used the word "black," and Beth interpreted this usage negatively. Beth didn't help the conversation when she called Brian "insensitive" and "clueless." These judgments and accusations contributed to Brian's disengagement.

In the second example, the conversation took a turn for the worse when the tired spouse was accused of "never wanting to talk" (although, if we could hear his tone, that might have been the starting point).

In these situations, you need to recognize what is happening. When you spot a reactive interaction, you can manage the dynamics more effectively than simply reacting negatively. Spirals usually end badly—without the results you are looking for—because you attack the other person rather than discussing the issue at hand. Then it takes even more time and effort to repair the damaged relationship. Visually, a downward spiral is shown in Figure 2.1.

All this reacting is based on negative interpretations and emotions that challenge the interpretations, judgments, and assumptions of the other person. When both parties spiral, the results are not good: the conversation dissolves; nothing is resolved; rationality is absent; people disengage; and anger, frustration, and bitterness are left in the wake of individuals' withdrawal.

FIGURE 2.1 Downward Spirals

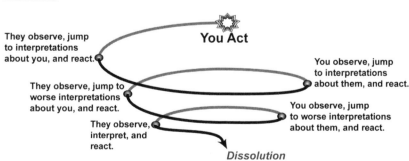

Engaging in Upward Spirals

To stop a downward spiral you want to create an upward spiral, elevating or lifting the conversation by asking questions that will increase understanding and learning. Although asking questions sounds relatively easy, it is difficult for some people because they are afraid to find out that they may not be right or that their thinking is inaccurate or incomplete. We don't like it when we discover that our reality—or at least the way we see reality—isn't really real.

Consider, for example, how the conversation between Beth and Brian would have been different if, in response to Beth's initial reaction, Brian had said, "Help me understand how I offended you?"

Perhaps Beth's response would have been, "Well, I just don't like the use of *black* in the way you used it, or maybe it was your tone of voice. I just took your comment as a slam, I guess." Then Brian could have said, "Although I didn't intend to be demeaning, I can appreciate your sensitivity to my choice of words. I apologize for offending you. I'm also wondering if I've done this kind of thing before. Or is there something in my behavior that I need to be more aware of?"

Had Brian taken a moment to be more aware, this interaction could have unfolded in an entirely different direction. "Upward spirals" are conversations that are characterized by respect in word, tone, and demeanor; increased understanding or learning; and improved problem solving. Graphically, the conversation is shown in Figure 2.2.

The process for lifting the conversation toward a place where you both get results begins with asking questions as soon as the other person interprets an aspect of the interaction either positively or negatively. Asking questions is an attempt to understand what's behind the other person's action or reaction.

When we put the two spirals together (Figure 2.3), it's easy to see how a conversation can head above the line or below the line, *depending on how we choose to act.* The choice for action exists

FIGURE **2.2**   **Upward Spirals**

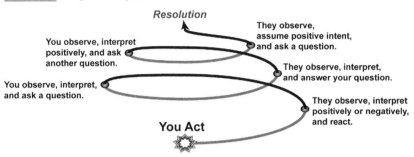

at the moment in time when the other person does or says something. When we negatively judge the person, feel a "hot" emotion, or begin to act defensively, we know we are on the road to ruin.

Most of us recognize that we are better off when our conversations remain above the line, but our choices sometimes take us below the line. To help us make better choices, there is a simple method for increasing your awareness of the dynamics present in all our conversations.

FIGURE **2.3**   **Spirals Above and Below the Line**

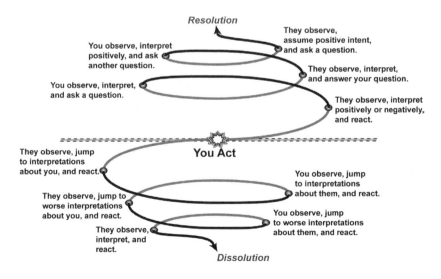

What Is "Walking the Line"?

We *walk the line* in every conversation that we hold. The line represents the choice we make to take the conversation above the line or below the line. *Above the line* and *below the line* are accounting terms that represent the outcome in a financial endeavor. You can make the same evaluation of every conversation you hold: are the results of your behavior positive or negative? Recognizing where the conversation is or where it is headed enables us to manage the conversation's dynamics more effectively to achieve the desired results.

REAL Conversations Are About Discovery

REAL conversations are respectful and include behaviors such as asking, listening, sharing, and learning from others. They also demonstrate positive intent as well as reasonable assumptions and responses, and they usually lead to learning and change, even if it is simply a change in perspective. REAL conversation is conducted in a positive, respectful tone. Individuals ask questions to try and understand differing points of view. Their physical demeanor is attentive, and their body language remains relaxed, with ample physical space between individuals. REAL conversations always end in resolution or with a specific outcome achieved—even if it's just that both parties agree to disagree.

Counterfeit Conversations Are About Defense

Counterfeit conversations are usually disrespectful and include behaviors such as denial, deference, criticism, self-justification, and blame. Individuals who are conversing below the line generally demonstrate avoidance, negative intent, unreasonable assertions, and reactive behavior.

Counterfeit conversations happen below the line. These conversations usually take a sarcastic, cynical, or accusatory tone. It is common to witness tempers flaring, wild gestures, accusations, and name calling. In most cases, both parties are usually more interested in convincing the other person that they don't have a clue about what that person is talking about. These conversations lead to dissolution—the breaking down or disintegration of the conversation altogether. Meanwhile, results suffer.

Aware individuals recognize what is happening in a conversation and choose not to be drawn into a downward spiral by others' defensive behavior. Even though many people may approach you from below the line, you can move those conversations above the line—*if* you can see what's going on right in front of you.

Keeping the above-the-line or below-the-line analogy in mind will help you spot what is happening in a conversation so you can take steps to stop it from slipping below the line. I've seen people stop and say, "I just noticed we've slipped below the line. Let's back up for a minute and have everyone share what matters most to them in serving this client. Can we do that?" Describing the process of the conversation in this manner helps everyone avoid blame and accusation, and everyone's attention is focused on the process rather than on the individuals involved.

In Figure 2.4, notice that the arrows are labeled *Act* and *React*. Conversations above the line are based on an individual's deliberate acts or choices, whereas conversations below the line are reactionary—and happen when individuals are not thinking rationally or are just interested in defending themselves. Because a REAL conversation is deliberate, individuals need to consciously practice, use, and choose those behaviors or skills that will lead to specific, desirable outcomes.

What Are "Deliberate Acts"?

REAL conversation is deliberate—it is conscious and involves a choice of action. The conversation is not simply left to chance, but

FIGURE 2.4 **Above and Below the Line**

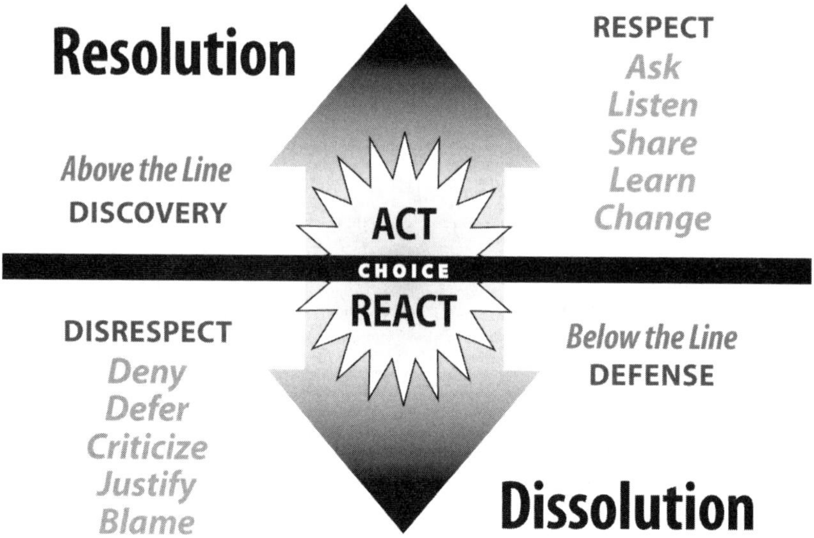

is a matter of choice. Specific behaviors and skills can be used to create desired results. Consider any of the following situations:

- You need to talk to your spouse about the family finances.
- The boss wants to talk about your challenges of his project.
- An employee has done something inappropriate or illegal.
- Your 14-year-old daughter wants to go with a friend to an out-of-town rock concert.

How would you respond to these situations? Would you respond immediately, or would you take some time to deliberately consider what you want as an outcome? Would you take time to think about what you are going to say and how you would say it? Would you try and plan a time and place for holding the conversation?

In all of these situations, you have a choice to make about how to hold the conversation and whether you will take the conversation above or below the line. Unfortunately, we usually don't stop to think about what to say and how to say it, and the result is conversations that get us nowhere (and often do much damage). Or, worse, we choose to say nothing and live with the misery of our thoughts. Consider this story:

NO VACATION?

Frank is a hard-working internal marketing specialist. After his manager, Sue, gives him a long to-do list, she leaves his office with this parting shot, "You're going to be a busy boy this summer, Frankie." Frank immediately goes ballistic because Sue said the same thing last summer. Then she gave him a ton of work and refused to let him take his vacation. Frank immediately assumes that Sue will pull the same stunt this summer.

After a reflective moment, Frank realizes that he is making some negative assumptions. He calls Sue and asks if he might come to her office to ask her some questions about scheduling. She invites him to come right over. Once in her office, Frank asks if it would be helpful to schedule his summer vacation before the work becomes too daunting.

"The sooner the better!" Sue affirms.

Frank then asks, "Could I ask why you made the comment about me being a 'busy boy' this summer?"

"Given that so many people keep asking me how the company is doing and how the economy might affect their jobs, I thought you'd like to know that your job is more than secure," Sue replies. "I didn't offend you, did I?"

"No! Not at all, but I was wondering if your statement meant that I wouldn't be able to take my vacation again this year," Frank answers, relieved!

Choosing to hold the conversation and to keep it above the line maintains respect for the individual while you maintain your own sense of integrity. It also allows the individual to reflect on the consequences of his or her thinking and behavior while building a positive relationship.

The "93/7 Rule"

In addition to improving our self-awareness and the dynamics of our conversations, let's identify other factors to which we often pay little or no attention. In bookstores and online, we see no shortage of communication books and seminars on how to hold conversations that enable us to improve our personal and professional relationships; so why do we still struggle to do so? The answer to that question resides in the research of Albert Mehrabian.[1] He stated that when people are talking about feelings or attitudes, they form their **perceptions** in a conversation in three ways:

   55% from body language
   38% from tone of voice
    7% from choice of words

These percentages suggest that 93 percent of communication occurs through nonverbal behavior and tone; only 7 percent of communication takes place through the use of words—thus the "93/7 Rule."

Obviously these percentages don't apply in every conversation. Nor do they apply to communication in general. For example, the context and content in any conversation may affect how the message is delivered and perceived. However, when conversation is discussed today, the focus is usually on using the "right words" and the "framework" or the prescribed steps for holding a conversation. Stated differently, if we only focus on 7 percent of the message in a conversation, that leaves the other 93 percent of the dynamics of a conversation open to individual interpretation. When you consider the disproportion of this ratio, it is easy to see why, if you only focus on word choice or a step-by-step process, the conversation easily goes below the line.

If you focus solely on choosing the right words and following a certain step-by-step process in conversation, you are far more likely to engage in fake talk. If you leave the other 93 percent of the conversation to chance—93 percent which should focus on results, respect, and relationships—is a potential recipe for disaster. So why take the chance? Being able to effectively recognize, manage, and use 93 percent of conversational dynamics to your benefit will greatly improve the power and quality of your conversations and your results. But to effectively manage this 93 percent of conversation, you must distinguish between the "said" and the "unsaid" in conversation.

The "Said" and the "Unsaid" in Conversation

The *said* part of a conversation includes the words and the framework or recipe that we use to hold any conversation. The *said* is what is spoken and the process for holding a conversation, or the 7 percent of a conversation that is the most obvious. Although the percentage is low, these elements of a conversation are important, particularly with conversations we would rather avoid. The words that we use hold real power in discussing certain topics; however, focusing solely on the words and the "way" you might say or deliver your message are overrated.

THE CARD IS *NOT* THE CONVERSATION!

Decades ago, I worked in a company that wanted us to improve our communication skills. We took a course that provided us with a cue card for each lesson—to help us review and remember the specific concepts and skills taught in each module. We were encouraged to keep the card with us at all times and to review the card during the day, especially before holding a difficult conversation.

One day I sat in a meeting where things began to get heated. The manager held up his hand and said to the group, "Hold on just a minute everybody." He then took the card out of his pocket and began to read the script on the card to the group.

While he read the script, eyes rolled, people snickered, and others just sat there in a state of shock and awe with their mouths agape. Although at one level he did succeed in stopping the growing anger and frustration of the people on the team, his credibility as a leader and a communicator was shot. Unfortunately, people then turned their anger toward him rather than the issue at hand. The meeting ended quickly.

I later spoke with him to help him realize the impact of what he had done, but he refused to acknowledge that he had done anything wrong by just reading the cue card—the mechanical recipe for handling this tough conversation. Because he failed to handle the critical issues in the meeting, he frustrated people and lost all credibility with this team.

Scripts or recipes all by themselves are not the conversation! Just focusing on the *said* part of the conversation doesn't work. The other 93 percent of communication comprises the *unsaid* part of the conversation, the part of the conversation that is communicated without words. Even without words, we can help our conversations a great deal if we recognize the meaning of what is being communicated but is not said. Consider the following example:

ARE YOU ANGRY?

When I began my career as a workshop leader, I came in on the second morning early to set up my laptop and to prepare the room. A participant was waiting for me. "Can I ask you a question?" he queried.

"Sure! What's up?" I asked him.

"Well, yesterday at about 4:30, just before the workshop ended and you were answering our questions, were you mad at us?"

"No! Why do you ask?" I asked in disbelief.

"Well, you were frowning, your brow was furrowed, and you just looked really upset. A couple of us got together after the workshop, and we all commented on how we thought that maybe you were angry with us or we had done something to offend you," he offered.

I initially discounted his feedback, until I received the same feedback from another workshop participant. I had taken one of the many a personality assessment where I scored high in the "thought" category. This second round of feedback helped me to realize that my frowning face was misinterpreted as anger when in reality I was just pondering more deeply. Although I didn't intend to portray this face to my audience, I learned that I had to make a deliberate effort to smile in workshops to not be misunderstood. Thank heavens someone gave me the feedback!

Notice that no matter what words I was using, the *unsaid* portion of my communication was more powerful. If you have been focusing solely on words and recipes, that might explain why so many of your conversations haven't worked. Unfortunately, you only find out in retrospect—after you don't achieve the desired results—that you missed something in the *unsaid* portion of the conversation.

Most of you have seen this illustration (Figure 2.5) by Leonardo da Vinci, which he entitled *The Vitruvian Man.*

In his drawing, da Vinci used the circle and the square to represent the blending of art and science in considering the proportions of man. The square represents science and the circle represents art. The image also applies when understanding the creation of *REAL conversation.* We would see a blend of science and art—the

FIGURE 2.5 *The Vitruvian Man* **by Leonardo DaVinci**

35

said and the unsaid. Counterfeit conversation usually results when an individual fails to recognize the unsaid aspects in a conversation. In order to create REAL conversations, we need to understand and manage 100 percent of the dynamics present in any conversation.

Why Is the "Unsaid" So Important?

Even more than just the visual and vocal aspects of conversation, as Mehrabian suggested, the mental aspects of a conversation have a huge impact on how the conversation is delivered and received. Aside from the said aspects, the unsaid parts of a conversation would include any of the following:

- **Awareness** of what is happening in a conversation helps us determine where it is headed. Lack of awareness leaves us adrift in the conversation.
- **Knowledge** of the skills and the process enables us to hold any difficult conversation. Without this knowledge, conversations inevitably suffer.
- **Interaction style** differences may cause us to offend others who are not like us.
- **Nonverbal messages** are displayed by the eyes, lips, hands, and body and offer messages that go unrecognized or misunderstood.
- **Mental models** we hold of how things are or how the world works impact how we deal with each individual, topic, or situation.
- **Protective-reactive brain function** protects us from potential threats by shutting down our thought process and all rationality at the same time.
- **"Hot" or negative emotions** become a major barrier to conversation when we let our thoughts run wild and our feelings get the best of us.

- **Assumptions** include the perceptions, opinions, and judgments that we hold about the individual with whom we are about to speak.
- **Intent** determines the purpose or desired outcome for holding a conversation.
- **Context** encompasses the situation in which the conversation occurs.
- **Tone** or word inflection changes the meaning of messages.
- **Pauses** impact message meaning by giving emphasis to certain words and phrases.
- **Tempo** or pace of the message determines whether the message can even be understood.
- **Energy** encompasses the life or vibrancy that resonates within a message.
- **Relationship status** influences how we converse and includes all of our past history with an individual.
- **Attention** from the listening audience determines the amount of understanding and presence given during the conversation.
- Your **intuition** in the conversation that warns you, "You'd better not say that!"

These unsaid aspects are present but usually go unnoticed in our conversations. The challenge is to learn to recognize and use these powerful dynamics to deliberately create REAL conversations and achieve what you want. Only then will your conversations work for you.

In Summary

We need to increase our awareness of ourselves and the dynamics present in all conversation, and take responsibility for what we create. Being aware of what is happening in a conversation will help us manage our conversations more effectively. Unfortunately, most of us don't recognize when our conversations begin to spiral downward and out of control until it is too late. Being able to recognize downward spirals is the key to creating upward spirals.

We created the above-the-line versus below-the-line methodology as a simple means of helping us become more aware of where our conversations are and where they are headed. Increasing your awareness of what is said versus the messages that are unsaid and communicated will increase your ability to achieve results, create respect, and build the relationships you desire.

Get REAL: During the next week, start noticing whether your conversations are going above or below the line. Also notice when, where, and with whom your conversations start to go awry. When you notice the below-the-line dynamic, try asking questions to lift the conversation above the line. Note what behaviors you engage in that take the conversation below the line.

Gentle Reminders

- Because you can't manage what you don't see, start looking for what you have never seen before.
- Be both a participant and an observer in conversation by listening to the content of the conversation and noticing the behaviors and process of the conversation.
- Recognize that what goes unsaid in your conversation will have more impact than what is said.
- Look to identify how your thinking is driving the unsaid aspects of your conversation.

You can find more information about this topic at
www.overcomingfaketalk.com/gentlereminders.

CHAPTER 3

What Are REAL Conversations?

The Knowledge Principle— Do to Know

When I was first hired as a whitewater guide on the Colorado River, I was overwhelmed by the prospect of having to learn 288 miles of river—every rapid, rock bar, back eddy, sandbar, whirlpool, hydraulic, and any other obstacle that could do great harm. So I went out and bought a couple of Grand Canyon River maps and made a notebook detailing everything I thought I would need to know. The older guides even helped me draw pictures of each rapid, identifying all the major challenges and obstacles in the rapid.

I soon realized that I had some good knowledge—and great drawings—but absolutely no experience. My first time in the middle of a rapid, I couldn't recognize anything that I had drawn on paper. Even months later when I really knew more of what I was doing, the river would still grab my boat when I least expected it and push me somewhere I didn't want to go.

My understanding only became knowledge when I had to put what I thought I knew into practice. It took me quite a while to recognize and feel the flow of the river and use my knowledge to take me where I wanted to go.

Developing Conversational Intelligence

Conversational Intelligence requires that you have knowledge of all the skills of effective conversation as well as a process for holding any conversation and *applying* that knowledge. To gain the requisite knowledge, you must engage with others. Only then will you sense what to do when something unexpected occurs, which happens often because—like the rapids—no two conversations are ever the same. Think about a conversation you've had more than once with a spouse, a child, or a coworker, and then reflect on how that "same" conversation has been different every time. The differences may be subtle or dramatic, but the dynamics are never exactly the same.

So, once you *know*, by *doing* you learn what you know and what you don't know yet. It's highly unlikely that you will get it right every time—but you will learn as you go to feel the flow of the conversation and to maneuver in its current. Conversational intelligence demands that you do something!

What *Don't* You Want?

No one starts their day with the intent of crashing and burning. In fact, most of us actually prefer avoiding such disasters. Then why do we spend so much time cleaning up messes and putting out fires? More often than not, the cause of our frustrations resides in everyone's inability to hold the REAL conversations that bring about specific intended results. So, without the proper know-how, we either avoid engaging altogether or we just do what we've always done, even though neither course of action works.

Self-Preservation Behavior

Whichever course we choose, a lack of usable knowledge leads us to communicate from the perspective of self-preservation. Self-preservation involves saving face or self-protection whenever our results, respect, or relationships are called into question. Ironically, our value for self-preservation is sometimes greater than what we say we value most—results! So we value one thing and act in a way that sabotages our desired results.

THROW ME UNDER THE BUS!

Marge was a director of project management. One day, without warning, her VP called her in and told her to let all the hourly union employees know that no vacations would be allowed during the month of August in order to meet a project deadline. With some reservation, Marge communicated the VP's edict to her employees.

One disgruntled employee approached Marge and told her to take a flying leap, went on vacation anyway, and filed a grievance with the union against Marge. The VP did nothing about the situation, so the grievance was placed in Marge's personnel file. Marge then confronted her VP.

"Why didn't you back me up? All I did was carry out your directive, and you couldn't support me?" Marge queried.

"Well, you know how it goes, um, well . . . I'll see what I can do," the VP muttered.

Marge left the VP's office without any kind of an explanation for the VP's behavior. The VP did nothing. And soon after, Marge—who had been a valued employee—left the company.

In a nutshell, the VP chose not to engage, not to discipline the rebellious employee, and not to come to the aid of one of her direct reports. Why did she act this way? In a word, *self-preservation!* Why? Perhaps the VP wanted to avoid confrontation with the union. Perhaps she issued the directive without the support of upper management and didn't want to draw attention to her decision. Or maybe she just didn't like confrontation. Whatever the reason, she chose to virtually throw a valuable director under the bus.

We will never know why the VP responded the way she did, but we do know that her behavior created a lack of respect, lagging support, mistrust, and a lack of credibility for herself, not to mention the loss of a good employee. The VP made a conscious choice to *not* handle the situation and to *not* communicate effectively. Results, respect, and relationship suffered. When we fail to communicate appropriately, our behavior always has consequences.

Sometimes self-preservation strategies show up with even more aggression:

OUT TO PASTURE

The plant manager of a major defense contractor discovered that the contracted project was $300 million over budget and three months behind schedule. Furious, he called a meeting with over about 150 directors, supposedly to get their take on the problem. But he began the "discussion" by standing up and yelling at the top of his lungs, "Do you idiots know why this is happening? What do I pay you for? Would someone please explain what is happening?"

He continued in this manner for more than 20 minutes. Finally, one brave individual took the stage and explained what had happened, what problems they were currently experiencing, and what they all needed to do to make the project successful. The plant manager yelled, "Thank you!" Then he promptly left the hall.

The next day when this brave soul came into work, his office had been cleared out except for a desk, a chair, a telephone, and a few of his personal items in a box. For three months, the man sat at the desk and did nothing, having been relieved of his responsibilities. Finally, his conscience got the best of him, so he quit.

Although aggressive self-preservation is not always this extreme, this plant manager typifies the behavior of not really wanting to know what is wrong, and aggressively making a point with the hope that the rant will inspire or scare the troops to new heights of achievement and motivation. Although this plant manager did succeed in communicating the need for change, he also succeeded in creating less openness, more distrust for management, more turf protection, less teamwork and collaboration, and more water cooler talk about "who would be next."

Our reasons for engaging in self-preservation boil down to a simple concept: Cognitive dissonance. In the late 1950s Leon Festinger formulated the theory of *cognitive dissonance*, which explains the disconnect that occurs between an individual's beliefs and what actually occurs. For example, let's say that I thought I had done a great job on a project. Then my manager tells me that I did a terrible job. In anger and disbelief, I lash out and come up with every excuse I can think of that will restore or reestablish the validity for my own perception of reality.

When confronted with this gap in reality, an individual will resort to any number of behaviors that they believe will create what they want or need. In the case of the plant manager in the previous story, his aggressive behavior was an attempt to improve performance and motivation in order to complete the project on time and under budget—neither of which occurred. Likewise, those who are more passive in their approach to tough topics usually say nothing.

Self-Preservation Leads to Fight or Flight

Self-preservation usually manifests itself in conversation as "fight-or-flight" behavior. In fact, fight or flight is symptomatic of fake talk because such behavior produces less-than-desirable results, decreases respect, and impacts relationships. Granted, aggressive communication can bring about results, but the outcomes are generally short-lived, and the attack usually leads to either "attack back" or some form of flight.

"Flight" or passive communicators are usually more interested in removing themselves from the heat of the moment than engaging in a vigorous exchange. Consequently, much of the conversation goes unsaid or is avoided. In addition, passive communicators usually are less open, direct, or specific in expressing their expectations or ideas. Consequently, their conversations are more subject to misinterpretation or to a lack of clarity—another form of fake talk.

Why Resort to Fight or Flight? Fight-or-flight communication is about saving face. When we feel threatened, embarrassed, or unsafe, we resort to some form of self-preservation in an attempt to control the outcome of the current situation.[2] A fight communicator believes he or she can control outcomes by being aggressive, even to the point of being disrespectful or abusive. The flight communicator expresses control by avoiding engagement or confrontation. By not engaging, flight communicators just kind of hope the whole situation will go away or magically improve. This tactic also allows them to not entirely reveal their thinking and to partially avoid taking responsibility for outcomes. Unfortunately, these behaviors seem to work in a variety of situations or people wouldn't use them. But in the end, these ways of dealing with tough topics always lead to less-than-desirable results.

Deliberately engaging in fight-or-flight behavior may be appropriate within certain contexts. For example, during my years as a river guide, if it looked like the boat was going to flip, I never quietly said, "I believe we should hold on really tight. What do you think?" Instead, I yelled, *"Everyone move to the left side of the boat. Now! Now! Now!"* However effective these behaviors seem to be in some instances, you will diminish your ability to achieve results if you use them on a regular basis.

Some people freely acknowledge they are routinely abusive to others and claim they get the results they want. Such comments serve the purpose of identifying their intent—outright manipulation. Let's break these patterns of behavior down even further.

"Fight" or aggressive behavior might include any of the following:

Denial involves excusing your behavior or the lack thereof out of ignorance.

"I didn't know. . . . It wasn't my fault!"

Justification is about bolstering your position or creating a logical rationale for an outcome.

"Yeah but, given the amount of
money we've spent, I thought . . ."

Blame is simply passing the buck or transferring your responsibility to someone else.

"She told me to do it her way!"
"I'm sorry you didn't understand what I said."

Belittlement is demeaning another person by name-calling, stereotyping, or generalizing.

"He is such an idiot!"
"That team is clueless when considering the feelings of others."

Threat is manipulating a person's behavior through impending negative consequences.

"Do it or else!"
"If you know what's good for you, you'll . . ."

"Flight" or passive self-preservation behaviors are represented by the following behaviors:

Deference is simply going along to get along.
"I agree. Whatever you say is fine with me!"

Evasion involves using evasive tactics such as humor, sarcasm, or outright lying.
"I thought Chuck said the project was due next Friday."

Avoidance is going out of one's way to not have an exchange or interaction of any kind.
To yourself: "See if I ever speak to
you again!" as you duck into a stairwell.

Disengagement is withdrawal from an interaction in hopes that whatever is happening will just "go away."

—SILENCE—

Retaliation is about getting even or malicious compliance. Getting even involves not quite doing what was asked, knowing full well that the manager will suffer the consequences for poor or incomplete performance. Malicious compliance involves doing no more or no less than what is required.

"That is what you want?
Okay, I'll give you exactly what you want!"

Although we have separated these behaviors into fight-or-flight categories, individuals from both sides of the aisle may use a variety of these behaviors interchangeably. However, we ordered the specific behaviors to demonstrate how one behavior might naturally lead to another. Here's how several behaviors might show up in a single interaction.

MARKED FOR DEATH

Tim is a young graphic designer. Recently, he had trouble getting one of his coworkers to complete his part of a work assignment. After several requests, and with an important deadline looming, Tim went to his group's manager to ask for assistance. The manager got after Tim's peer to complete the work. The peer completed his work, and Tim got what he needed to finish his part of the project. A few weeks later, Tim received an e-mail from his manager telling him he was "difficult to get along with."

Shocked by this feedback, Tim went to seek more specific feedback from his manager.

"Tell me, what did I do?" Tim asked.

"You know, sometimes you are 'interpersonally challenged,'" replied his manager.

"What does that mean?" Tim queried.

"I don't know, but you are doing it right now! And it is bothersome, so get over it! You figure it out because the only people who are still working for me are people who can work and play well together!" his manager blurted out.

"Can you please just give me something that I am doing specifically?" Tim persisted.

"I told you! You really don't know how to listen, do you? Ask your peers!" the manager yelled.

And with that, the conversation ended. Tim then went to his peers to seek feedback. They offered nothing more specific than, "You're just difficult to work with."

Then a coworker took Tim aside and told him he was "marked for death." When Tim asked what that meant, he was told, "They've already decided to get rid of you, but they are waiting for you to do something that will justify firing you."

On two separate occasions, Tim returned to his manager to ask for specific feedback or examples of things he could work on to improve. Each time, he was rebuffed with the same generalities.

Not only would no one provide the feedback that Tim was seeking in this example, but the manager actually moved back and forth between fight and flight. One moment he was rather nasty, and the next moment, he clammed up and refused to engage. What is most unfortunate in this situation is that Tim was an employee who repeatedly tried to move the conversations above the line—he wanted to learn, improve, and grow. And yet everyone refused to give him the feedback he was so desperately seeking. Instead, Tim's manager and peers left him filled with doubt, discouragement, and despair.

Figure 3.1 illustrates the dynamics of fight and flight. Notice that "Results" shows up both above and below the line. Sometimes we can get results by being aggressive or passive, but those results are a mere reflection of what we could have achieved if our conversation had stayed above the line.

The arrow pointing to fight and flight below the line represents the interrelationship between these two styles. Fight creates either more fight or flight. Flight usually gives rise to fight when the flighter refuses to engage the more aggressive fighter. Finally, when a flighter engages another flighter, the interaction inevitably leads nowhere. It is ironic that both of these dynamics result in wasting huge amounts of time and energy as people create what they really don't want. In the end, *Results* are what suffer, either by what is said or by what is left unsaid.

FIGURE 3.1   The Dynamics of Fight and Flight

What Do You Want?

You want to quit using the behaviors that don't work and start using behaviors that create REAL conversations. This statement may sound quite obvious, but most people don't know what skills are required to create REAL conversations, nor do they have a process for holding these types of conversations.

What Is Dialogue?

The concept of REAL conversations is based on the work of David Bohm, who introduced the concept of "Dialogue": a mode of communicating that emphasizes the necessity of everyone involved placing their "meaning" on the table or into the "shared pool of meaning."[3]

Bohm believed that if people could openly and authentically share their thinking and were willing to explore a diversity of perspectives, then learning would take place. He used the analogy of a "shared pool" of meaning where everyone involved felt safe to put their perspective or "meaning" into the pool. Where greater shared meaning is achieved, learning is more complete; change is more easily accomplished; problem solving is improved; decision making is more timely, appropriate, and effective; and accountability is created.

Consequently, "dialogue" is REAL conversation and is defined as follows:

REAL conversation is the unrestricted creation of shared meaning, borne of shared respect, authenticity, and the desire to learn for increased capacity.

In our definition of REAL conversation, "shared meaning" does not imply that we necessarily agree, but that we are open to sharing all of our experiences, ideas, and opinions with others without fear of repercussion in order to achieve the results we seek. The "unrestricted creation of shared meaning" suggests that we purposely do not behave in ways that would cause anyone to feel or think that they cannot safely add their meaning to the "pool."

Shared meaning is also supported by "shared respect"—how we treat, speak, or act toward each other. "Authenticity" encompasses honesty, sincerity, and truthfulness. The "desire to learn" is the drive or motivation to engage in conversation and understand others—without the desire to engage one another, nothing happens. "Increased capacity" is the result of everyone's participation in the conversation toward a mutually beneficial end.

Given that shared meaning is vital to the outcomes we desire, let's take a deeper dive into the elements of respect, authenticity, and desire.

What You Give Is What You Get—Respect

Of the three elements, *respect* is the most important. Respect touches every conversation we hold. A lack of respect or blatant disrespect will take any conversation below the line.

At the heart of **respect** is the reflection principle. We often don't realize that we reflect the respect we have for others. In other words, when people react disrespectfully to you, you might take a look at the degree of respect you are reflecting toward them. Experience shows that the respect we receive from others is a reflection of what we gave to them.

Everything we say and do conveys respect or a lack thereof. Our facial expressions, eye contact, physical gestures, and body language all convey messages to our listeners. Our choice of words, tone of voice, tempo, word inflection, and emphasis signals our level of respect. And the way we listen to and even think about a person also sends a strong message. Any degree of disrespect or ambiguity in the way we reflect each of these behaviors, and our listeners will usually interpret our behaviors negatively by assuming the worst about us or our message.

Of course, you may have good reason to not respect certain individuals with whom you speak. Perhaps your history with them shows that they do not warrant your respect.

THE GRANDSTANDER

Years ago, when I practiced law as a criminal defense attorney, I always had a difficult time dealing with one particularly obnoxious prosecutor. To put it mildly, the guy was a grandstander. In short, he was the kind of person who did everything to make himself look better than everyone else. That's right— he was a real showboat!

One day, another attorney pulled me aside and stated, "I've noticed that every time you have to deal with Ed, you let him get under your skin. I recommend that you find something you really like about him, even if it is just the color of his tie!

"Why?" I queried.

"I believe that, on some level, people pick up on what we think and feel about them. So if you'll just hold a 'happy thought' in your mind while speaking with him, I believe your interactions will be much smoother."

At first, I thought my friend had attended one too many "power of positive thinking" seminars. But I decided to follow his suggestion and was shocked at the results. Although the prosecutor didn't give up being a "showboat," he became more calm and rational in his demeanor and dealings with me, particularly in a courtroom in front of a jury.

Again, we can't hide our thinking—it comes out in the way that we speak and act. And since we know our thinking drives our feelings, on some level this prosecutor picked up that I disliked him immensely. His behavior was the result of what I was reflecting to him; all he was doing was reacting to my reflection and the thoughts and feelings that I was conveying.

What Is the Cost of Disrespect?

The answer to this question is simple—retaliation. It's the *Law of Returns*: what we project to others returns to us in multiple ways.

GETTING EVEN

Once I was standing in line at the airport, attempting to check my luggage for the flight home. An elderly woman was at the head of the line and was having some difficulty with her reservation. The "suit" behind her was clearly in a hurry. He was obviously a seasoned traveler, and it became more and more clear that he had no tolerance for those not accustomed to flying—not even old ladies. Before long he was swearing, fuming, and stomping the floor, as though his tantrum controlled the departure of the flight. Then he started dropping one-liners to the woman and the ticket agent in front of him.

"Too old!" "Too slow!" "You're making me late!" "Get the lead out!" Through all of these mutterings, the ticket agent remained cool, calm, and collected, while the rest of us grew more disgusted with this guy's absolute insensitivity and rudeness.

Finally, when the elderly woman finished and it was his turn, the man exploded and launched a tirade of blame and accusation leveled at the ticket agent, who continued to remain calm. As the guy ran off to catch his plane, I asked the ticket agent, "How could you maintain your cool while dealing with that moron?"

"Oh that's easy!" he replied. "That guy's going to New York City, but his bags are going to LA!" Everyone in line howled with delight.

Most of the time, retaliation is not so extreme. But when people feel disrespected, they won't give you their full effort, and sometimes they even turn hostile, overtly or otherwise. Loyalty, initiative, trust, respect, and relationships go out the window—and so do your results.

How Do You Increase Respect? Pay attention to the respect people reflect to you. Notice your own assumptions about people that may influence the way you speak and act toward them. Make a concerted effort to be more respectful toward those who are disrespectful to you, and notice what they give back in the exchange. Pick out something to admire or appreciate in everyone you deal with, and take the time to express appreciation. Simply put: love your enemies—it will drive them crazy!

It's the Real Thing!—Authenticity

Authenticity is about being real, honest, truthful, and sincere. Authenticity is not something you are, but something you choose. When you understand how much power comes from the heart, you work harder at being authentic. Being authentic is an unspoken aspect of conversation. Authenticity has a certain frequency that resonates with people. When you really care about a person's well-being, they get it—your authenticity permeates your conversation—and the results are often amazing.

Of course, you need not tell the *whole truth* about everything all the time; sometimes that is just not feasible. Some information is privileged, and some personal observations are not worth sharing. But you can ensure that when you open your mouth, what comes out is the real thing.

If you are not authentic, people will know it, perhaps not consciously or immediately, but at some level they will have a gut feeling that what has been said is not true. What is not authentic will sound hollow. Besides, in most cases, the truth eventually comes out in some way or another. Is it any wonder why so much cynicism and distrust can be found in the workplace?

You have likely had the sad experience of working for or living with individuals who are not authentic, who tell you one thing and do another. It's like riding an emotional roller coaster that leaves you exhausted and relieved when you get off the ride. You sense that something is going on beneath the surface. And if you are still for a moment, something inside will tell you whether the person is up to something. When you don't trust another person, you might ask questions to discover more of what is going on. Remember, saying one thing and then doing something else is classic fake talk.

TAKING THE TIME TO GET IT RIGHT

One of our clients was going through a cost-cutting effort. We watched as a plant manager made an impassioned plea to his people for support and assistance.

He began, "The company is considering closing this plant. I'm trying to make the best business case I can for keeping us up and running, but I can't do it alone. I need your help."

Someone from the crowd yelled, "Yeah, we've heard that before. The last two plant managers said the same thing, and nothing came of it."

Another chimed in, "If we bust our butts for you, what guarantees will you give us?"

The plant manager responded, "I'm sorry about what happened in the past, and I can't make any guarantees about the future. All I can say is that I'll do my best to make this plant viable, and I'll be straight with you about what we all need to do to make that happen!"

The meeting continued for another hour as the plant manager answered the employees' tough questions and addressed their concerns.

Afterward, as we debriefed the meeting in his office, we were interrupted by a phone call. After the call, this manager exclaimed, "So much for taking off for vacation tomorrow."

"Why is that?" we asked.

"The corporation just signed a contract to outsource all of our shipping. They found a company who will package and ship our product for $17 an hour. It is costing me $38 an hour to do the job in-house. I don't want the workers to hear about this from anyone but me! So we'll meet tomorrow with everyone, and I'll postpone my vacation."

This leader understood the power of authenticity. He knew he had to deal with this difficult issue himself for people to believe him. He didn't let the rumor mill deliver the message or wait for some e-mail from corporate headquarters to break the news.

Rather than avoid the tough questions or vaguely tell people what he thought they wanted to hear, he confronted current realities head-on to maintain his authenticity and integrity.

How Can You Increase Your Authenticity? Take time to consider the authenticity of your conversations, and allow time at the end of the day to reflect on and assess your authentic effectiveness. Being authentic may also require some preparation on your part when you are dealing with potentially difficult conversations or tough subjects. Think of all the possible nasty or irritating issues or questions you might be asked and take the time to think through how you can respond authentically and respectfully.

Being authentic requires thought and preparation; most of us can't just shoot from the hip and expect to hit the mark in tough situations. If you don't know the answer to a perplexing issue, tell people you haven't had sufficient time to think about it. Then get back to them with the answers they need to do the work and to move forward with commitment and dedication. Don't avoid the tough issues. People want answers, so give them what you can, but be authentic.

It Takes Two to Tango—Desire

Sometimes the challenge in a conversation *is* the other person and not you. If someone can't or won't dance, you're stuck out on the dance floor by yourself (an unpleasant feeling). Recently one of my assistants declared, "You can try all the communication stuff you want on me; but if I'm angry, having a bad day, or in a foul mood, nothing will work. So back off!" You can't force a person to engage in the conversation you want to have if they can't or won't participate.

Some people simply do not have the skills to engage. Others have so much going on in their lives that they may be incapable of engaging at a certain time. Still others are hampered by physical handicaps, emotional trauma, psychological issues, or sleep deprivation. Whatever the reason, some people are not able to engage. We should respect the situation until they can.

Still others refuse to engage in conversation. It is difficult to make people talk or engage when they're not willing. Once we had a skilled facilitator who was told after a training session that "her services were no longer needed." That was it. No feedback or explanation. All the client would say was, "We choose not to talk about it." This facilitator had consulted with this company for a decade. She tried repeatedly to understand what she had done that warranted her dismissal—to no avail. You cannot force people to talk about what matters most, but you can increase your chances.

How Can You Increase Desire—in Yourself or Others—to Engage in a Particularly Difficult Conversation? Begin by learning the skills you need to hold tough conversations (skill increases desire). Also, you might candidly identify your life's deficiencies as the motivation for mastering the skills to create more successful outcomes. *Knowing* and then *doing* are the keys to creating different results because *doing* is *knowing*.

Creating desire in others is more difficult. You may need to give people space and time to process or think through tough issues. Increasing engagement is also about creating enough safety in the interaction that others will want to engage. Sometimes people just don't feel safe, so you need to be patient and work to build the respect and relationship that will improve your results. Consistency of respect on your part builds trust and sends the message that you value the person and what they have to offer. There is no magic wand you can use to create more desire in others, but consistent respectful behavior will go a long way to helping your cause.

What Is REAL Conversation?

REAL conversation is the process of creating dialogue. **REAL** is an acronym for Recognizing and Suspending to Uncover, Expressing Your Intention, Asking to Reveal, and Listening and Attending to Connect. These behaviors and characteristics, shown in Figure 3.2, are found in all effective conversation.

- *Recognize and Suspend to Uncover* is the ability to notice how your thoughts affect your behavior in conversation. If the conversation is not working, then you need to make a different choice. Stop what you are doing and do something different. The Suspension skill is the ability to set aside your thoughts, purpose, or agenda in order to hear and consider other points of view. Recognition and suspension require a person to be both a participant and an observer in the conversation.

FIGURE **3.2**   **The REAL Conversation Model**

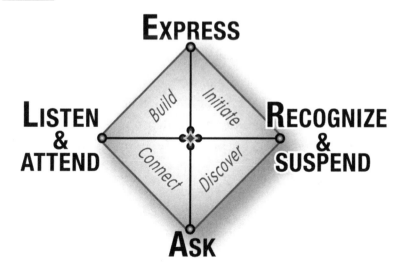

- *Express Your Intention* is sharing your point of view or your ideas from the mindset of "we" rather than "me." Sometimes we become so passionate, assertive, and even aggressive, we turn off others with our delivery. The challenge is to express ourselves in a way that invites cooperation and contribution rather than confrontation and rejection. Expression reflects intention; you must identify your intention.

- *Ask to Reveal* is the skill of asking questions to understand and explore other points of view. Asking great questions increases our understanding, creates respect, and improves engagement. The more we seek discovery, the broader our perspective becomes and the greater our learning. Answers are revealed in the asking.

- *Listen and Attend to Connect* requires that we not only *listen* to the words of a message, but that we also *attend* to all the aspects of what is not being said in the conversation. While we listen with our ears, we attend with our eyes, heart, intuition, and body. Attention in conversation is being present. We really listen and attend with all of us, and we listen past what we think we know!

The Framework for Holding Any Difficult Conversation

In addition to understanding the skills of REAL conversation, you will want to learn a simple framework or the process for holding any difficult conversation. The framework is created by combining the behaviors of dialogue into a four-step process of *initiate, discover, connect, and build.* These steps are illustrated in Figure 3.3.

What Is Initiation?

Initiation is the beginning phase of any conversation. During initiation, you want to gain the attention of your listener and then

FIGURE 3.3   The REAL Conversation Framework

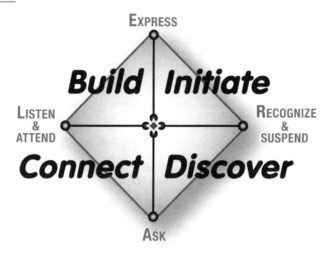

share the data of the situation as well as your interpretation of those facts. For example, you might say,

> "I'd like to talk about something that is important to me. Could we do that? *(Attention Getter)* I've noticed you haven't spoke to me for three days. *(Data)* I'm wondering if I have offended you. *(Interpretation)*"

What Is Discovery?

Discovery involves asking questions to confirm your thinking or to learn of another's perspective. In combination with the preceding statements you might ask:

> "Is that true?"*(Confirm)* or "What has been going on?" *(Learn)*

What Is Connection?

Connection occurs as you summarize what you believe you have heard and understood, any differences in values that may surface, and any expectations and consequences that are important to clarify. For example, you might clarify by saying:

> "If I understood correctly, you thought . . . ; and yet, I thought. . . . Is that right?"

What Is Building?

Building in conversation is about establishing accountability by finalizing a plan and gaining commitment to that plan. Simply, you want to build a plan, gain commitment, and increase individual accountability to achieve results. In the building phase of the conversation, you might ask these questions:

> "What could we do?" or "What could you do?" *(Plan)*
> "Can you . . . ?" or "Will you . . . ?" or "Do we agree that . . . ?" *(Commitment)*

Putting It All Together

In holding any difficult conversation, we want to initiate by describing the situation, which includes what we are observing and thinking. We discover by asking questions to gain understanding. We connect by summarizing to clarify our understanding, and we build by creating a plan and gaining commitment to improve accountability. This process is illustrated in Figure 3.4.

These are the skills and phases you will learn to create the REAL conversations that will help you achieve results, create respect, and improve relationships—conversations that are above the line. Using them will help you avoid the fake talk that occurs below the line and fails to achieve desired results.

To assess your current use of the skills for creating REAL conversations, you can take the self-assessment on our website at www.overcomingfaketalk.com/assessment.

FIGURE 3.4   Detailed REAL Conversation Framework

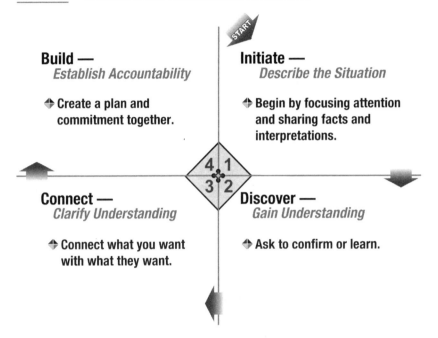

Build —
Establish Accountability

✦ Create a plan and
commitment together.

Initiate —
Describe the Situation

✦ Begin by focusing attention
and sharing facts and
interpretations.

Connect —
Clarify Understanding

✦ Connect what you want
with what they want.

Discover —
Gain Understanding

✦ Ask to confirm or learn.

In Summary

So What *Don't* You Want or What *Do* You Want?

We *don't* want to engage in conversations that go below the line. We also don't want to engage in self-preservation strategies of fight or flight in an attempt to create what we think we want while saving face. These behaviors result in fake talk—conversations that simply do not create what you want.

We *do* want to know all the skills of REAL conversation— Recognizing and Suspending, Expressing, Asking, and Listening and Attending. We also want to internalize the simple four-step framework for holding any difficult conversation. We want the knowledge of the skills that comes by using them anytime, anywhere, with anyone. But you must do to know!

Get REAL: Take the self-assessment (www.overcomingfaketalk
.com/assessment) and learn which of the REAL conversation skills
you need to learn how to use or which skills you need to brush up
on. Start to notice whether you engage in fight-or-flight behaviors.
Once you notice what behaviors you resort to without thinking,
make a conscious choice to do something different and then
notice the results that a change in behavior creates.

You might also journal your insights as you become more
aware of what you are doing with certain people. Note what helps
your conversations and what hinders the creation of the results
you desire. Engage in this activity in the context of your strengths
and opportunities you identified by taking the DialogueWORKS
Self-Assessment.

Gentle Reminders

- Recognize when people resort to self-preservation anytime they
  feel threatened or embarrassed, and realize that you are one
  of them.
- Notice the degree of respect people reflect to you, and notice
  what you are reflecting to them.
- Tune in to your authenticity, and be still as you quietly measure the authenticity of others.
- Notice the measure of your own desire to talk about what
  might be most difficult but would produce the greatest
  satisfaction.
- Identify your conversational weaknesses and do something
  daily to turn each weakness into a strength, and then capitalize
  on your strengths. Be deliberate in what you do!

You can find more information about this topic at
www.overcomingfaketalk.com/gentlereminders.

CHAPTER 4

Do You Ruin Everything by Being You?

The Reflection Principle— Reflect Reflections

You already know that the water in a river reflects what's underneath the surface. To navigate, you must see the current in the surface of the water and then match the movement of the current. If you don't match the current, your progress downstream is hindered. If you are running a motorized rig, you will use up all your gas and wear out your arm motoring outside of the current. If you are rowing, your back will give out before the day is out. You must reflect or "match" the current's flow to move downstream easily.

What Is Reflection in Conversation?

We reflect ourselves in conversation. What we reveal to people, they reflect back. For example, if you ask questions, your listener will usually ask questions back. Remember the first time you shared something really personal with a friend, and they responded by sharing something really personal about themselves? Did you wonder what happened? People will reflect what you reveal to them.

Likewise, respect in conversation is either a reflection of our own respect reflected back to us, or a reflection to us of how people want to be treated.

Generally we don't set out to intentionally sabotage conversations or interactions with others. We simply want to be ourselves . . . but so does the other person. We are different from one another, and those differences in style can often cause problems we would rather avoid.

Rather than treating people the way *we* want to be treated, we should treat them the way *they* want to be treated. It often happens that people become irritated or defensive because of the way they are treated or spoken to. Reflecting a person's reflection puts us into the flow of the conversation.

Sometimes individual differences are even interpreted as poor communication skills. Some people attending our training sessions have told us that their managers have sent them to our program to "get fixed." When we ask what that means, we hear that their managers find them to be too direct, too blunt, or too cold. This difference is a matter of style, not a "fixer-upper"!

How do we learn to recognize our differences? Much has been written about personality, behavioral, social styles, or "types." Just enter "personality styles" into an online search engine, and 15.5 million citations appear. Worse, search for "social styles" and 227 million web citations pop up. Few of these web citations pull all the different elements of communication style together. This chapter summarizes these individual styles as "interaction styles" and explains them in a way that will make it easy for you to use them to improve your communication.

Why Does All This Matter?

Research on first impressions indicates that it takes from 1/10 to 15 seconds for your brain to make an assessment about a person's trustworthiness.[4] At the same time, your brain is making judgments about the person's integrity, respect, and loyalty—based solely on the way they converse and interact. And those snap judgments are often inaccurate.

The field of social neuroscience has revealed that human brains are "wired to connect" with others.[5] Hence, the *way* we interact in fact *creates* the interaction—our behavior is reflected back to us by the receiver.[6] These reflections either help us to connect and understand each other, or they become a barrier that inhibits and stifles the effectiveness of our conversation. Being able to identify individual interaction styles will help you recognize and adapt your style—or match their style—keeping you from ruining the interaction by just being you. Simply put, if you deliberately reflect a person's reflection back to them, you will improve the conversation.

Isn't That Manipulation?

Not at all! We instinctively adapt our message to the particular context in which we find ourselves. You wouldn't speak and interact with your friends at a funeral on Saturday the same way you interacted at the Friday night football game, and when visiting a foreign country you would adapt somewhat to the customs and communication practices common in that area—to do otherwise would be considered rude and disrespectful.

When the context of our communication changes, our communication style should change to match it! Adapting to match the styles of others helps you connect with them, and creates the REAL conversations that yield the results you desire.

Of course, none of us displays purely one style. We have a *primary style* that we use frequently, and a secondary style that we learn to adapt in order to work and play with others. We may even use traits of additional styles when necessary. We make a variety of different style adaptations in different contexts from work to home, person to person, and from topic to topic.

In addition, we may also use a variety of behaviors from other styles to accompany our primary style. Don't worry—it's not that complicated, and it is well worth learning the various styles. You can recognize your style and those of others and then match their style by being both an observer and a reflector in your conversations.

What Are Our Differences?

Because our behaviors are driven by the way that we think, we need to understand the individual styles from the *mental, vocal, visual,* and *verbal* aspects that occur in all conversation. The *Interaction Styles Model,* shown in Figure 4.1, identifies four

FIGURE 4.1   Interaction Styles

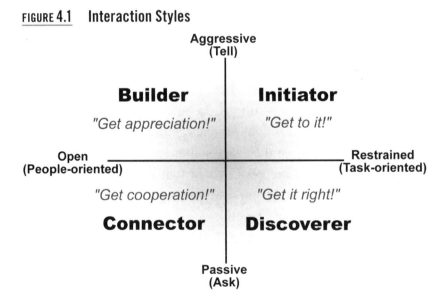

distinct styles: Initiator, Discoverer, Connector, and Builder. I'll describe the styles, explain which ones have difficulty in dealing with one another, relate how you can recognize the styles, discuss matching, and provide some tips for connecting with the individual interaction styles of others.

Let's review the different interaction styles to understand how different our styles are.

Initiators—"Get to It!"

Initiators have a mental focus that impels them to seek results and action, and they like to be in control. Although they delegate, they tend to micromanage others. To Initiators, victory or "getting things done" isn't everything, it is the *only* thing. They take charge and are driven to achieve the goals they have set. They are exacting in what they demand. They resolve issues quickly, making bold decisions in spite of apparent risks. They are typically task-oriented, not people-oriented, so they don't readily express appreciation to others. In fact, the only time they may speak to those who work for them is when they give assignments or provide negative feedback. They cannot stand weakness and are frustrated by people who are unprepared or who lack motivation. The saying *"Fire, Fire, Fire, Fire, and Fire!"* may apply to them.

Vocally, an Initiator's tone is characterized as forceful, aggressive, or arrogant. They are often accused of being too blunt or direct. As an Initiator, I once said to our marketing director, "Bryan! Note your hours. Bill me!" My spouse, overhearing the conversation, asked, "Do people like to work for you?" She was drawing my attention to my style, which is definitely not her style.

Initiators are fast, direct, to the point, and impatient in terms of tempo or pace. Their volume is emphatic, meaning they make or emphasize their points with an inflection of voice or a change in volume on a certain word. These vocal qualities can cause others to feel defensive if they perceive this behavior as a personal attack or demand.

Visually, Initiators are frequently viewed as being aggressive. Their eye contact is sustained, direct, and usually serious. They have no space limitation, so they might get right up in a person's face. They use gestures to make a point, so they may begin by whipping out their index finger and pointing at you. Or, they may make a karate-chopping motion with their hand in the air to emphasize certain words or phrases.

Initiators will face the person directly with their body and will lean in toward the person when making a point. Their facial expressions are limited but serious. They show little emotion except when angered by issues of nonperformance or a lack of results. They usually meet confrontation with coercion or describe impending consequences to the person.

When one Initiator is speaking to another Initiator, none of these behaviors comes across as imposing or aggressive, but when speaking with people who have other interaction styles, any of the Initiator's behaviors might derail the conversation.

Verbally, the Initiator uses the following types of phrases to emphasize the need to take action and achieve results:

The bottom line is . . .
Point
I need it ASAP!
Results
Get to it!
Solution
What's the deadline?
Win at all costs!
Finished
Action
Handled

Achieved
Goal
Purpose
Target
Get it done!

Initiator—Dialogue Cues and Do's

Initiators can improve their conversation skills by observing the following cues and do's:

- *Recognizing and Suspending.* Initiators are not usually open to the ideas of others because they have already decided that they are right or they know what needs to be done. They do respond well to the ideas of others that focus on completion of the task at hand.
- *Expressing.* They tend to be forceful, to the point, and even demanding. It may seem like they are giving orders.
- *Asking.* Initiators ask questions to get solutions or results, but they don't often ask questions to ensure that they have been clearly or accurately understood or to solicit different opinions.
- *Listening and attending.* They tend to listen only for agreement and support for what they demand because they believe they already know what is best.

Do's to Improve

Because Initiators are the poorest listeners of all the styles, they need to slow down, recognize that what they *know* is really what they *think* they know, and ask questions to improve and clarify their understanding. Then they need to solicit ideas from others and listen to what others have to say rather than assume they always know best.

Builders—"Get Appreciation!"

Builders' mental focus impels them to seek appreciation, recognition, and respect through their performance. Consequently, they typically like to be the center of attention. They prefer interaction with others. If they have the stage, they are in their element. They are outgoing, optimistic, and enthusiastic, and they always have a lot of ideas for getting things done. Being long on ideas, however, sometimes leads them to be short on follow-through or finishing a task. They tend to be easy-going and impulsive in how they approach the completion of tasks, so they often take more time to make decisions. The phrase *"Ready, Ready, Aim, Aim, and then Fire!"* could apply to them.

Builders tend to be persuasive and engaging. They are excellent at enrolling and motivating others toward goal achievement because they are people-oriented. They can be very talkative and are usually excited about what they are saying. Sometimes their excitement about their ideas or aspirations is interpreted as egotism or overconfidence. Their talkativeness is the result of thinking out loud as they process information vocally. Talking things out aids in their thinking process. Builders are not motivated by work that is routine because they like their tasks to be challenging and fun. They are also intuitive about what they perceive. Builders are frustrated by people who do not listen to them or who reject their ideas out of impatience.

Vocally, Builders display a varied, expressive, and upbeat tone. Their tempo is quick and fast-paced, and they often interrupt others who are speaking. They talk a lot and use metaphors, analogies, or stories to make a point or explain an issue.

Visually, Builders use varied, less-sustained, intermittent eye contact, but they are comfortable looking people directly in the eye. They move closer in proximity when speaking with others. They often touch an individual with whom they are speaking—they may touch the person on the back or shoulder or use a light touch on the forearm. Builders use many large and small gestures when speaking. They talk with their hands by "drawing" or gesturing in the space in front of themselves.

Builders will position their bodies to face individuals frontally, and they display a casual posture. They lean in when making a point, and their hands are usually open, with the palms facing upward. Their facial expressions are animated and varied. They may smile one minute and then show "questioning" or furrowed eyebrows the next. A Builder's facial expressions can often be an "open book" into what they are thinking.

They usually display a positive, optimistic emotional demeanor, but they can become defensive—even aggressive—when their ideas are rejected, maligned, or ignored.

Verbally, Builders tend to use metaphorical language, such as these phrases:

Great idea
This is "big time" over-rated.
Concept
Give it to me—off the cuff.
Cover our bases
Give me the big picture, don't sweat the details.
I'm sensing that . . .
Hit the ball out of the park!
I feel like . . .
Dazzle and baffle 'em.
I have the impression that . . .
Take the weight off your shoulders.

Builder—Dialogue Cues and Do's

Builders could improve their communication skills by recognizing the following cues:

- *Recognizing and Suspending.* Builders are often so focused on their own thinking that they fail to recognize other people's ideas. They have their own agendas, and interrupt others to occupy public airtime or to offer their own spin or perspective on what someone is sharing.
- *Expressing.* They usually express too much, too often, anywhere, on any subject, and at any time. They also think out loud and use analogies to make their points.
- *Asking.* They ask questions for approval or validation of their ideas.
- *Listening and Attending.* They listen and attend fairly well because they want to be liked. However, they may tend to "one up" and interrupt the person they are listening to.

Do's to Improve

Builders should work on being precise and concise in making their points and expressing their ideas. They should also ask questions to be sure that people have understood them correctly or that they have expressed themselves clearly. They can also improve respect and trust with others by consistently allowing others to share their perspectives and listening and giving their full attention—not interrupting—when others are speaking.

Connectors—Get Cooperation!

Connectors' mental focus moves them to seek cooperation and collaboration with others, so they like to work in teams. They prefer an environment of peace and harmony where everyone gets along. They are relationship-oriented and like the stability of doing routine work with people they can count on and who count on them. The phrase *"Ready, Ready, Ready, Aim, and Fire"* would apply to them because they want everyone to be on board and in agreement about what they are going to do before they move forward.

Connectors will go along with the crowd, even if they disagree with a decision that has been made. They rely on others to make the big decisions, and avoid drawing attention to themselves by speaking up or disagreeing. They are consistent, supportive, and well-organized; they are persistent and hard-working, and they like to be assured that their work is acceptable.

Connectors are uncomfortable with change—unless the change improves a relationship. They also want to know the rationale for any change and how it might impact them and others. Because they need to understand change, they don't like to be pressured or forced into doing things they have not fully explored. Connectors are often quiet, slower-moving, sensitive people who are frustrated by pushy, aggressive, insensitive people. They are often perfectionists so they can avoid conflict.

Verbally, a Connector's tone is friendly, mildly confident, and somewhat contemplative. Their tempo is slow and easy while their volume ranges from quiet to soft-spoken. Consequently, sometimes they are hard to hear when speaking in groups, if they talk at all!

Visually, Connectors are viewed as timid but warm and friendly. Their eye contact is intermittent if any, and they may look around the other person rather than maintaining direct eye contact. They may even look down at the floor while speaking. In terms of proximity, they like to keep at least "two arms' lengths" distance unless they know the other person.

Connectors use few gestures and are not demonstrative. They usually display a casual body posture that is slow in movement; they will lean away when speaking in a sitting position. They display a warm, gentle, demeanor with varied facial expressions. Connectors tend to be emotionally subdued; they express their feelings openly to others, but they do not show emotional peaks and valleys. They meet confrontation with deference to avoid conflict—they "go along to get along."

Verbally, Connectors might use the following words or phrases:

Team
Could you please explain that to me?
That's too risky!
Let's slow down and consider . . .
Let's work together.
Don't be in a hurry—we have to get this right.
That change is uncomfortable for me.
Everyone is an integral part to what we're doing.
What's the impact of that to the people on the team?
I'd like to hear everyone's ideas first, if that's okay.

Connector—Cues and Do's

A Connector would benefit by using the following communication cues:

- *Recognizing and Suspending.* Because they are resistant to change, Connectors can be stubborn in considering different ways of thinking or doing things. It is important that they get answers to their questions and have opportunity to address their concerns.
- *Expressing.* Connectors will not speak up to share their ideas unless everyone else in a group setting has spoken first. They tend to withhold their views or opinions unless they feel it is safe to share.
- *Asking.* They may remain relatively silent until they know it is safe to ask questions. Connectors will usually use questions to discover the opinions of others before they share their own perspective.
- *Listening and Attending.* Connectors are the best listeners of the four styles, even though they may not appear to be listening. They are empathetic and sensitive people.

Do's to Improve

Connectors need to speak up to express their views and share their expertise. If you notice that there are individuals in a meeting or a group setting who are not contributing, you may suspect that they are Connectors, and directly solicit their participation. Connectors usually have a broader view of what is required to get a job done, and they need to realize that this is valuable insight from which everyone in a group or team can benefit. Connectors should recognize their discomfort with change and take the initiative to ask questions in order to get the information they need.

Discoverers—"Get It Right!"

Discoverers' mental focus causes them to seek precision and accuracy. They are thorough about compiling and analyzing data and information that would lead them to logical conclusions and decisions. In their quest for precision, Discoverers usually prefer to work alone. They are deliberate in their efforts to accomplish assigned tasks.

Discoverers seek answers for everything in an attempt to prioritize and create solutions they have been asked to develop. They love the order, clarity, and accuracy that are required to "get it right" or to "be right." In fact, Discoverers would rather "be right" than be in a hurry. Consequently, they seek perfection in an attempt to offer the best possible solution to a problem. They do not like rendering an opinion that may reflect poorly on their capability. The phrase *"Ready, Aim, Aim, Aim, Aim . . . Fire!"* would describe Discoverers. In fact, they often suffer from "analysis paralysis."

Discoverers are wary of the decisions of others until they have completely analyzed those decisions. Their wariness might be construed as negativity, sarcasm, or cynicism. They are patient, hardworking, well-organized, and accurate, and they are frustrated by

75

people who want to make quick decisions, refuse to answer their questions, or become too personal.

Vocally, Discoverers' tone is cautious and formal, but may become skeptical or cynical if their ideas or opinions are challenged. Their tempo is deliberate and slow—as if they are carefully choosing their words or the arrangement of their ideas. Volume is usually calm and measured, and can often be monotone.

Visually, Discoverers look away from their listener when thinking, but they will give direct eye contact when they are challenged and think that they are right. Discoverers prefer to maintain ample space—at least an arm's length—when speaking with others. They become uncomfortable if their personal space is invaded.

Discovers do not usually use hand gestures when they speak. Their arms remain at their sides, with the hands down. They lean away when sitting, and they may hold their bodies in a stiffer, rigid, formal posture when standing. Discoverers demonstrate controlled facial expressions, usually referred to as a "poker face"—they can be difficult to read. They demonstrate little emotion unless they are being criticized, and then they become defensive. They meet confrontation with evasion unless they think they are right.

Verbally, Discoverers might be heard using the following words or phrases:

Figured out
Precisely
Effective
Give me the data!
Hypothesize
What is the issue?
Evaluate
What is the procedure?
Problem
What is the plan?
Logistically

76

What happened? Why?
What are our choices?
That will never work!
Whose idea was this?
We've tried that before!

Discoverer—Cues and Do's

Discoverers should pay attention to the following cues that occur in their conversations:

- *Recognizing and Suspending.* Discoverers are preoccupied with what they know or what they want to know. This preoccupation does not predispose them to being open to hearing new or different ideas unless they gain the information they seek.
- *Expressing.* They usually don't share their opinions or their thinking unless they believe they are right or have thoroughly analyzed the data.
- *Asking.* Discoverers ask well-thought-out questions to gain understanding or to seek data. They may also ask questions to scold or challenge their listener. Simply, they ask a lot of questions.
- *Listening and Attending.* They listen for the facts and answers to their questions, so they are often oblivious to the visual and vocal cues coming from other people.

Do's to Improve

Discoverers need to do a better job of recognizing and suspending their thinking when working with others, particularly when they are in a collaborative setting where the intention is for individuals to share in order to broaden the number of ideas. They should also invite others to share their views by asking questions that will get others involved. They would benefit from slowing down their own questioning, so that others have time to think and formulate responses, which will keep people from feeling like they are being interrogated.

Who Frustrates Whom?

Each of the interaction styles has the potential to frustrate the others. No one style is right or wrong; we're all just different. Let's take a look at how our differences might get in the way.

Initiators become frustrated with Connectors who are more methodical—even though they are consistent workers who persevere. Initiators may also become frustrated with Connectors who don't *appear* to be listening to them. Initiators need direct eye contact to believe they are being heard. Initiators may become impatient with Builders who take a long time to explain themselves or to get to the point. Finally, Initiators are often irritated by Discoverers whom they believe ask too many questions and who are reluctant to offer opinions or make recommendations or decisions before they are ready.

Builders have a hard time with Initiators who want them to get to the point when they may not have figured out what the point is—yet. Builders may also become defensive with Discoverers who off-handedly dismiss their ideas because of the absence of data to support their thinking. Finally, Builders may be frustrated by Connectors who go along with their ideas to please them, but do not offer any ideas of their own.

Connectors are often put off by Initiators who are forceful and aggressive. They dislike being given orders or commands, which Initiators tend to do. Because Initiators are task-driven and Connectors are people-oriented, Connectors tend to see Initiators as insensitive and uncaring toward people in general. Connectors are put off by any style that comes across as insensitive and uncaring of others.

Discoverers are frustrated by Builders who don't respond to their questions with supporting facts. They are also frustrated by

Builders' proclivity to get personal. Discoverers tend to see Builders as exaggerating buffoons or entertainers who want their attention and waste their time. As mentioned previously, Discoverers are frustrated by and frustrating to Initiators who try to force a decision that appears to have no logical explanation or rationale. Discoverers might see Initiators as reckless risk takers in the way they make decisions. Finally, Discoverers become frustrated with Connectors who try to avoid conflict by not answering the Discoverer's questions—which increases their frustration and may result in more conflict.

Bottom line: *Who we are* plays a big role in sabotaging our conversations because we are offended by styles unlike our own. So where *can* we begin? By learning to identify *who is what.*

Identifying Who Is What

The key to identifying whose interaction style is whose comes by understanding the axes that divide the Interaction Style Model into the four quadrants shown in Figure 4.2.

FIGURE 4.2   **Expressiveness and Forcefulness Axis**

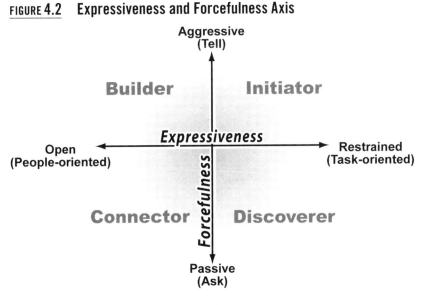

The Expressiveness Axis

The *horizontal axis* demonstrates the spectrum of individual *expressiveness*: people who are *expressive* are open in what they display to their listener; people who are *restrained* reveal little about themselves when speaking with others. Initiators and Discoverers are generally more restrained, while Builders and Connectors tend to be more expressive, more self-revealing, about their thinking and their feelings.

The restraint of **Initiators** and **Discoverers** shows up in their *tone*, which is deliberate and monotone. They make their point by sticking to the facts as they demonstrate an orientation to task. Rather than speak openly about their feelings or relationships, they focus on solutions and logic.

Builders and **Connectors** display the opposite characteristics. They are varied in their tone, use metaphor and analogy to make their points, and are people- or relationship-oriented.

The chart shown in Figure 4.3 compares the distinctions in the manner of expressiveness.

FIGURE 4.3   Expressiveness Axis

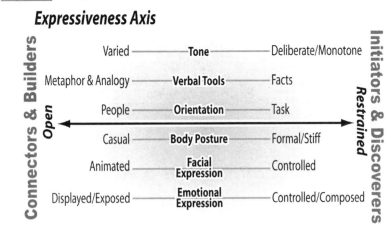

80

To identify people who are more expressive, simply ask, *"Is this person more open or more restrained in what they show or express about themselves?"*

The Forcefulness Axis

The *forcefulness* axis shown in Figure 4.4 runs from *active* to *passive* in the behaviors that participants display in influencing a conversation. Builders and Initiators are more active; whereas the Discoverers and Connectors are more passive. Consequently, Builders and Initiators are more into *tell*, *demand*, or *explain*, while Connectors and Discoverers are more prone to *ask*, *understand*, or *explore*. Let's review the characteristics of these pairs of interaction styles.

Builders and *Initiators* speak with a fast-paced tempo. They are often loud and use hand gestures to make their points with emphasis. They lean forward, give direct sustained eye contact, and move into a close physical proximity to their listener. They also use a greater quantity of words to illustrate or explain themselves— they just have a lot to say.

FIGURE 4.4   Forcefulness Axis

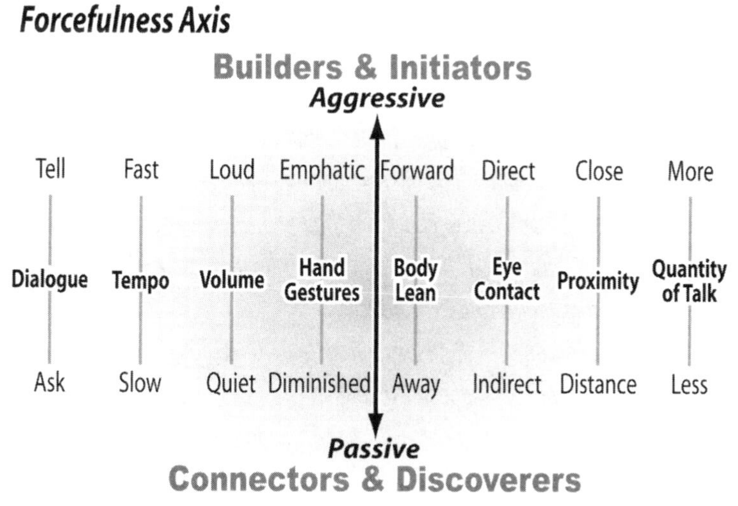

Forcefulness Axis

Builders & Initiators
Aggressive

Tell	Fast	Loud	Emphatic	Forward	Direct	Close	More
Dialogue	Tempo	Volume	Hand Gestures	Body Lean	Eye Contact	Proximity	Quantity of Talk
Ask	Slow	Quiet	Diminished	Away	Indirect	Distance	Less

Passive
Connectors & Discoverers

Connectors and *Discoverers* display more passive tendencies. Their tempo of speech is much slower. They are generally quiet or soft-spoken, displaying few hand gestures. They lean away from their listeners and give indirect, if any, eye contact. They like their personal space and require a distanced physical proximity. Finally, they use far fewer words to communicate their messages.

To identify forcefulness, ask yourself, *"Is this person more active or more passive in his or her delivery?"*

Builders and Initiators are more aggressive and forceful in their conversations. They get right to their point and push for what they want. This type of approach usually "turns off" the Connectors and Discoverers. On the other hand, Builders and Connectors are more open or personal in speaking to others about themselves and their feelings. Their candor and openness may frustrate or embarrass Initiators and Discoverers. To identify *who is what*, you might practice by doing some "mall watching." This exercise will help you to identify the interaction styles and to connect with those to whom you are speaking. Let's see if you can identify which style the characters in the following scenario portray. Ask yourself, **"More open or more restrained?"** or **"More active or more passive?"**

WHO IS WHAT?

Jack is the director of sales for a major retail company. Human Resources just hired Susan to replace one of his retiring managers. Today is Susan's first day on the job. Jack has called a meeting with Susan and his other manager, Jim, but he has asked Susan to come a few minutes early so they can talk. Susan enters Jack's office on time.

"Good you made it!" Jack exclaims, looking serious. Smiling, Susan extends her hand, but Jack doesn't take it.

"I am so glad to be working with you," Susan proclaims. "Can you tell me how you got started here? What do you think my greatest challenge will

be with my group? Could we go to lunch to discuss our department?" Susan asks in rapid-fire succession.

"Stop! Please sit down. We don't have time for this. Look, you need to know three things if you work for me. First, be on time; second, keep your commitments; and third, do whatever it takes to do what I ask."

Susan's eyes widen while inwardly she thinks, "What did I sign up for?"

"Got it?" Jack retorts.

Looking frustrated and glaring right at Jack, she says "Got it!" She pulls out a note pad and prepares to take notes. Just then Jim walks slowly through the door.

"Oh, am I late?" he asks, looking at the ground.

"No, just sit!"

Jim sits down slowly and begins to raise a concern. "You know, I've been looking at the numbers for our sales in the western region over the last couple months, and I believe we need to reassign some people to different territories. The numbers in the West are down. Have you noticed?" Jim asks as he moves his chair away from Susan's.

"Yes I have noticed. That's why I called this meeting. Oh Jim, Susan. Susan, Jim," states Jack.

"Good to meet you, Susan," Jim states timidly.

"Likewise," Susan responds, extending her hand. Jim shakes her hand quickly while averting his eyes and smiling faintly.

Jim then asks, "So what's the plan? Have you visited with anyone in the field about their problems? What do you want us to do?"

"Look, Jim, the plan is the plan. I just want you to execute it!" retorts Jack.

Jim starts, "But . . ."

Jack cuts him off with a look at his watch. "No 'buts.' I've got another meeting. Bring Susan up to speed on the problem and schedule another meeting with my assistant for this afternoon at 4:00 p.m. And please come with solutions to the problems in the field—not questions. Thank you!" Jack quickly gets up and hurries out of his office leaving Susan and Jim still seated looking at each other in awe.

Identifying Who Is What

Jack is an Initiator. He is direct, blunt, and not very personable. He wants a solution to a problem and is focused on results.

Susan is probably a Builder. She wanted to make a personal connection with Jack, which he refused, and she wanted to know about him as a person before discussing challenges with her group. She also reached out to both men by extending her hand

Jim is a Discoverer. He is concerned about problems and solutions, and wants answers to questions in order to solve challenges. He looked down when entering the room and moved his chair away from Susan, increasing his personal space. Although he did shake Susan's hand, he did so quickly while averting his eyes. Jim's behavior puts him on the passive half of the Forcefulness quadrant.

Taking the time to learn and notice the interaction style behaviors is the first step to connecting and effectively conversing with others. You can do it if you just take the time to practice observing others while they are talking to you.

To gain insight into your own interaction style, take the short self-assessment entitled "Understanding Different Styles" found in the Appendix.

Match, Don't Mimic

Matching is not a gimmick. Remember that our brains are made to connect, so rather than leaving it to chance, let's make it a deliberate act.

To form a connection and make the speaker feel at ease, you want to match his or her behavior or style. It is NOT about mimicking their behavior. If they touch their left temple with the left index finger, for example, you don't do the same thing a second after they do. More importantly, if the person you are speaking with goes below the line, you don't want to follow him or her there. In other words, if the person stands up, moves into your personal space, and starts yelling at you, don't return that behavior. Obviously, that would just make matters worse. So what do you do?

Notice the other person's general posture or the way their body leans, the kind of eye contact they give, the nature of their gestures, the tone of their voice, and the tempo with which they speak. Then gently emulate those behaviors. Once you master the nonverbal, start to notice what they speak about by asking yourself, Are they task-oriented or do they focus on people and relationships? Do they want answers to questions, proposed solutions, clarity about change or to share their ideas about the big picture? Once you understand a person's individual style, speaking to that style will increase the effectiveness and results of your conversations with that person. Your people will get that you get them.

WHY DON'T YOU CARE ABOUT ME?

Early in my consulting practice, I received a message from the VP of Organizational Development that he wanted to speak with me immediately.

I broke off what I was doing and called him. He answered the phone in a casual manner, asked how I was doing, and then proceeded to ask about my spouse, my children, and business in general. When he finally took a breath, I jumped in with, "Tell me what was so important that you need my help!" To which he responded, "Hey, I asked about you and your family, aren't you going to ask me about mine?"

What he was really saying was, "I took time to demonstrate that I care about you, so you should take the time to care about me!"

This experience with the differences in interaction style could have been costly if that VP hadn't been so forgiving. For the decade we worked together, I always took his lead and matched his Connector interaction style, even though I am an Initiator. We developed a long-lasting business relationship, and he became a close personal friend who exemplified integrity, diligence, loyalty, and service to others. The matching was well worth the effort.

Can Anyone Be All Four Styles?

You may readily adapt to different styles given appropriate context. For example, if my manager was in my face and was yelling at me, I would adopt a *Connector* stance: I would just listen because I know that the display of extreme emotion signals that the person is irrational at the moment and is not in a frame of mind to have a rational conversation. I would wait until the emotion had subsided before addressing that person's concerns and frustrations.

In identifying your own style or the style of others, I would look for consistent patterns of behavior. I would ask, "What behaviors am I seeing most consistently?" In this way, you are trying to identify clusters of behaviors to identify their style. For example, you might ask, "What are they doing with their eyes and hands? What kinds of words are they using? What tone of voice are they using?" Learning to recognize clusters of behaviors a person consistently uses will help you identify that person's interaction style. Learning to recognize and match another's style will create safety and respect and encourage them to engage in conversation.

In Summary

We are all different and have different styles of interacting and communicating with each other. Increasing your ability to recognize individual differences and then matching those differences not only improves the power and effectiveness of your conversations, it also communicates to your listeners that you care enough to "get it right," to connect, to understand, and to be understood. You would never deliberately ruin a conversation by being yourself, therefore, you need to increase your awareness and motivation to improve your conversations with others by recognizing the dynamics that may inhibit you from understanding them.

Get REAL: Start by noticing what behaviors you display in conversation, then what others are doing, and match their interaction style to improve the quality of the conversation. Remember that matching is about establishing connections with people so that personal engagement is increased and understanding improved.

If you work with a team, have a team meeting where everyone takes the simple self-assessment and then shares his or her personal style with the group. This activity would help everyone on the team to recognize interaction style preference and improve the team's ability to work together more effectively.

Please refer to Table 4.1 for a complete description of each style as well as a number of suggestions for improving your dialogue skills.

Gentle Reminders

- No one sets out to purposely offend others. Our unique differences only get in the way when we think that everyone should be like us.
- No one's style should be viewed as a liability. Everyone's style can be utilized for maximum team effectiveness or for individual development opportunity.
- Recognizing and matching the style of others will increase connection, personal engagement, and mutual understanding.
- To reflect reflections, you must learn to be a participant and a reflector in conversation.

You can find more information about this topic at
www.overcomingfaketalk.com/gentlereminders.

TABLE 4.1   Interaction Style Distinctions

ASPECTS		INITIATOR	BUILDER	CONNECTOR	DISCOVERER
MENTAL	SEEKS	Results, action	Appreciation, recognition	Cooperation, collaboration, harmony	Decision, accuracy, data
	NEEDS	Control	Interaction	Stability, approval	Thoroughness; respect for expertise
VOCAL	TONE	Forceful, direct, aggressive, confident, blunt, cold	Varied range, expressive, upbeat	Friendly, less confident, contemplative	Cautious, skeptical, cynical, formal
	TEMPO	Fast, direct, to-the-point	Varied, speaks quickly, interrupts	Slow	Deliberate, careful, chooses words
	VOLUME	Emphatic	Loud, demonstrative, warm	Quiet	Calm, monotone
VISUAL	EYE CONTACT	Sustained, direct, serious	Varied, less sustained, intermittent	Intermittent, if any; looks around or down at floor	Looks away when thinking; looks directly if they believe they are right
	SPACE	No space limitation; in-your-face	Touches when talking, puts hand on others' back, shoulder, or forearm; close	Two arms' length	Arm's length
	GESTURES	Points finger for emphasis or "chops" with hand	Many gestures; moves quickly; draws in air with hand	Few gestures; not demonstrative	None; arms to the sides, with hands down.
	BODY POSTURE	Leans in; faces front; formal posture	Leans in, faces front, casual posture	Leans away: casual posture; slow-moving	Leans away: stiff posture; rigid
	FACIAL EXPRESSION	Serious; limited	Animated; varied, smiles; an "open" look	Warm; gentle; varied	None; "poker face"; controlled
	EMOTION DISPLAYED	Little; angers easily; frustrated by nonperformance	Positive; optimistic; emotional when rejected	Subdued	Defensive when criticized
	MEETS CONFRONTATION WITH	Coercion	Aggression	Deference	Evasion, unless they think they are right

VERBAL	WORDS OR PHRASES USED	Tell me; ASAP; handled; solution; bottom line; finished; win	Idea; concept; I feel . . . . Metaphorical language: from the hip; cover our bases; big-time overrated	Slow down; team; impact on others; together; too risky; don't be in a hurry	Precisely; evaluate; problem; figured out; what's the plan?; procedure; Give me the data; What's the priority?
DIALOGUE BEHAVIORS	RECOGNIZING AND SUSPENDING	Not open; focused on task	Not open; interrupts; has own agenda	Resistant to change; maintains status quo	Preoccupied with what they know or want to know
	EXPRESSING	Forceful; to-the-point; gives orders	Too much, too often—anywhere, any subject, always has an opinion to share; thinks out loud	Non-initiating; must be invited to express	Expresses only if they think they are right
	ASKING	To get answers or proposed solution	For approval, validation, or need for understanding	Remains silent, asks for opinions of others	Asks to scold or challenge or in search of data
	LISTENING AND ATTENDING	For agreement; doesn't listen	May do "one-up"	Excellent listener; may appear not to be listening	Listens for facts and answers to questions
IMPROVE		Listen and attend: ask questions for clarity and understanding; suspend judgment	Ask questions to check for understanding; listen to the views of others	Express: speak up to contribute expertise	Recognize and suspend: explore other perspectives

CHAPTER 5

How Do You Get Out of Your Stinking Thinking?

The Perception Principle— Recognize and Suspend to Uncover

O ne of my most memorable trips on the river in Grand Canyon came at the expense of another person's thinking. Before every trip, I always provided an orientation and a clear set of rules that I wanted everyone to follow to ensure their safety. I always warned them that the rules for normal living did not apply on their Grand Canyon adventure, and our situation included some new rules that I wanted them to obey. One such rule was, "Thou shalt not put any part of your body where you cannot see!" People always laughed, and then I clearly reiterated that the rule was not a laughing matter.

A few days into this particular trip, a passenger did not look before she sat on a rattlesnake that managed to bite her rear end seven times before she realized what was happening. I will never forget the drama that unfolded. Later I asked her why she didn't follow my rule; she said that she didn't think it was that important!

In conversation, we often fail to recognize that our thinking is to blame for our results.

Why Should I Recognize and Suspend My Thinking?

We are continually making assumptions and interpretations about people and situations. In fact, our *thinking* is a main culprit in creating fake talk. For example, we *think* we've been clear, but we don't find out until we get poor results that we weren't. We *think* there will be negative consequences for speaking up, so we don't. We *think* we come across well intended, yet people take offense where none was given. We *think* that if we ask questions, we'll look stupid, so we don't ask and end up looking stupid anyway. All of these scenarios are the result of how we think.

Our thinking impacts how we speak, deal with, or treat others in everything that we say and do. Because the brain has a *mind of its own*, it influences us and drives our reactions outside our conscious awareness. So we often regret what we said or did to others while saying to ourselves "That's not me!" or "I really didn't mean that."

Finally, sometimes people's emotions seem to rule the day. We speak and people seem to become defensive for no apparent reason. When all the negative or "hot" emotion starts flying around, rationality departs—our emotions have us, rather than our having them.

To improve our conversations, we need to *recognize* how we think and why we think the way we do and *suspend* our thinking in order to examine its accuracy. Recognizing and suspending our thinking is key to increasing self-awareness and understanding others.

What Is Recognition and Suspension?

Recognition is recognizing what we are thinking and how we are behaving. **Suspension** is noticing our thoughts and setting them aside to be more objective or open to others' points of view. It is impossible to suspend if we can't recognize what we are thinking. These skills go hand in hand. To create REAL conversation, you need to understand how your thinking impacts how you feel, what you say and do, and what results you create.

Interpreting What We See

Our thinking occurs as the *Process of Perception* from data to results, which is illustrated in Figure 5.1.

Notice that **data/event** is on the far left. The person in the illustration observes through the five senses—seeing, hearing, touching, tasting, and feeling—while making observations through the lens of his or her mental models. The person in the illustration in Figure 5.1 is observing some kind of a tree.

FIGURE **5.1** **The Process of Perception**

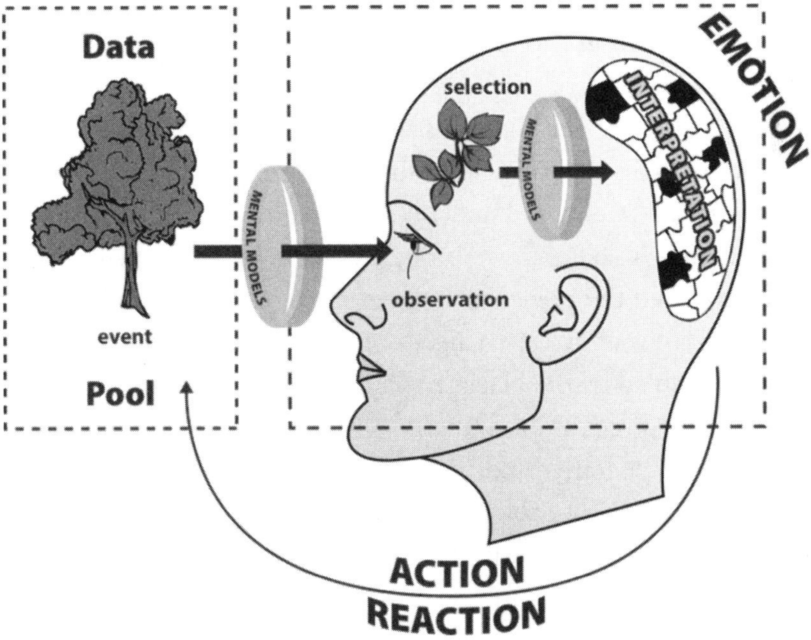

Our *mental models* are the perceptions, assumptions, pictures, or stories we hold of how things are, or the way the world works.[7] In essence, the lens of our mental models is a reflection of our own personal reality. Consequently, what is reality to us may not really be reality to others. Unfortunately, we have a hard time even considering that what we see or think may not be what we think or perceive it is.

After making observations, we engage in the process of *selection*. In this example, the person looking at the tree through the lens of his or her own mental models sees a group of leaves, but anyone looking at the same event might see the trunk, the shape of the tree, the kind of tree, the color, and so on. In short, we don't all experience the same event in the same way.

We then take our selected piece of data and filter it through our mental models again. Often we unconsciously add data from a piece of our history, experience, or perceptions to the selected data. We also may subtract or ignore the observable data that is outside the realm of our thinking or experience.

Then like pieces in a puzzle, we take our selected data and build our *interpretations* or assumptions by placing our selected observations of the data where we think they fit. We just assemble the data in a way that helps us make sense of what we are experiencing. What is quite interesting, however, is that the way we make interpretations is usually incomplete or inaccurate. If there is any chance of being misinterpreted, count on it, you will be.

Notice that the pieces of selected data in the figure's head are assembled in such a way that gaps or blanks in that person's thinking (represented by the black spaces) are evident. Those blanks signify that the pieces around them really don't fit, but we ignore how the pieces fit together and the gaps that exist and make them fit anyway. We are simply blind to any inconsistencies that signal that the way we have assembled our selected observations and made interpretations is inaccurate. We all have "gaps" in our thinking.

Here is an example of *gap thinking*. Suppose someone tells you they are from California. How would you describe people from California with a one-word adjective? You might describe them as "healthy," "broke," "liberal," or "surfers." Overall, these terms are overgeneralizations about the people in California, and not all Californians fit these particular labels. In this example of *gap thinking*, we decide *what or how something is and ignore any data to the contrary.*

The *cloud* around the person's head represents **emotions**. Sometimes the way we interpret data causes us to become **emotional**. If our emotions are "hot" or negative, such emotionality hijacks our rationality and clouds our ability to assess the accuracy of our thinking. Then our *interpretation* of events drives us to **react** or **act**. We **react** when our emotions hijack us, and we are unconscious of our thinking. And we **act** when we are cognitively conscious of the choices before us—we deliberately choose what we want. So our thinking drives our feelings, which in turn drives our actions and creates our results. Whether those results are what we wanted is another matter. Consider the following less-desirable results.

COLDCOCKED AT AN OFFICE BIRTHDAY PARTY

Jillian was headed to a bar to attend a surprise office party for her husband's thirty-fifth birthday. She was running about 20 minutes behind and knew that she would be arriving later than the others.

At the bar, her husband, Jim, was patiently waiting with three of his friends and their spouses. After having a few beers, the boys excused themselves and went to the restroom, leaving Jim seated at the table at the entrance to the bar with his friends' wives. Jim was sitting in the middle of these very attractive women, laughing and talking and enjoying himself. These gorgeous women were gathered close to Jim and were laughing, talking, and cuddling up to him. Then, one of the women gave Jim a big kiss on the cheek.

95

As she was doing so, Jillian walked through the front door of the bar, flushed red in the face, and shouted, "Oh no you don't!" Jillian marched straight toward the woman who gave Jim a kiss, reeled back, and punched her right in the nose, sending her flailing to the floor and knocking her out cold. Luckily, Jim jumped up and blocked her path to the other two women, for whom Jillian was headed.

What's going on here? Simply, Jillian observed a stranger kissing her husband and in the moment she assumed the worst, became angry, and reacted without thinking.

We're not so different from Jillian—sometimes we interpret and react emotionally. When our feelings emerge, we may even go so far as to say to someone, "You made me mad." What we should realize is that *they* can't make *you* mad; *you* make *you* mad by the way you filter and process the incoming information through your mental models and by the interpretations that you draw. This process occurs so fast that we are not really aware of what we are thinking. Then you add a strong emotion, such as anger or frustration, and your emotions obscure the thinking that created them. Consequently, our emotions overshadow our interpretations, so our thinking never sees the light of day.

Our thinking process yields a variety of results on many levels. Our feelings result from this process, along with the consequences from our behavior—our reactions or actions. What we must remember is that our emotional reactions, our behavior, and our results say more about us than anything else. Why? Because we created our results, actions, interpretations, and emotion by the way we processed the information through our process of perception.

Do Events Create Emotion?

No! You do, by the way you think. That's why offense may be taken when none was given. People's emotional reactions are of their own devising and are not within your control. Granted, an event is the point of departure in the way that we process information, but the event does not create the emotion. Your emotions are fabricated by the way that you *select* and *interpret* the data in combination with your existing mental models.

Yes, you are responsible for your feelings. For example, suppose instead of placing a tree under the label *data/event*, you place a photo of the New York City Twin Towers on September 11, 2001. How many different emotions did people experience on that day? Shock, anger, frustration, horror, bewilderment, and contempt to name a few. However, on the other side of the world, people were expressing and displaying joy, excitement, and jubilation. They were dancing in the streets. How can such a spectrum of emotion result from a single event? People with different mental models make different interpretations, resulting in different emotions.

There is good news about our emotions! Please don't think that becoming emotional is a bad thing. Having feelings is part of our human experience and frame what is important to us. The good thing about negative or "hot" emotions is that they are the bridge to self-understanding—***your emotion is the cue to*** **you**. When you become emotional, something is going on in your head—you are *interpreting*. Your challenge is to uncover the thinking at the root of your emotional reactions.

How Does This Emotion Stuff Happen?

The brain has a mind of its own, and the brain's physiology contributes to our emotion reactions. One great challenge in staying above the line and in creating REAL conversations has to do with the way the brain processes incoming messages. Your brain thinks and processes incoming messages at a "precognition level" or outside of your awareness.[8]

Becoming more aware of what happens within the brain is a key to understanding your reactive behavior and improving the effectiveness of your conversation. Neuroscience research reveals that we have a two-track mind: a purposeful, analytic *"high road"* and an automatic, reactive *"low road."*[9] The brain processes information in a two-road circuit simultaneously. Let's begin by reviewing how the brain handles incoming messages while elaborating on the different functions performed by parts of the brain, which is illustrated in Figure 5.2.

All incoming messages from our senses come into the **thalamus**, which translates information into the language that the brain can understand. In the example in Figure 5.2, the image of the spider moves through the retina along the optic nerve to the **thalamus**.

In the *"high road"* aspect of our thinking, the information about the spider travels from the thalamus to the **visual cortex**, which analyzes and categorizes the information for meaning and appropriate response. From there, the information moves to the **neocortex**, the "logical/rational" portion of the brain. The

FIGURE 5.2   **The Role of the Brain in Emotion**

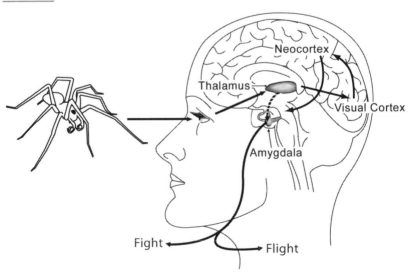

neocortex, or the thinking brain, functions as the center for conscious thought that encompasses planning, strategizing, envisioning, problem solving, decision making, or analyzing.

From the neocortex, the information about the spider is transferred to the **amygdala**. The amygdala acts as a "reactive-protective" mechanism to ensure our survival. Within six seconds of being activated, the amygdala signals the adrenal glands on top of the kidneys to secrete norepinephrine, epinephrine, adrenaline, and cortisol for an appropriate fight-or-flight response.[10]

Simultaneously, the *"low road"* circuit of our brain is also activated. Notice in the diagram, the *"low road"* circuit sends a signal directly from the thalamus to the amygdala in 12 milliseconds.[11] This "light speed" response protects us from danger by triggering a reactive response. In addition, the amygdala also triggers our emotional reactions to the event that are stored in our emotional memory. So, when individuals are triggered by their amygdala, they not only display "hot" or negative emotions, but they also engage in reactive behavior. This response is why we said that a person's emotion says more about them than it does about you. People who are *emotionally charged* are irrational and act without thinking.

How Do You REACT Without Thinking?

It's a physical thing. Your brain's "reactive-protective" mechanism is the culprit. Outside your awareness, the amygdala, commonly referred to as the primitive or "reptilian" brain, is constantly scanning your environment for potential threats. In fact, the reptilian brain is always asking three questions in this order about your current experience:

- Can it hurt me? If not, then . . .
- Can I eat it? If not, then . . .
- Can I mate with it?

The amygdala's responses to these questions are so automatic that a reaction occurs before the rest of the brain even has time to rationally process the incoming messages. Complicating matters further, the amygdala orders the secretion of chemicals that shut down the neurons in the brain that keeps it from storing and processing new information or learning. Obviously this process enables us to focus and react quickly when driven by a perceived danger.[12]

Consequently, you cannot hold a respectful, rational conversation in this part of your brain. The amygdala is not a "thinking place." Even if you are not in your amygdala, if someone who confronts you is in a state of high emotion, you know they are in theirs. Because most of us do not understand the physical nature of emotion, we usually respond in one of two ways: with emotion (*fight*) or with disengagement (*flight*). In either case, individual rationality is absent.

To make matters worse, once the amygdala orders a chemical dump into the blood stream to prepare you for fight or flight, it takes up to 48 hours before the chemicals exit the body. In other words, some people are reactive all the time. They are always in reactive-protective mode, and their emotional reactions make it difficult to speak with them about issues that really matter. So, what's the point? "Hot" or negative emotions derail conversation. Your emotional reactions are a barrier if you want to talk about what matters most.

Is There Any Good News?

Emotional intelligence involves recognizing and managing emotion in conversation. The good news is that the *"high road"* of our thinking enables us to recognize our reactions and create conversations that are above the line. If you stop and deliberately think, you can choose the outcome for the conversation you desire—you can increase your emotional intelligence.

Low road thinking also has a bright side. It is the "low road" that allows us to make natural assessments of situations as we communicate with others. These natural assessments are made by the amygdala for our protection and include assessments of the physical size, spacing or distance, volume, similarity, mood, and physical demeanor or posture of the person with whom we are speaking.[13]

Everyone always talks about wanting to be a *body language* expert. Interestingly, our brain is unconsciously making natural assessments about whether it is safe to proceed with a particular conversation or person. Consequently, our emotional reactions or feelings of discomfort serve to signal us that some assessment or interpretation has been made outside of your conscious awareness. Your challenge is to understand the nature of the assessment and its accuracy.

Recognizing your emotional reactions is a cue that you need to examine your own thinking. Let's look a couple of different skills to defuse your emotion and surface your thinking.

How Do You Recognize and Suspend Your Emotions?

Our emotions are the bridge to self-understanding. Recognizing and suspending is the process of looking to learn from our feelings as the cue to the thoughts hidden by our emotions before we react to them. Adopting the posture of looking to learn from our emotions helps us to suspend them and to surface our thinking. In suspension, we gain the freedom and clarity to see and discover the perspectives that we hold. Here is a skill that will help you to recognize and suspend your emotions and surface your thinking. I refer to this skill as SOS—an acronym for **S**tate your emotion, **O**bserve your thinking, and **S**elect the positive.

You use SOS to defuse your emotions while surfacing your thinking.

State Your Emotion

To understand the meaning or thinking behind our emotion, we first must *acknowledge the emotion.* Such acknowledgment tends to defuse the energy of our emotional state. We articulate it by writing out or voicing our feelings by finishing sentence stems.

Recipe: "I am _____."
(Fill in the blank by identifying your emotion:
angry, sad, frustrated, etc.)

Completing this sentence enables you to objectively observe the emotion that you are experiencing while releasing the energy of the emotion. The next step is to ask yourself *why* you're feeling what you're feeling. We identify the *why* by finishing the next sentence stem in the "observe your thinking" phase.

Observe Your Thinking

Next, you need to surface your thinking in order to objectively assess its accuracy. Voicing or writing out your thoughts enables you to hear and see them and become more aware of what they are. To do that, we complete the recipe below:

Recipe: "I am _____ because _____."
(Fill in the first blank by identifying the emotion
and then finish this sentence with whatever comes to mind.)

Using this process allows you to identify the emotion that you're experiencing and the thinking behind it. We often encourage people to finish the second sentence stem as many times as they can without thinking about it. Just keep writing whatever comes to mind.

This process may be completed privately by writing these sentences on paper. Or you may choose to finish the sentence stem out loud privately or have someone take notes so you don't have to think about what you are saying. What is important is to finish the sentence as many times as you can.

Suppose somebody promised you a report by the end of the day, and they never delivered the report and kept their promise. You would complete the first two steps of this process by finishing the sentence, "I'm angry because . . ."

For example:

- "I'm angry because they never follow through."
- "I'm angry because they said I could count on them and I couldn't."
- "I'm angry because it is the third time this has happened and we talked about it."
- "I'm angry because people don't seem to take their commitments seriously."
- "I'm angry because no one seems to listen to me around here."
- "I'm angry because I've only been here six months and the honeymoon is over."
- "I'm angry because I'm having my first major performance review next week, and I'm sure I'm going to hear about this."
- "I'm angry because I just don't like looking bad."

Notice that a whole lot more is going on than just a report that being late. Finishing sentences allows a person to surface his or her thinking and examine its accuracy. This process is essential in discovering what we think and learning whether it is even accurate. After all, most of us don't see past what we know let alone know what we know.

Select the Positive

Notice that all of the completed sentence stems are *negative* assessments of blame or accusation either of ourselves or the person who failed to deliver the report. Because we naturally jump to interpretations and assume the worst about people and situations that negatively affect us, we need to approach potentially difficult conversations with curiosity rather than the dogged assertion that what we see and think is reality. Finally, we want to shift ourselves out of the emotion that we are feeling by answering this question:

> ### "What would explain this person's behavior in a positive or logical light?"

Yes, we're asking you to create a *positive* or *logical* explanation for what you may have experienced with an individual, because to identify something positive, forces you to give a person the benefit of the doubt. In essence you're doing what we call **"negative thought detection, positive thought selection."**[14] This approach will shift your emotions in an instant.

Why give someone the benefit of the doubt? We realize that often you may have ample history with some people who have already proven to be jerks, idiots, or morons. This way of thinking isn't about making excuses for people. It is about your return to rationality—your improving your emotional intelligence. Consequently, using SOS helps you to acknowledge your emotion, observe your thinking, and return to rationality before trying to talk to an offending party. If you can't control your emotions in a difficult conversation, then they will control you and the outcome of the conversation.

SUSAN SAVES HERSELF

Susan is the director of Human Resources. Occasionally, she has the unsavory task of providing performance feedback to senior managers. Today is one of those days. It seems Bill, a director in product development, has made comments to some of the female employees that are unprofessional and inappropriate; in fact, it is the second time she has had to speak with

Bill. She begins, "Bill, I'd like to visit about what happened yesterday with Millie. Can we talk about it?"

"Oh, give me a break! Nothing happened! She is totally out to get me. Besides, she's the stupidest employee I've got!" Bill states sarcastically while rolling his eyes.

Susan feels her blood begin to boil as her face flushes crimson. Her internal voice screams "You pig! You are the most insensitive uncaring leader I have ever met. I'd like to fire you, right out of here, right now!"

*Catching herself, she quickly asks herself, "**What am I feeling? I am incensed. I am incensed because** . . . he is trying to avoid this conversation at all costs in an attempt to keep his job by blaming Millie! **What would explain his behavior in a positive or logical light?** Maybe he has amnesia!? Perhaps he thinks that women like his attention. Or, maybe he really doesn't know how he comes across. Maybe he still doesn't understand "'Inappropriate.'"*

"So Bill, what happened?" Susan asked more calmly and rationally than she can believe.

"I told you! Nothing happened," Bill retorts.

Choosing to stay above the line, Susan asks, "Bill would you like me to read to you my notes from your file of what happened last time? Or I would be happy to call in Millie and the other people who witnessed your behavior yesterday. Maybe that would be of help? What would you like me to do?"

"Uh, well, umm, uh, I seem to remember now as I think about it, that I said. . . ."

Susan was able to keep her emotional composure while moving the conversation toward rationality. She did try to give Bill the benefit of the doubt while not letting her feelings get the best of her. Her choice kept her above the line and helped lift Bill above the line. This approach is what you follow if you are going to address challenges and create satisfactory resolutions.

In summary, we interpret everything we see. Usually we interpret incompletely, inaccurately, or incorrectly. Our emotional reactions are the result of our thinking. When we use SOS, we defuse our emotion, surface our thinking, and select the positive or logical to shift our feelings. ***Bottom line: If you want to change your feelings, change your thinking.***

Unfortunately we are also challenged because we only see what we interpret.

Seeing What We Interpret

Not only does our brain's perception get us into trouble, but our perceptions limit us from expanding our perceptions. This concept is referred to as *self-fulfilling prophecy* and was coined by Robert Merton, a professor of sociology at Columbia University. In Merton's work, *Social Theory and Social Structure*, he said this phenomenon occurs when individuals take a false premise and then behave in a way that makes the false premise become true.[15]

For example, in our training sessions we hear, "This stuff works great if everyone's had the class!" Notice such a comment places the individual's responsibility for effective communication on everyone else. Nice try! The real "responsibility" for improved conversation falls to each of us because we all possess the ability to choose a response.[16]

However, if the individual's belief is "This stuff won't work!" then that person probably won't spend the time necessary to learn the content or practice the skills. The person's perception of the usefulness of the course content actually becomes the impetus for its failure.

This concept of self-fulfilling prophecies becomes even more disconcerting when applied to our relationships. For example, let's suppose that you believe Martha, one of your teammates, is not carrying her fair share of the workload. When you try to talk about the situation, she becomes defensive and shuts down. You come to believe that Martha is lazy and difficult to deal with. Consequently, in all your dealings with Martha you communicate and treat her in a way that reflects your thinking: demeaning non-verbal behavior, sarcastic tone, interrogating questions, and harsh criticism. Your behaviors then result in her not taking initiative, doing less work than before, and avoiding any kind of conversations with you.

Her behavior then leads you to declare "Yes, I knew I was right. She is lazy!" You want to blame Martha when all the while, your behavior toward her elicited the very behavior or characteristic you decided she already possessed. In a real sense, we create the behavior that we expect to experience.[17] People reflect to us what we give to them. It is impossible for you to look in the mirror and say, "That's not me!"

Just realizing that we interpret what we see ought to make us challenge the accuracy of our thinking. But because we see events the way we do, we just assume that's the way they are because that's the way we see them. Consequently, we don't communicate as effectively or as openly as we should because our perceptions are constantly reinforced by the thinking that created them. We must realize that there is always more than what we think.

Why Does Our Thinking Affect Results?

Our perception is a function of our selection. Our mental models influence what we select and the way we see the world. The vast assemblage that makes up our paradigms or mental models includes our values, beliefs, assumptions, interpretations, and conclusions from all of our past experience. Our upbringing, education, family, friends, peers, religious values, health, age, gender, ethnicity, culture, geography, and more all affect how we see and interpret our experience. Indeed, we never actually see reality in totality because we project all these elements of our perception onto the current reality. That should be enough to make us stop and think!

Several challenges contribute to our unconsciousness when it comes to seeing and assessing our thinking: invisibility, fundamental flaws, and negative interpretation.

Seeing the Invisible

How is our thinking **invisible** to us? We just don't stop to examine what we think—we all have blind spots. Aside from using the SOS skill that allows you to surface the thinking behind your emotion, taking time to look at your results—wanted or unwanted—should lead you to also look at the thinking that created them.

SIT ON YOUR HANDS

Beth, a manager of a group of HR generalists, took her team to a corporate conference to review new developments in the law for human resource issues. The group attended the conference meetings together. Halfway through the afternoon meeting of the first day, Beth turned to her team members, who were asking many wonderful questions, and said, "Just shut up and sit on your hands!" Everyone was dumbfounded. Not one of her team spoke up the rest of the afternoon.

Later that evening, they went out to dinner together with numerous conference attendees from other companies. When the waiter came to take drink orders, Beth told her team, "There will be no alcohol, not even beer!" Again people were shocked and surprised, but no one said anything nor did anyone on her team order alcohol.

When the meal was about over, Beth stood up, excused herself, and said, "I am taking my problem children home!" Beth hurried out of the room. Because everyone had come with Beth, they also had to leave when she departed. When the team reached the car, Beth had locked herself in the car and wouldn't let anyone in. She just stared straight ahead.

In frustration, her team waited and mulled outside the car for at least 30 minutes before Beth finally unlocked the car doors. Once they all squeezed in, she looked straight ahead and refused to talk to anyone. This "silent" treatment continued for the next two days. Even though she was asked several times, she never would tell anyone what her frustration was.

Within two weeks, two people on Beth's team had quit the company.

Why a leader would act in such an embarrassing manner is incomprehensible. But obviously, Beth's behavior or how she came across was not so obvious to her. *All of us have blind spots.* Taking a closer look at our results may help us to see the behavior—our behavior—that created our results. Making the invisible visible and learning to see ourselves as we are seen is a great way to start. Our results can help us to look at what's obvious.

Being Fundamentally Flawed

Our mental models become *fundamentally flawed* when we do the all-for-one-and-one-for-all thing! We want to apply the same mental model to every situation. As the saying goes, "Once you have a hammer, everything else becomes a nail." Even though our mental models don't apply in every situation, we apply them anyway. Sometimes the reason they don't fit is because they are overly broad, or we fail to recognize that times have changed. When the latter happens, we stay stuck in the past.

"You'll never amount to much!"

That's what my father used to tell us around the dinner table, "You'll never amount to much unless you get a good college education." By "amount to much," he was saying "You won't be able to make a living." Now, is it true that you have to have a college degree to make a good living? No! But that's how we were raised. No wonder we can claim 13 college degrees among myself and four siblings—we were programmed.

Why was education so important to my father? His father had died when he was nine. His mother, who had no formal education, was forced to take in boarders, wash floors, and work as a short-order cook during the Depression. My father went to college, served as a pilot trainer in World War II, went to law school on the GI bill, and served as a judge for the State of California for 49 years.

On the evening of his funeral, we were going through some of his personal affects. We found a small, red leather journal that

109

he had kept when he was 12 years old. On the very last page, he had written his name and under it he wrote, "The boy with a future." Then we understood his mental model about education—education meant freedom and the opportunity to live a better life. His mental model, although helpful, is no longer completely accurate today, nor does it apply to everyone or in every situation. I have a lot of friends who have made a lot of money—legally, and without any degree.

Making Negative Interpretations

What causes us to make up data and then interpret them in the worst way? Our brain is hardwired to fill in the gaps of our thinking. Unfortunately, the way we interpret events causes us to interpret the data in *the worst possible way*, partially because only 10 percent of visual information reaches the visual cortex, which leaves the brain to make up the other 90 percent.[18] Additionally two-thirds of our brain is programmed to protect our person and our ego or sense of self. So any time the brain perceives a potential threat, it starts making negative interpretations as the basis for our survival.

SEEING, BUT BLIND

Jenny was flying from Seattle to San Francisco. Unexpectedly, the plane was diverted to Sacramento. The flight attendant explained that they would experience a delay, and if the passengers wanted to get off the aircraft, they could reboard in 50 minutes.

Everybody got off the plane except for Jenny, a passenger who was blind. Stan had noticed her as he walked by and could tell she was blind because her seeing-eye dog lay quietly underneath the seats in front of her throughout the entire flight.

Stan could also tell she had flown this flight before because the pilot approached her and, calling her by name, said, "Jenny, we are in Sacramento for almost an hour. Would you like to get off and stretch your legs?

Jenny replied, "No thanks, but maybe Buddy would like to stretch his legs."

Check this: the people in the gate area came to a complete standstill when they looked up and saw the pilot walk off the plane with a seeing-eye dog! The pilot was even wearing sunglasses. People scattered. They not only tried to change planes, but they were trying to change airlines!

The way you deal with certain individuals and the conversations that you need to hold are directly affected by the way you think. Recognizing that your mental models and the assumptions behind them are often *invisible, flawed,* and *incomplete* because of the negative spin your brain provides should serve as the motivation to slow down, stop, and assess the accuracy of your thinking. Such assessment is the start of improving the quality of our conversations with others.

What Mental Models Affect Us the Most?

Not all mental models are created equal. Some mental models are of little importance while others can have a real impact on results. Recently someone in our office was struggling to make a certain piece of software perform. I overheard her agonize under her breath in utter frustration, "Arrghh! Why can't I get this right? Enough already!"

I find it fascinating to consider the assumptions underlying her statement. Consider the following mental models behind her statement:

- There is a way to get this to work.
- There is a "right" way and a "wrong" way.
- I can't get this "right."
- I am done trying to figure this out.
- I am to blame for this.

Other mental models or assumptions were probably going on but weren't divulged, but I thought it was interesting how this person saw herself mostly as the problem. Recognizing our mental models or assumptions is the beginning of understanding how we create our results and the choice to create different results. There is a mental model behind everything we do and say.

What's the Point?

Your thinking drives your behavior. If you think that you're always "right," then you probably don't solicit input and ideas from others. When you think you "can't," then you usually "don't" even try to do something about your goals. After all, you've already decided. If you always have to be in "control," you probably micromanage others and go ballistic when the unexpected occurs. All mental models come with a corresponding behavior. Here are some statements and the resultant behaviors.

Mental model: *"That will never work!"*
Behavior: The idea goes unexplored.

Mental model: *"You don't know what you're talking about!"*
Behavior: People quit listening to them.

Mental model: *"We've done it this way forever."*
Behavior: People don't explore the necessity of change or look for ways to improve.

Mental model: *"That's not my job!"*
Behavior: The person won't take the initiative to help out or learn something new.

Mental model: *"It can't be done!"*
Behavior: No one will try to implement a new process.

Making our thinking more visible, looking for flaws in our thinking, and recognizing negative interpretations let us create what we really want.

Assessing the Accuracy of Your Thinking

Assessing the accuracy of your thinking is the key to improving your results. The *Process of Perception* becomes the means for taking a look at how we think or process information. To assess the accuracy of our thinking, we need to distinguish between *data* and *interpretation*. When holding a difficult conversation, we always begin by sharing the facts, then our thinking. We'll put *data* and *interpretation* together in a minute, but let's be clear about the distinction.

What Are *Data*?

Data are "observable" or "verifiable" facts or information—events or situations that anyone might observe: "I notice you are wearing a blue shirt," or "Yesterday, I said 'Hello!' to you in the hall but you kept walking and didn't look up."

The data may show up as the Facts of the Situation, as the Facts of Expectation or Agreement versus Occurrence, or as the Facts of Behavior and Resulting Consequences.

Facts of the Situation—"You told the waiter that your fish was still frozen in the middle."

Facts of Expectation or Agreement versus Occurrence— "You agreed to be on time for our 8:30 meeting, and you came in at 9:45."

Facts of Behavior and Resulting Consequences—"The report wasn't completed on time, so I couldn't do the analysis before I met with our VP. I received a verbal reprimand."

113

Understanding how to identify the facts helps us to understand how we arrive at our assumptions and interpretations.

What Is *Interpretation*?

Interpretation is the meaning we assign the facts. For example, I might say, "I notice you are wearing a sweater today. I bet you thought it would be cold outside." It's a fact that the person is wearing a sweater, but the meaning for wearing the sweater was the result of the interpretation or meaning I assigned to "wearing a sweater."

An interpretation, then, is defined as any inference, judgment, opinion, conclusion, assessment, or assumption that is drawn by the individual from the observable facts. Putting data and interpretation together might sound like this: *"You agreed to be on time for our 8:30 a.m. meeting, but you arrived at 9:45 (data). I'm concluding that something else took priority over our meeting (interpretation)."*

The interpretation in this example is nothing more than an interpretation the speaker created from his or her own thinking, which gives meaning to the experience.

Making the distinction between *data* and *interpretation* is not easy, because people tend to see their thinking as the *facts* simply because they thought it.

Get REAL: Try this simple exercise. Watch the news, listen to talk radio, read a few paragraphs in a newspaper, or eavesdrop on someone else's conversation, and listen for the distinction between data and interpretation. You will be surprised at what you hear, but it will help you make the distinction. Don't laugh out loud, and keep your thoughts to yourself.

Why make the distinction? Because the next time you become emotional and judgmental over the actions of others, you need to force yourself to get clear on your thinking. In doing so, you may discover that there are no facts to support your *stinking thinking*. Then you'll have to admit that perhaps you make it all up—emotion, thinking, and action—inaccurately.

How Do You Assess the Accuracy of Your Thinking?

We already learned how to recognize or suspend our emotions and identify the thinking behind it by using the SOS skill; however, we didn't talk about challenging our thinking for accuracy. The *SEE* skill is the basis for assessing your perspective and moving past what you originally thought. **SEE** is an acronym for **Surface** Your Thinking, **Examine** Your Accuracy, and **Explore** Your Understanding.

Surface Your Thinking

At times our thinking is hidden from us because the amygdala switches us into reactive-protective mode. By taking the time to slow down, you can stop and surface your thinking, even during a conversation, as an effective way of keeping your thinking above the line. You surface your thinking by simply asking yourself this question:

"What am I thinking about this situation?"

This question helps you to recognize your thinking. Being aware of your thinking is the beginning of objectively examining what usually goes unexamined.

Examine Your Accuracy

When our amygdala causes us to react and become emotional, we do not see present circumstances accurately. Because the brain is in reactive-protective mode, it is trying to predict what is going to happen in the future. Consequently, the brain is skipping ahead, adding information based on past experience and making up information to rationalize our reactions. In addition, the brain excludes information it deems to be unimportant. We examine the accuracy of our thinking by asking either of these two questions:

115

"Is my thinking absolutely true?"

or

"Is my thinking what I want or need to believe is true?"

The first question forces us to focus on the relevant facts or details in the situation. The second question is a self-reflective question that challenges the repetitive nature of our thinking as well as our openness to new or different perspectives.

Explore Your Understanding

Once you have identified the accuracy of your thinking, you are in a position to clearly take a look at what you know and don't know. Asking yourself the following questions should heighten your awareness and assessment of what you really understand and where you might need to reevaluate what you think you know. To explore your understanding, you ask yourself these questions:

"What do I know?"

or

"What do I not know?"

or

"What do I need to know?"

Why does it matter that we SEE our thinking? Consider the following example that we have all experienced in some way or another.

GRANDPA'S BRIEFCASE

When Daryl got his first big promotion at work, his father gave him a wonderful leather briefcase. The briefcase had originally belonged to Daryl's grandfather, who had given it to Daryl's father when he had received his first big promotion at work.

116

One day when Daryl came home from work, he found his four-year-old son in the garage vigorously scrubbing his grandfather's briefcase in a bucket of hot sudsy water. Daryl was horrified when he realized what his son was doing.

Immediately, Daryl grabbed the boy by the arm and started yelling, "Are you dumb or what? You are such a bad boy! You are in your room for a week! Right now!" Daryl whacked his son on the rear end and carried the crying boy up to his room, threw him on his bed, and slammed the door.

Three hours later, after Daryl had calmed down and felt a little guilty for yelling at and spanking his son, he decided to try to understand what the boy had been thinking that caused him to wash his grandfather's briefcase. He entered his son's room, sat on the edge of the boy's bed for a minute and then asked him, "Son why did you wash my leather briefcase?" The boy looked up through reddened eyes and said, "I know this is your favorite briefcase, Daddy. And I love you so much that I wanted to make it really nice and clean it for you."

Ouch.

Our thinking process assembles bits and pieces of information, and before we know what we're even thinking, our emotions take over. But there is hope! The reason both the SOS and SEE skills work so well is because asking and answering your questions force you out of your amygdala and into your neocortex. This process kicks you out of *reactive-protective* mode and into *logical-rational* mode while defusing your emotions. Using these skills on yourself will help you to become more rational in heated moments and less likely to be emotionally hijacked by your brain's reactive processes. The more you practice the skills, the easier they become.

In Summary

Our *Process of Perception* causes us to interpret everything we see. Our brain doesn't help us any in its attempts to protect us from what it perceives as a source of potential harm. The brain's reactive-protective mode is what creates defensiveness before we even have a chance to stop and think about anything.

The challenge then becomes to defuse our emotions and to get to the thinking that is hidden from view. The mental models through which we see the world are often incomplete or inaccurate, which affects how we interpret what we see. Making the distinction between data and interpretation and taking the time to defuse emotion and to assess the accuracy of our thinking are the first steps in creating REAL conversations.

Get REAL: Identify a conversation that generated some emotional heat. Use SOS to identify the thinking that created the emotion. Identify as many interpretations as you can to explain why you were so emotional. As you create alternative logical explanations for the results that you received, notice if the feelings associated with the conversation subsided or shifted.

Use the same conversation to explore the accuracy of your thinking by using the SEE skill. Identify any data that would support your thinking. Write out your responses to the SEE questions so you can view them objectively.

Gentle Reminders

- Don't believe everything you think. Just because you think something doesn't make it so.
- We all have a difficult time seeing past what we think we know.
- Emotion is the bridge to understanding.
- You can defuse emotion—your own and others'—by asking questions.
- Stop, slow down, and think.

You can find more information about this topic at www.overcomingfaketalk.com/gentlereminders.

CHAPTER 6

Can You Talk About What Really Matters?

The Preparation Principle— Prepare or Beware

n the Grand Canyon, the water in the Colorado River no longer rises and drops based on the Spring runoff. The water flow through the canyon is determined by the number of air conditioners turned on in Phoenix and Las Vegas. The greater the power demand, the more water is released from Glen Canyon Dam.

Rising water makes some rapids bigger—and more dangerous. Lower water levels make some rapids smaller—and more dangerous. Running the rapids is further complicated because the water is rising and dropping at different times and in different locations on the river. The changing river dynamics demand that whenever possible you stop, scout ahead, and prepare for the rapid you plan to run.

Scouting a rapid is about looking for all the obstacles you might encounter—all the rocks and "holes." In some rapids, rocks lurking just beneath the surface can hang up your boat or even slice it in half. "Holes" are created in spots where water pours over gigantic boulders and then explodes back on itself, creating giant "haystacks." The irony of this dynamic is that the rock is always in front of the wave. You have to know which holes you can "crash" or ride and which ones you have to avoid.

Preparing to hold a REAL conversation about a difficult topic likewise is about identifying the potential barriers that will impede your success. Some people are like rocks or holes, you can't remove them from the conversation, but you can identify the dynamics they create and plan how to successfully navigate them in order to move forward.

What Really Matters?

Whatever keeps you up at night is what really matters! Any of the issues that you need to confront, such as violated expectations, broken promises or commitments, poor performance, low accountability, difficult people, and poor attitudes, demand your attention.

Then you have all the personal relationship issues—money, sex, health, in-laws, and other competing issues—that disrupt your peace and harmony. If you have children then you know that they also present challenges by not doing their homework, trying drugs, and doing everything else on the planet to drive you insane.

Even though we know what keeps us up at night, we often avoid talking about such issues because we just don't know what to say— we lack confidence in our ability. Others fear the outcome of the unknown, so it's easier to turn a deaf ear and hope everything will just "go away" or fix itself. But it doesn't go away. In fact, it may get worse unless you choose to talk about your "*Undiscussables.*"

What Are "Undiscussables"?

Have you ever heard the voice in your head? Sometimes it provides insight, inspiration, and hope. At other times it is full of doubt, accusation, and blame. This "headspeak"—as we call it— is ongoing and it keeps us from talking about what matters most by offering a never-ending laundry list of negative consequences should we even venture an attempt.

More often this internal voice is judging, criticizing, editorializing, and analyzing everything we are observing and experiencing. These mental musings are nothing more than our interpretations. We call everything that we *think* and *feel* and *don't say* our Undiscussables.[19] Why undiscussable? Because we keep these thoughts to ourselves along with the feelings that they create. Then they fill us up, and we act them out. Likewise, we also possess an external voice that includes everything that we *say*. Consequently, we are always running two conversations: the one in our head and the one coming out of our mouth. If we only listen to the one in our head, we don't hear anything else.

Why Prepare?

We already discussed how our amygdala or "unconscious" brain acts as a reactive-protective mechanism. Likewise, our "subconscious" runs a "protective-illogical" mechanism to protect our ego or sense of self. When these parts of our brain manage the conversation, problems arise. When we don't prepare, our subconscious reacts to protect us, and thoughts suddenly burst out of our mouth with accompanying emotion and nonverbal behavior. Such conversations don't represent our best intentions. Consequently, the lack of preparation leads to fight-or-flight responses in conversation.

If we take the time to think about the conversation we want to hold and give a potentially tough topic deliberate, purposeful preparation in our "conscious" brain, then we are literally creating a different reality. By thinking through a difficult issue, you prepare your mind, heart, and the conversation to increase the likelihood of success.

Why Don't We Speak Up?

Most people avoid talking about important issues whenever they think they might feel threatened or embarrassed for doing so.[20] If people perceive negative personal consequences then they are less likely to speak up. What keeps us from talking about difficult topics is that we project onto others what we think they think and feel, and even what they will do or how they will respond. All of this projecting is nothing more than our perception of what we think will happen. Consequently, important issues go unexplored because our perception is reality.

Holding REAL conversations takes courage to speak up and tell it like it is—telling the truth. This is a scary proposition for even the most competent and brave-hearted souls. We just don't know what the results or consequences of speaking up will be. We are afraid. One well-known entrepreneur, Wilson Harrell, tells of his confrontation with fear.

BURIED ALIVE

"As a fighter pilot in World War II, I was shot down behind enemy lines and was picked up by members of the French Underground. They devised a unique and cynical way to hide me from the Germans: they buried me in a cornfield with a hose stuck in my mouth so I could breathe. The first time they buried me, I lay there for four hours—time enough to consider all the bleak possibilities. I figured the Germans would (1) stick a bayonet through the dirt into me; (2) riddle the ground with bullets; (3) accidentally kick the hose; or, worst of all, (4) hook up the hose and turn on the faucet. For eight days in succession, I was buried; for eight days, I lived with a new and unwanted friend—stark, raving fear."[21]

Harrell's fear was the result of imagined scenarios. Although none of these outcomes became reality, the fear that he experienced was created by his thought process in this situation.

Predictably, people act out of self-preservation—in accordance with what they believe or perceive to be true. Is perception reality? It is to the person who perceives it! Hence, the word *fear* aptly serves as the acronym for **F**antasized **E**xperience **A**ppearing **R**eal. Our fear of the negative consequences and our inability to manage our fear inhibits our speaking up.

Over the years, we have asked thousands of individuals, managers, and leaders what they believe will happen if they talk about difficult topics. Here are their feared consequences.

1. *"I could lose my job!"* Why do we jump to such extremes? Such a statement makes a person wonder what has happened in the past. Has the individual seen others lose their jobs for sharing a different perspective or speaking up? If they have, then such thinking may be justified. On the other hand, such an overstatement is an easy way to avoid taking responsibility to share what might lead to solving major problems and making necessary changes.

2. *"I don't know what to say."* This situation implies a "right" or "wrong" way for what needs to be said. Absent an understanding of "how" to say it "right" or what should be said, most of us avoid saying anything. We need to understand that sharing a perspective in the spirit of learning and improvement rather than criticism and blame will carry the day. It's the feeling, not the words, that matters.

3. *"I don't want to hurt their feelings."* Why do we equate giving others feedback with hurting their feelings? Does it mean we would accept poor performance rather than run the risk of "hurt" feelings? This statement feels like some semblance of a relationship is more important than results. Most of us actually want to know when we have broccoli in our teeth or when we are not meeting expectations. When we know what is

wanted, we can change, improve, and deliver what is expected. And yet, we assume everyone is too thin-skinned to hear the truth.

4. **"I'm uncomfortable with how the person might respond."** This statement is political speak for, "I hate dealing with conflict, emotional reactions, or defensiveness in any form." People feel this way because they don't know what to do when emotion shows up and smacks them in the face. Still others are afraid of how they might respond when they have a short fuse. Most of us go to great lengths to avoid confrontation or conflict.

5. **"I want people to like me."** This consequence assumes a negative cost associated with speaking up, telling the truth, or expressing our opinions. Rather than tell it like it is, we feel it's just easier to keep our thoughts to ourselves. After all, who wants to be labeled a "trouble maker," a "naysayer," or the "devil's advocate"? Part of wanting to be liked is also about wanting to be viewed as capable or competent. Some may think, "If I speak up and reveal how little I know, then perhaps people won't like me."

All of these consequences have two elements in common: they are all projections about what people believe will happen to them in the future, and each consequence leads to silence—no one speaks up! Paradoxically, these fear-based stories we tell ourselves may create the outcome we are trying to avoid. For example, if I think, "If I say that, I'll lose my job," then I choose to say nothing. Later, my manager finds out that I knew about the issue and chose to say nothing, so I lose my job. We assume that we can't change our forecast of the future by how we act in the present. Unfortunately, how we act in the present may create the future we are trying so desperately to avoid.

What Is the Cost of Silence?

No results is the cost of silence! You may get more of the same, or things may get worse. The advantages for speaking up far outweigh keeping your mouth shut and your head in the sand.

Today, more people are not speaking up for fear of the consequences. Recently, Towers Watson, a consulting firm, completed its "Communication ROI Study" that noted: "Effective employee communication is the leading financial indicator of financial performance and a driver of employee engagement. Companies with highly effective communication have a 47% higher return to shareholders over the last five years."[22] The study specified that employees really want to know what tough decisions are being made and what feedback customers are providing. The study emphasizes that companies need to have courage, step up, and "tell it like it is."[23] People respond to the truth.

Many business reasons support the need to speak up: to increase learning, to solve problems, to improve performance and motivation, to increase productivity and profitability, to manage change, to accelerate decision making, to express appreciation, to enhance teamwork, to increase respect, and to build trust. We can ill-afford to underestimate the cost of silence. Speaking up and telling the truth is critical to professional effectiveness.

CLOSE DOWN THE COMPANY AND FIRE EVERYONE

An Irish trucking company recently purchased a local U.S. company. An executive from Ireland arrived to hold a meeting to review what would happen to the company in the near future. The first thing she did was ask to see a map of all of the company's distribution centers.

After going over the map for several minutes, she announced, "These distribution centers are much too close to each other. We need to make plans to close at least half of the centers and lay off the employees who work at the centers." No one said a thing.

She spent the next half hour calculating how much the company would save by laying people off and saving money by being more efficient. Still, no one said a thing.

Finally, someone asked, "How close are your distribution centers in Ireland?"

"Well, we've found that having distribution centers within 10 miles of each other helps us to efficiently serve our customers," she answered. "Why do you ask?"

"Well, I don't know if you noticed the key on our map, but none of our distribution centers are closer than a 100 miles from each other," responded an employee.

"Really?" she asked.

Someone finally asked questions and spoke up before the decision was made that would have significantly affected the profitability and efficiency of the company. Remaining silent is a common practice. No one wants to challenge management, look bad, or open his or her mouth and remove all doubt. It is just easier to say nothing than run any kind of risk. Our fears can rule the day.

What Supports Our Fear?

All our fears of the consequences are the product of our thinking. Neuroscientists believe that we have approximately 60,000 thoughts a day, and 80 percent of those thoughts are negative.[24] That's about 1,920 negative thoughts an hour—42,080 negative thoughts a day! No wonder we often allow our fears—our negative thoughts—to determine whether we speak up and create different results!

Our fears arise out of our history, mental models, and past experience—whether real or imaginary—and are supported by our justifications or assumptions and our inability to objectively identify our thinking.

Supporting Justifications

To support the fear-based assumptions that we adopt to avoid speaking up, we rationalize our assumptions with justifications for not engaging others. Some justifications are well founded. Other times we fabricate them to excuse or to justify our inaction. We've captured several of these justifications for your consideration.

1. *"There's not enough time."* Sometimes this justification is true. We are behind. We are overworked, so we tell ourselves we don't have the time, we can't make the time, or we won't make the time. A corollary to this justification is "I need to simplify."
2. *"It doesn't really matter."* Since when does not talking about improving anything not matter? It's just easier to make such a statement and move on. If it doesn't really matter, then no one need do anything.
3. *"No one cares about that."* What a great way to make a judgment for everyone else, keep it to yourself, and never find out whether others do care about it. Excluding everyone from the problem-solving process doesn't create a better solution.
4. *"It's not my place."* This justification is akin to "it's not my job" or "I'd better stay on my own turf." It allows you to limit your responsibility to whatever you deem your responsibility to be. How convenient!
5. *"Something else is more important."* This justification is about priorities and determining that something else "matters more." In a sense, this statement rationalizes an unwillingness to engage and be responsible.

So what do our fears of the consequences and these justifications have in common? Both are interpretations—stuff we make up in our head. Both contribute to silence and inaction.

Get REAL: Think of an issue that you need to discuss but have been avoiding. Ask yourself: "What might the consequences be if I bring up this topic?" Now take an honest look at the justifications you are using to avoid holding the conversation. Finally, check your thinking about these justifications. Are your assumptions accurate? Do you have any supporting data?

Can You Recognize Undiscussables?

Undiscussables are easy to recognize, whether they are your own or someone else's. When you see negative emotion, hear blame stories, or notice that everyone is talking about a problem *except* the person who needs the feedback, you know that undiscussables are in control.

THE PATIENT IN 2033

A hospital administrator was visiting the floors of his hospital to make observations. As he was passing one nursing station, he stopped briefly to eavesdrop on a conversation a group of nurses were having. Here is what he heard:

"That patient in 2033 is a major pain!" one nurse whined.

"No kidding! She calls me in just to turn on her TV and then wants me to turn it to her favorite channel. Why doesn't she do it herself?" another groaned.

A third nurse contributed, "Yeah, she's lazy. She always wants help to go to the bathroom. She is able-bodied enough to do it herself, so I take my time."

"Sometimes she asks me to open her milk carton. Honestly, some people are pathetic!" announced another.

By this time, the administrator was about ready to lose it. The patient in 2033 was a longtime family friend who had only been admitted the previous day.

Calmly, he walked up to the nurses and said, "Excuse me, I've heard enough, thank you. It might help you to know that the patient in 2033 is a friend of my family. She is blind! I'm sorry it was omitted from her chart." With that, he turned and left.

We tend to be quick to make assumptions and judgments about people, assign blame, and get emotionally worked up over things. Recognizing these behaviors in ourselves and others signals the presence of Undiscussables. We would do well to adopt a more objective perspective while exploring and testing what we think we know.

Get REAL: Think of a conversation that didn't go particularly well. Take a piece of paper and draw a line down the middle of the page. Try to recreate the conversation in the right-hand column by writing everything that was said by both parties. Then on the left-hand side of the paper, write down everything that you **thought** and **felt** but didn't say. Review your thinking and feelings and ask yourself what the benefit might have been for sharing and exploring what you kept to yourself. Did remaining silent keep you from getting what you really wanted?

Should You Always Share Your Undiscussables?

It depends! If you find yourself complaining about the same issues, blaming the same people, or experiencing emotional drama, and you never talk to the parties involved, then perhaps it is time to do some serious self-reflection. We're not saying that you should always share your undiscussables. Some things are better left unsaid. However, you need to decide if sharing what plays over and over in your head is worth the cost. Consider asking yourself the following question:

"What will it cost me to share or withhold my thoughts?"

This question is intended to help you stop, think, and make a conscious choice about what you want to create for yourself. Only you can count the cost. Only you can decide what the cost for sharing or withholding your thinking might be. If you believe speaking up will create a rift in a relationship, diminish respect, or get you fired, then keep your thoughts to yourself.

Exploring Undiscussables requires the courage to self-reflect. The intent in identifying your undiscussables has always been to surface and challenge your thinking and your feelings as a measure of improving your results. Once you have determined that sharing your thinking is worth the effort, you are ready to begin your preparation.

Preparing Your Mind and Heart

Few (less than 5 percent) leaders prepare to hold potentially difficult conversations. No wonder those conversations go awry! No matter what you *think* you are projecting, what is *really* in your head leaks out in your feelings, words, and actions. If you don't establish a clear-cut path through a conversation, who knows where you might end up!

Prepare your mind and heart by clarifying your assumptions and identifying your intent.

What Are Your Assumptions?

We all make assumptions, judgments, and evaluations about certain people in certain situations. They are influenced by our mental models and our history with the individual. These opinions are our *undiscussables*. Take a moment to surface and challenge your assumptions. (You might use the previous exercise.) This process enables you to examine your thinking more objectively before the conversation. If you don't look at your thinking, you risk having invalid assumptions influence the entire conversation. Identify your assumptions by doing an **Assumption Check**.

Clarify Your Assumptions. To check your assumptions, ask yourself: *"What am I feeling, thinking, or believing about this person in this situation?"*

130

Once you have identified your assumptions, ask yourself the next question: *"What is the other person in this conversation feeling, thinking, or believing about me in this situation?"*

The first question allows you to take a look at your feelings and the thoughts that drive them. Then you can think about whether your thoughts are accurate. Suppose, for example, that someone who works for you is constantly asking you to validate or acknowledge her positive performance. The behavior has become quite annoying, to the point that you wonder if she really *does* know what she is doing. You decide to hold a conversation to understand what is going on with her. As you begin to prepare, you answer the first Assumption Check question like this:

> *"I am angry and frustrated. Ingrid has worked for me for eight years. I'm thinking that she's absolutely clueless!"*

The thought that Ingrid is clueless will come across in the way you speak and act toward Ingrid, especially in this conversation. If you want the conversation to be respectful, you need to clear your feelings and thinking—you have to recognize them and suspend them. If you do nothing more than identify some data that supports your thinking, you may get yourself out of "attack" mode. Bringing your feelings and beliefs to the surface creates newfound awareness that allows you to challenge your thinking and shift out of your current frustration. Simply answering the question aloud clears a space for new thoughts and a more focused intention.

Next, you could answer the second question from Ingrid's perspective like this:

> *"She is probably feeling insecure about the manner in which she does her work and maybe a bit fearful about having a conversation with me. She might be thinking that she has done something wrong or that I don't appreciate the value she adds."*

Considering the situation from Ingrid's perspective forces you to get out of your own skin and into hers. Admittedly, we are asking you to *guess* at the other person's feelings and thinking, but it is a wonderful opportunity to see the situation from a different perspective. This question also allows you to anticipate how the other person might respond when you engage in the conversation.

Even though your guesses about Ingrid's thoughts and feelings may be off the mark, your attempt to look at the situation from her perspective will help you be more respectful during the interaction. You are more likely to ask questions to try to understand any negative emotions she may bring to the conversation, and you can better help her surface her own version of reality. Remember, just because you think something about another person doesn't make it true! Asking respectful questions is the only way to understand what is really going on with someone.

Once you have checked and cleared your assumptions, identify your intention.

What Is Your Intention?

Your intention is the **purpose** you want to achieve in holding the conversation. Identifying your intent will focus the conversation and keep it on track.

When talking about tough subjects, people will often employ several different tactics to derail the conversation. For example, one employee we had always emphasized his latest résumé of accomplishments whenever we tried to hold a constructive feedback conversation with him to improve a few substandard behaviors. It seemed to us that his feeling was that if he emphasized all of his great work, it would be difficult or impossible for anyone to bring up his poor performance in other areas. It felt like he was trying to talk his way out of a traffic a ticket!

Blaming is another common tactic people use to derail conversations. Once I approached an employee about a deadline she had missed. Before I could even begin the conversation, she shot out, "If your instructions had been more specific and emphatic, I would have realized how important it was to meet this deadline!" In her mind, I was to blame for her poor performance!

Holding a tough conversation can sometimes feel like trying to herd cats. No matter what derailing tactic a person tries to use, stay at ease, maintain your composure, and continually refocus the conversation on the topic at hand. In the conversation with my blaming employee, I responded, "I'll be happy to talk about how I can improve my directions after we are done here. Right now, I'd like to talk about what kept you from meeting your commitment and what you will do going forward to keep it from happening again."

Identify Your Intent. To identify your intent, do an **Intention Check** by asking yourself, "*What do I want?*" or "*What is my purpose?*"

Several years ago, I used an Intention Check to prepare for an uncomfortable conversation with my son about his grades. To my surprise, I responded to these questions with, "I want him to feel so guilty for getting a 'D' in Chinese that he will never dare to not do his homework again!" I realized that this conversation was doomed from the beginning. Because I identified my intention, I was able to stop and rethink what I wanted from our conversation. (If you don't know what you want out of a conversation, then you will never know what you might get.)

Also, try asking these questions from the other person's perspective. You might come up with some ideas that will help you be prepared to maintain the focus of the conversation.

The Challenge in Identifying Your Intent

To focus your intent in a conversation you must be clear about what you *want* as opposed to what you *need*.

WHERE ARE YOU?!

Sally, a director of sales, was visiting a client with one of her salespeople about an hour away from their corporate office. Her cell phone rang, and she answered the call from Erin, her new boss.

"Where are you?" demanded Erin.

"I'm visiting a client's site! Why?" asked Sally.

"All the directors of sales are sitting in front of me for a very important meeting—everyone except you! Why aren't you here?" she demanded.

"Gosh, I never received notification of your meeting, and your assistant didn't put it on my calendar," Sally responded.

"That's no excuse! You are supposed to know what you're doing. I need you here—now. So what am I supposed to do?" screamed Erin.

"I'm sorry. I didn't know. Hold the meeting, and I'll catch up on what I missed," Sally replied.

"Fine! Did I really promote you to director?" Erin hung up the phone.

What did Erin want? She *wanted* Sally to be at her meeting. However, Erin's *needs* are different—in this case, she needs to be in control and to be right. She also needs to send a message to the other directors listening from the meeting room that she expects them to read her mind or anticipate her every desire.

When you identify what you want, but then act incongruently, you know your *needs* are overriding your *wants.* Being clear about your purpose or intention for a conversation will help you to stay focused and increase the likelihood that you will achieve your desired results. Unfortunately, we usually do not discover that we have not been sufficiently clear until we get results that we did not want.

Context Helps with Intent

In addition to asking yourself questions about your assumptions and intent, you might want to ask yourself some of the following questions that will help you identify the context of the conversation. (Context includes anything that might have an influence on the conversation.) These questions will help you clarify your intention and formulate what you might say to the person. You will want to consider the purpose of the conversation, the person involved, the current status of your relationship with that person, past events or behavior, and the plan for moving forward. Consider these questions:

Purpose
"What is the topic of the discussion?"
"What do I want? Why?"

Person
"Who is the person?"
"What position do they hold?"
"How do they usually deal with this topic?"

Relationship
"What is the current status of our relationship?"
"What is the current level of trust?"

Perception
"What happened/is happening?"
"What are the facts in this situation?"

Plan
"What are we going to do?"
"How will we get there?"

Your reflection on these topics will help you prepare to hold the conversation more effectively. You will find value in *attempting* to answer these questions, even if you are in doubt as to how this person may actually respond. Your answers to these questions determine the mindset with which you will approach the conversation. If you are prepared, you need not beware.

Preparing the Conversation

We are frequently asked, "How do you begin a conversation like this?" Begin a conversation by using an **Attention Check** to focus the attention of your listener and increase that person's engagement. The Attention Check is not complicated: clearly **state your intention** and **ask permission** to proceed. Putting it together could sound like this:

> *"I'd like to talk about the report you*
> *presented at yesterday's meeting."*
> (Intention)
> *"Can we do that?"*
> (Permission)

Beginning the conversation in this way is like "sign-posting" or framing the conversation to follow. It is like saying, "This is where I want to go. Will you come along?"

Watch Your Words

Use positively charged words rather than emotionally charged words. The words you use should enable people to hear your message and not put them on the defensive. Table 6.1 provides a partial list of emotionally charged words you should avoid, along with possible positive replacements.

Words that are emotionally charged create defensiveness. Using them will often defeat your purpose because the individual will likely resort to his or her own thoughts in self-defense.

When you begin a potentially difficult conversation with an Attention Check, keep your words neutral by keeping your tone of voice and nonverbal behavior neutral as well. If you have clarified your assumptions to prepare for the conversation, this part will be relatively easy. If you are still holding on to negative feelings

TABLE 6.1   Choosing Positively Charged Words

EMOTIONALLY CHARGED	POSITIVELY CHARGED
Stupid	Uninformed
Problem	Challenge
Poor	In need of change
Cowardly	Careful
Loud	Extrovert
Cheap	Frugal
Objections	Concerns
Lied	Misspoke
Lazy	Uncommitted
Pushy	Assertive
Didn't do it right	Unprepared
Unacceptable	Redo

and thinking, then the words you choose will be irrelevant—your energy will color your meaning despite your neutral words.

Be Neutral or Positive

Your Attention Check should be a neutral or positive statement. You would *not* want to say this, for example: *"I'd like to talk about how your leadership style is like Attila the Hun. Do you have a minute?"* A more effective, simple, neutral Attention Check could be: *"I'd like to talk about your leadership style for a minute. Can we do that?"*

To make it even more positive: *"I'd like to talk about how you might capitalize on the strengths of your leadership style. Can we do that?"*

Your statement of intention should create interest, not resistance. We suggest you follow an old river-runner adage, "When in doubt, pull it out." **Bottom line: If you wouldn't want someone to say it to you, then don't say it to them!**

Finally, notice that the questions at the end of the statement are not necessarily creative. Simpler is better: *"Can we talk about it?" "Is now a good time?"* or *"Do you have a minute?"*

Get REAL: Think of a conversation you need to hold and craft an Attention Check. Begin with "I'd like to talk about. . . ." Then end in a question that invites them to engage, such as "Can we do that?" Read what you have written out loud so that you can get a feel for what you have created. If you do not like how it sounds or feels, then rewrite the sentence. Or try the Attention Check you create on someone else and see how it strikes them.

Using the REAL Conversation Framework

Once you have prepared yourself to hold the conversation, you are ready to use the conversation framework to prepare the conversation itself. The REAL conversation model shown in Figure 6.1

FIGURE **6.1   REAL Conversation Framework**

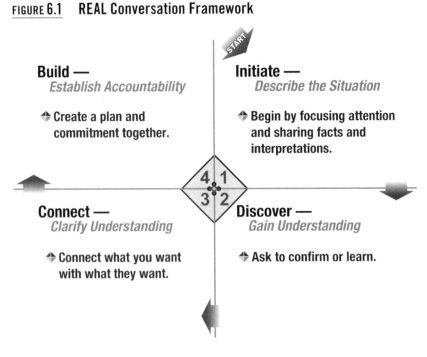

will help you navigate any difficult or undiscussable conversation. Before we review the model, let's apply the framework to a story to help you understand how it works.

CAN'T YOU GET IT RIGHT?

Mae has been promoted to manager in a graphic design department because none of the other designers want the responsibility. Mae knows practically nothing about leadership or about managing. To make matters worse, Mae used to work under some of the designers in the department before she was promoted.

Mae is not good at setting clear expectations, nor is she proficient in prioritizing assignments for others.

One day Mae assigned Sue to build a set of presentation slides for the director of professional development. She gave Sue an older set of slides that the director had created sometime previously to use as an example.

Mae told Sue, "Make the new slides like these, but upgrade the photos and content to match the manual he created."

Sue completed the assignment and submitted the slides to Mae.

In Mae's weekly staff meeting, Mae took Sue to task in front of the entire team.

"Why couldn't you get these slides right?" Mae demanded.

"What do you mean by that?" Sue protested.

"There are too many slides. The director will never be able to get through them all. This is the second time you've done this, and it's frustrating!" Mae announced in front of everyone.

Sue asks, "Mae, could we talk about this after the meeting?"

"I guess." Mae confirmed as she moved on to another topic.

Obviously, no one wants to be put on the hot spot in front of others. Sue's challenge now is to prepare a REAL conversation that will improve results while maintaining respect and building the current relationship. Let's review the four phases of the REAL conversation model in this context: ***Initiate Discover, Connect, and Build***.

Initiate to Begin

Sue ought to begin the conversation by using an *Attention Check* to engage Mae, sharing the *facts*, and then her *interpretation* of those facts. These three components will help the conversation to begin well.

Attention Check. The Attention Check introduces the intent for holding the conversation while positively engaging the other person. Sue might begin with this Attention Check: *"Mae, I'd like to talk about increasing my work efficiency. Can we do that?"*

Notice that Sue has chosen to address how tasks are given and completed, not the lack of Mae's respect by criticizing her in the meeting—that issue is a different conversation.

Share Facts First. The facts are the verifiable data that are the subject of the conversation. The facts in this conversation might sound like this: *"When you gave me the assignment to build a graphic presentation for the director, you gave me the slides he had created and asked me to upgrade the photos and match the content to the manual he created. I completed the assignment and submitted the presentation to you. Then in our meeting you said, 'There are too many slides.'"*

Notice this statement is nothing more than a repetition of exactly what happened—the facts.

Share Interpretation Second. The *interpretation* is the meaning you assign the facts. The challenge in sharing an interpretation is to do so in a way that is respectful. The easiest way to sabotage a conversation is to share your interpretation or assumptions "as if" they are the truth or the facts because this approach immediately creates defensiveness. When you push your reality against someone else's reality, you create resistance.

140

It is also important that the interpretation not blame or accuse the other person. Sue should not say, for example, *"I believe you are a lousy manager because you don't have any idea what you're doing!"*

Instead, Sue would be more effective if she shares the following interpretation: *"I'm thinking that you have received some feedback about the number of slides—some feedback that I did not receive."* Notice that this interpretation gives Mae the benefit of the doubt.

Now, you might think that this statement is not really what Sue is thinking, and that what she would really like to say is something like, *"I believe you have a difficult time giving clear and specific directions."* This interpretation accuses Mae of being a bungling, incompetent manager. If Sue goes this direction, the conversation will almost certainly spiral downward.

The principle of Initiation is that we begin well so that we will end well. *Ending well* in this case is about changing the way Mae and Sue work together to improve results, not about making Mae bad, stupid, or wrong . . . or even about Sue defending her "right" position.

Discover to Learn

The purpose of Discovery is to increase understanding and to discover the perspective or thinking of the other person. Asking good questions will increase respect and help us to identify solutions that will improve results. In Discovery, we ask two types of questions: questions to confirm and questions to learn.

Confirmation Questions. Questions to confirm are about "checking out" your thinking, so they should follow your interpretation. For example, Sue might say, *"I'm thinking you received some feedback about the number of slides—feedback that I did not receive. Is that correct?"*

The question, "Is that correct?" is simple. Your intent in this phase is to have the other person comment on how accurate or complete your thinking is. Similar questions might be:

- "Is that true?"
- "Is that right?"

These questions require a simple "yes" or "no" response. (Most people find it easier and safer to answer "yes" or "no" to confirm or correct someone's thinking than to provide a lengthy response.)

Questions to Learn. Questions to learn are open-ended questions that require more than a simple "yes" or "no" response. They require more thought to answer and are usually framed with the journalistic questions words "Who," "What," "When," "Where," "Why," and "How."

When Sue asked Mae *"Is that correct?"* Mae might have answered, "No." Then Sue could have asked any number of "learning questions" to get to the bottom of the issue:

- "Why were there too many slides?"
- "How many are too many?"
- "What did you want?"
- "When did you know?"
- "What else would you like me to improve upon?"
- "What feedback did the director give?"

All of these questions require a detailed response—and would provide a more complete perspective. Once you have discovered what you need to know, you are ready to move to the Connection phase of the conversation.

Connect to Clarify

In the Connection phase of the conversation, you come to a mutual understanding by summarizing each other's perspectives and by sharing expectations and consequences. Connection is a crucial step in creating accountability and in improving results. Connection in conversation occurs when you ask questions and then listen and attend to the other person's responses—whether the person agrees or disagrees with you.

Summarize Perspectives. Restate what you learned from asking questions. You always end with a "confirming" question. Here's how Sue's summary might sound: *"So what I'm hearing was that you wanted fewer slides in the presentation as requested by the director. Is that correct?"*

Ending with a question in this manner invites the other person to acknowledge your perspective and add his or her own perspective.

Sometimes when summarizing, you want to summarize what other people value. Competing values frequently contribute to misinterpretation and violated expectation—what people believe to be important but has gone unaddressed. We summarize competing values by using "and yet" instead of "but" to give equal weight to both values. It would sound like this: *"I followed your directions and completed the project as assigned. And yet, the director gave additional requirements for the project that he said he'd address with me, but didn't. Is that correct?"*

Notice that Sue values following the directions given, while Mae wanted Sue to make changes to the slides based on the directions of the director. Don't worry about interpreting different perspectives incorrectly; if you do, your listener will usually correct you and you'll get points for trying anyway.

Share Expectations and Consequences. Clearly state specific outcomes or desired results. Adding consequences to the mix clearly establishes the potential implications if agreed-upon actions are not completed. For example, Sue might share expectations and consequences as follows: *"Going forward, we both agree* *that we need to clearly identify the parameters of each project.* (Expectations) *Doing so will heighten our creditability with our corporate customers.* (Consequences) *Following their directions will also demonstrate that we can be counted on.* (Consequences) *Do you agree?"*

Notice that the two statements of consequences are *positive.* People are motivated far more by positive consequences than by negative ones.

If this conversation were about poor performance, however, then you might want to share negative consequences that would result from a failure to change behavior or follow through with an agreed-upon plan. Even then, you still have a choice of using positive versus negative consequences: "continued employment" versus "separation from the company."

Let's talk about the final phase of the conversation—Building.

Build for Accountability

The fourth and final phase in the conversation framework builds accountability to achieve desired results. The components in this phase include finalizing executable plans and gaining commitment.

Finalize the Plan. It is important to include the individual in creating the plan if that person is knowledgeable and experienced. You can work together to create a plan by asking a number of questions that encourage the other person's participation. Here are a number of questions that Sue might ask her supervisor, Mae:

- "What could we do differently next time?"
- "What would you like me to do?"
- "How should we manage changing priorities?"
- "What might get in the way?"

- "What would you do if you were me?"
- "How can I best support you as my manager?"

Sometimes, of course, the other person may not be experienced enough to be instrumental in the planning process. In such a case, you will want to determine *who* will do *what* and *by when*. It is also helpful to explain the *why* behind what you are requesting because you may be addressing any questions that they may have, but are afraid to ask. Explaining "why" will also help others be more motivated and committed.

Once you have established a plan, you are ready to gain commitment.

Gain Commitment. Gaining commitment is the most frequently overlooked step in creating accountability! When you ask for a person's commitment, you firmly establish your expectations of performance and emphasize how important it is that the other person be accountable. It may sound simple, but when you want someone's commitment, you have to ask for it.

To establish accountability, ask questions that address a number of issues:

- "Can you do this?"—*addresses ability*
- "Will you do this?"—*addresses motivation*
- "Are we in agreement as to how you'll proceed?"—*addresses agreement*
- "Do you understand?"—*addresses understanding*
- "What else do you need from me?"—*addresses support*

The questions dealing with motivation and ability are the most important. Pay close attention to the way the person reacts, and to how they answer these questions. If the other person hesitates or seems uncommitted, ask questions to check out that hesitation. Explore and try to identify concerns he or she may have.

Finally, always express your support. People need to know that they can approach you with questions or concerns that they may have.

Sue could ask Mae any of these questions to create accountability with her supervisor:

- "I'll do _____, and you'll do _____. Do we both agree to that?"
- "Is there anything else you need from me?"
- "How will you let me know if your requirements or expectations change?"

The process of using **Initiate, Discover, Connect,** and **Build** is a simple and effective way to achieve results in any difficult conversation. After all, your purpose in holding the conversation in the first place is to create learning and change, right?

Once I asked individuals in a workshop to use the REAL conversation framework to craft a difficult conversation. One gruff older gentleman asked for my feedback about what he had written: "Honey, I have noticed that we don't talk any more. I'm wondering if there is still hope for us." Under his hard exterior was a heart that yearned to reconnect with his sweetheart. Was this a conversation worth holding? Yes! And it was probably long overdue.

Can I Do This on the Fly?

Once you internalize the model, you can prepare and hold any difficult conversation with anyone, anytime, anywhere. The framework will help you keep track of where you are in the process of the conversation and remember where you want to go.

You may be tempted to skip part of the process—to jump from Initiate to Build and omit the Discover and Connect steps—because some of us think in terms of "See the problem/ Find a solution." Don't do it! Discovery will help you more clearly understand the nuances of a problem, and Connection will ensure that everyone has clearly shared and understood the values, expectations, and consequences in play. These two phases are crucial for developing accountability to address problems in a more effective way. Each phase of the REAL conversation process is vital to achieving desired results.

In Summary

Preparing to hold a difficult conversation opens the door. Before you begin, you need to decide *what matters most* (it's difficult to resolve issues that never see the light of day). Usually your *undiscussables*—topics you would rather avoid—are *what matter most*. These issues are formed by assumptions that usually go unexamined, but which drive your behavior. When you recognize that you and others are acting out of assumptions, you can challenge the accuracy of that thinking. Once you have "counted the cost" and decided to share your thinking, the challenge becomes *how* to share—a quandary solved by using the REAL conversation framework of *Initiate, Discover, Connect,* and *Build* to prepare and hold a conversation that works.

Get REAL: In the Appendix you will find a **worksheet** entitled, "Putting It All Together!" that will help you prepare to hold an Undiscussable conversation. Start in the *Build* quadrant and work counterclockwise through the framework while you answer the questions to help you prepare. Then, without the worksheet, deliberately hold the conversation you have prepared using the Initiate, Discover, Connect, and Build sequence. Notice what worked well and what you can improve. The person you are talking to won't answer exactly as you expected, but you will find it easier to hold the conversation when you take the time to prepare.

Gentle Reminders

- People avoid talking about what matters most.
- Clarifying assumptions and identifying intent creates a different reality.
- Gain attention to increase engagement.
- Prepare the process, and then let yourself go.

You can find more information about this topic at
www.overcomingfaketalk.com/gentlereminders.

CHAPTER 7

Do You Open Your Mouth and Remove All Doubt?

The Expression Principle— Express Your Intention

The river rafts we used on commercial trips through the Grand Canyon were enormous—36 feet long by 18 feet wide. They were made of World War II pontoon rafts converted into floating barges powered by 35–40 horsepower motors. At night, we would tie up to anything on the shore directly in front of the boat. On a two-boat trip, we would tie the backs of the boats together and then run a side-line back upstream to hold the boats perpendicular to the shore. One night, I was so tired that I just left the boats tied to the shore. "No big deal," I thought. So I climbed on the boat with my helper and some friends and went to sleep.

Wrong! As I rolled over in the middle of the night, I saw the moon shoot across the sky and then I heard what sounded like a freight train echoing between the canyon walls. I shot out of my sleeping bag to discover we were in the middle of a rapid at 3:00 a.m. with only the moon for a guide. We started bouncing off rocks, smashing into walls, and dropping over chutes and water-falls. Finally, I got the motor into the water, started it up with a roar, and succeeded in ramming the boat into a sheer wall to which we tied off in the middle of the rapid.

We could do nothing until morning. I lay on a shuddering boat, unable to sleep in the dark, feeling like an absolute idiot. All the people on the trip were back upstream at our camp. Luckily, the second boat was still upstream where the rest of my crew was able to load everyone and all their gear and then motor downstream to where we had landed.

So what's the point? No matter what I said was important, the only thing that was really important was going to sleep—not the safety of our boat, our equipment, or ourselves. I was lucky no one was seriously injured. It is the same in our conversations. Intention is everything! Intention is the source of the force that dictates what we feel, say, and do. Interestingly enough, "conversation" is defined as "the action of living, associating, and dealing with others; our conduct or behavior; and the oral exchange of sentiments, observations, opinions, or ideas."[25] These definitions of conversation actually occur in this order and include how we speak to one another and everything we do.

Your expression is a reflection of your intention—the thinking aspect of conversation that is manifest vocally, verbally, and visually. You'll remember that our thinking is the result of everything that we selectively see and hear through the lenses of our mental models and is more a function of the projection of our past reality onto the present situation. What results from these internal processes is the external expression of our feelings, what we say, and what we do. Our internal musings are reflected externally. This process is illustrated in Figure 7.1.

One of the primary challenges in expressing ourselves in a respectful and effective manner in holding a REAL conversation is to deliver our message without creating defensiveness. You want

FIGURE 7.1   Internal Processes Are Expressed Externally

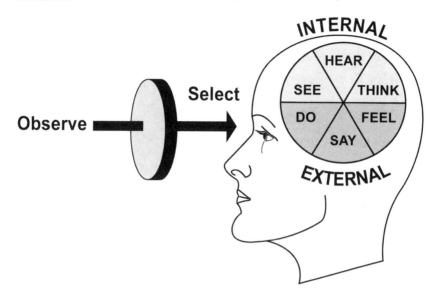

to deliver a message with power and clarity in a way that allows others to hear what you have to say and to increase the likelihood of their making a contribution to your perspective—you want everyone to share or add their meaning in the pool.

Effective expression requires that you know your intention and that you deliberately project it into the conversation. To do this there are a number of dynamics you must learn to manage.

Managing Your Energy

Energy is power. Your energy is the power you use to actively express your ideas, feelings, and actions. Because everything is made up of energy, everything has a vibration or frequency. Positive energy vibrates at a higher frequency; whereas, negative energy vibrates at a lower frequency.[26] Your thoughts, feelings, words, and actions have vibration or frequency that is detected by others on a subconscious level.[27] Sometimes people don't even have to say anything.

The silence speaks louder than words; and yet, not all silence is the same. When you walk into a room where an individual is silently seething, you know it. Although nothing is said, you can feel the energy of that person's anger or frustration. Sometimes after retreating from that space, you may even remark, "Boy, you could cut that with a knife!"

DON'T GET SUCKED IN!

Eve has a supervisor, Mary, who always seems to be having a bad day. Early one morning, Mary entered Eve's office and began criticizing the company, work in general, and some of the deadlines for the work that Eve had been completing.

Eve recognized that her blood was beginning to boil as she felt herself becoming angry. Instead, she started to think of some positive things Mary had done while waiting for Mary to stop her tirade. As Mary took a breath, Eve offered, "Mary, I want to thank you for all of your support these last three weeks. You have given me clear direction and well-thought-out timelines. When my work got a bit bogged down because I was waiting for other people to complete their assigned parts of the project, you covered my back when the director started to get on me in our team meeting. I really appreciate your management of my work on this project. Thanks!"

Mary was speechless. She stopped talking, smiled, turned to leave, and then offered, "You're very welcome Eve. I'm glad I stopped in this morning."

Eve was almost as shocked as Mary. But she was glad that she had managed her thinking, feelings, words, and actions to create a positive effect. She was surprised how her shift created a shift in Mary.

The only way this conversation works is if Eve is sincere. When she told me about her experience, she attributed her success to the positive intent that she had attributed to Mary. Eve's positive thinking, feeling, words, and actions had a vibration that were communicated to Mary. We have the possibility to create the types of conversations that we desire if we are deliberate in what we want to create. Even the ancients understood this concept. The word *abracadabra* used in magic incantations has Aramaic origins and means, "I create as I speak."[28] Understanding the power that belies how we express ourselves begins with what we think.

Managing Your Thinking

The heart of your expression begins with what you are thinking— what you are assuming and what you really want as an outcome for the conversation. Because your intention affects the way you share your opinions, ideas, and experience, your expressions should be clear, logical, and credible, and they should facilitate learning. Effective expression should increase the collaboration, cooperation, and contributions of others. The goal of expression is to create more expression—shared meaning and understanding of all involved. We begin to improve our expression by shifting our perspective from "me" to "we."[29]

Shifting from "Me" to "We"

If you want to increase the engagement and collaboration in your conversation, you can improve your results if you shift your perspective, your mindset, from a "Me" perspective to a "We" perspective. The "Me" perspective focuses on "What's in it for me?" while the "We" perspective focuses on "What's best for 'we'?" Notice the differences in the assumptions and intention of each perspective shown in Figure 7.2.

Notice that the "Me" perspective assumes that "I'm right and I want what is best." This assumption is reassured and often falsely selfless. Individuals with the "Me" perspective see others as wrong and selfish. Therefore, their intention is "to get others to do it 'my way.'"

The "We" perspective, on the other hand, holds the assumption that "I have a perspective, but it may be incomplete or inaccurate."

FIGURE 7.2 "Me" versus "We" Perspective

Assumption:		Assumption:	
Self:	"I'm right and I want what is best." *(reassured, falsely selfless)*	**Self:**	"I have a perspective, but it may be incomplete or inaccurate." *(reassured, open)*
Others:	"You are wrong, and you only want what is best for yourself." *(uninformed, selfish)*	**Others:**	"You may know things I don't, and your actions are logical, given your experience." *(informed, rational)*
Intention:	To get others to do it "my way."	*Intention:*	To collaborate and learn in order to improve solutions.

This assumption is also reassured but is open to exploring other perspectives. Individuals with a "We" perspective see others as holding a perspective they don't hold. They also assume that these people are rational based on their experience. The intention of these individuals is "to collaborate and learn in order to improve solutions"—in other words, to solve problems and make better choices.

Note that the "Me" perspective may result in confrontation, contention, and coercion, whereas the "We" perspective leads more to collaboration, cooperation, and contribution. The "We" perspective brings a different energy to a conversation. People feel the energy of this mindset. It resonates with them and says you care enough about them and their perspective to explore, understand, and address an issue together. When we shift our intention from "Me" to "We," real learning is created.

Now more than ever before we need to have a "We" rather than "Me" mindset. Unfortunately many of our elected officials regardless of political party in both the legislative and executive branches are so entrenched in the "Me" mindset and in supporting their individual ideologies that the ability to solve problems is nonexistent.

No one has more recently portrayed the "We" mindset better than Senators Orrin Hatch and Ted Kennedy. Orrin Hatch is a conservative Republican and Ted Kennedy was a liberal Democrat, and yet they found ways to work together and solve pressing problems. At Ted Kennedy's memorial service, Senator Hatch eulogized the late Senator Kennedy in the words of his brother John F. Kennedy: "We must think and act not for the moment but for our time." When we engage in a "We" mindset, we must truly believe that the other person has something to offer. I would go so far as to say we must believe that there is something that we can help the other person obtain and vice versa. Without "We," people remain intractable and everyone loses.

SAVE A DANCE FOR ME

In my first job out of graduate school, I was working late when the cleaning person came into my office and started to vacuum. For the first time, I noticed she was disabled. The vacuuming was distracting and annoying.

I stopped what I was doing, took a breath, and then said, "I noticed you've been vacuuming in here for a while. I wondered if there is something I can do for you?"

She stopped and sat down in the chair opposite me. I was a bit surprised at her decisive move.

"Are you going to the office Christmas party?" she asked.

"Yes," I responded.

"Who with?" she asked.

"A girl I've been dating. How about you? Are you going?" I asked.

"Yes, I'm going," she answered while looking at the floor.

"Who are you going with?" I asked.

"My mother," she answered.

"Why are you going with your Mom?"

155

"I don't have a Dad. He left us when I was young—probably because of me," she answered.

Then she began telling me about her life. I listened as she shared what it was like growing up, being different. I heard the sadness in her voice as she told me how she wished that she could be like "normal" people, have a husband and a family and even do something important. Then she abruptly stopped talking, stood up, and said, "Well, save a dance for me!" I nodded. As she left, I was glad that I had stopped working.

Six weeks later, we all gathered at the company Christmas party. After dinner and the awards were given out, the music started playing. No one budged. Then I felt a tap on my shoulder. I turned. There she was.

"Did you save a dance for me?" she asked.

"I did." I hesitated for only a second as I caught a sideways glance from my date, who was wondering what I was doing.

Out we went on the empty dance floor and began. A minute later, more than 100 people joined us.

"Thank you!" she said.

If I had not recognized and suspended my preoccupation with my work, expressed an interest in knowing and understanding her, and patiently listened, she would never have made the effort to share her perspective of her life. Listening to her that night taught me some sobering things about myself, my perspective, and my opportunities. I would have missed out on understanding this human being if I had been more into "Me" rather than "We."

Why "We"?

What if you just want what you want? How does "We" benefit you? The irony is that communicating from "We" will benefit you more than "Me" ever could. "We" increases contribution, innovation, problem solving, decision making, learning, and all of what we want to create for ourselves. The challenge in shifting from "Me" to "We"—in changing our mindset—is in how we approach

TABLE 7.1 "Me" versus "We" Mindset

"ME"	"WE"
"I'm right"	"I may be missing something"
Sees others as misinformed and selfish	Sees others as informed and rational
Autocratic	Collaborative
Competitive	Cooperative
Inflexible	Flexible
Uses "either-or" thinking	Uses "both-and" thinking
Defends reality	Explores reality
Judges	Investigates
Self-assuring	Self-examining
Listens for validation and agreement	Listens for data and assumptions
Forces solutions	Creates solutions
Excludes	Encompasses
Tells	Asks
Blames	Explores

our personal and professional lives. Table 7.1 lists of some of the distinctions in those mindsets.

The "We" mindset is outward-focused; whereas, the "Me" mindset has an inward focus. "We" is about learning and discovery, which are impossible to achieve without involving others. "Me" is about personal promotion at the expense of others, which may also lead to personal justification and blame. "We" takes deliberate effort and achieves more effective results. "We" is not an easy mindset to adopt if you're solely into yourself. Recognizing the quality of your results and trying something different could make a big difference. Increasing your awareness of which mindset you resort to may help you to make a different choice.

157

Get REAL: When you encounter resistance in a conversation, assume that the other person is both rational and well-intended. Understand the basis of his or her resistance by asking questions to uncover the other person's perspective and positive intent. Try a little "We" rather than "Me."

Managing Your Feelings

A whole school of thought supports sharing your "hot" or negative feelings during a difficult conversation. People who espouse this view believe that the offending individuals need to know how their behavior has been offensive. Although everyone wants to be listened to, more importantly everyone wants to be acknowledged and to receive an apology if they have been offended. Unfortunately, an acknowledgment and an apology may be a long time in coming if offending parties do not see themselves as the source of any wrongdoing. Part of the problem occurs because we judge ourselves based on our *intention*, not our *behavior*. So if the individual was well intended, he or she assumes that the offense falls to the offended party—the other person's feelings are not their problem. End of issue.

Before you even consider sharing your negative or "hot" emotions, you might ask yourself, "What is my intent?" Obviously, if you intend to shame, blame, or belittle the other person, sharing your negative feelings will end all rationality in the moment. Sharing negative or "hot" emotions usually creates more of the same. No one likes another person to throw up on them, and sharing one's negative feelings is closely akin to that. When we share our negative emotions with others, we don't know whether they are prepared or even open to receive them. Without this understanding, we risk derailing the conversation by sharing our emotions emotionally. It's like throwing a person a grenade and expecting them to know what to do with it (they won't know).

Another part of the problem in sharing negative feelings is the assumption of causation. For example, let's say someone said to you, "You agreed to attend our meeting this morning. You didn't come, and I am angry because I thought that we agreed that you would support me in the meeting." Notice that the underlying assumption is "your behavior is responsible for creating my feelings." Although the nuance is subtle, the message is still, "You are to blame!"

So what do you do? Check out the source of your emotions. Negative thinking creates negative feelings. Our negative feelings fill us up to the point that they overflow onto others. Then those negative feelings end up pushing others away or creating the same degree of emotional intensity in others. The challenge then becomes to rid ourselves of the emotional energy before we attempt to hold a conversation.

Our emotions are created by the attributions, judgments, or interpretations created by the unconscious and subconscious parts of our brain. For this reason, we provided the SOS skill earlier. However, if you want to get to the root of your thinking and shorten the process, simply finish the sentence stem, "I'm (*identify the emotion*) because (*finish the sentence with whatever comes to mind*)." Using this process will help you to surface the thoughts that are floating around in your subconscious that usually never see the light of day. Once you make them visible, you can challenge their accuracy.

Should you decide to share your feelings in a tough conversation, two concepts will serve you well:

- *Own your feelings* by couching them in the context of your thinking, "I felt _____ because I thought _____."
- *Avoid "hot" words* that seem to arouse emotion in others. Notice the different tenor of the words "angry," "upset," or "frustrated" versus "disappointed," "confused," or "let down."

Try using these different words in a sentence that you say out loud and you'll hear the difference.

Get REAL: In order to manage your feelings, decide what feelings or emotion you would like to convey during a REAL conversation. Pick one word that matches the emotion that you would like to convey (i.e., *confidence, enthusiasm, courage, urgency,* etc.). Hold that word in your mind as you hold the conversation and notice how doing so will change the entire tenor of the conversation.

Managing the Music of Your Message

You're like a musical instrument. The way you *"play"* or deliver your message and the vocal quality you give the sound of your words can greatly improve the quality of your expression.

The vocal quality of a message accounts for upwards of one-third of what is conveyed. You are your voice. Unfortunately, people will judge you by your tone of voice whether you are confident or nervous, energized or deflated, strong or weak, certain or uncertain, bold or timid. The great news is that you can change your vocal qualities to improve the power of your expression. We want to spend a moment talking about tone, tempo, volume, and pauses.

Voice Tone

Tone changes everything. Your tone is the emotion that fills you and manifests itself in the way words, phrases, and ideas are shared. Your tone is the music of your mind—it reflects what you are thinking, feeling, and intending. For that reason, focusing on the words in a conversation is not enough.

Your tone is a vibration that everyone understands. Your tone determines whether a person listens to you. You can alter a person's thinking, nonverbal behavior, and attitude by altering your tone.

You can say the same phrase over and over and convey different feelings—hate, love, disgust, frustration, curiosity, or sarcasm—by changing your vocal intonation.

Placing tonal emphasis on different words in the same sentence will change the meaning conveyed by the following sentences. See if you can catch the different meaning as you read these sentences emphasizing the bolded word.

> "**I** didn't say you were a bad performer."
> "I **didn't say** you were a bad performer."
> "I didn't say **you** were a bad performer."
> "I didn't say you **were** a bad performer."
> "I didn't say you were a **bad** performer."
> "I didn't say you were a bad **performer.**"

Giving tonal emphasis to different words changes the meaning of each sentence because people respond more to feeling than words. Your tone reflects the power of your thoughts and emotion, so that your tone is believed more than the words in a message.

Some individuals have a harsh, demanding tonal quality to their voice. Have you ever been accused of being *mad* when you weren't? I have found that you can lighten the tone of your voice by smiling. Smiling tightens your vocal chords in your throat and makes your tone "lighter" or more pleasing. I am not suggesting that you walk around with a "Cheshire Cat" grin on your face all the time. However, noticing the effect that changing your tone has in certain situations should improve the quality of your message.

STOP THE SARCASM

I recently wrote an article on sarcasm and pointed out that we often use sarcasm as a way of communicating contempt or disagreement with something that someone is doing, thinking, or proposing. Sarcasm is a veiled and vague attempt to show disagreement or displeasure.

161

Unfortunately sarcasm is a mixed message where the words that are used convey one message, but the tone of voice, the eyes and gestures, and the inflection of the words in the sentence convey a different meaning. Consequently, with sarcastic messages, the intent of the conversation is lost. Rather than stepping up and holding a REAL conversation, people use sarcasm as a means of communicating their disagreement as if it gave them permission to be rude or disrespectful if what they say can be interpreted as humor.

Interestingly, someone responded to my article with an e-mail message that made my point: "I disagree with your article. I use sarcasm when the party that I am conversing with delivers platitudes and meaningless drivel. In those cases, my words and the tone of my voice convey the message that if they insist on avoiding the meat of the subject by uttering generic, PC, and vague comments, I will opt to mock them. Consequently, your article does not address the possibility that sarcasm is not a sign of disagreement over a valid point, but an expression of contempt for inane words that do not pass the giggle test."

Mocking others or their ideas through sarcasm does not help the recipient to understand the message you wish to convey. Doing what the individual in the example is suggesting would lead most of us to wonder what was going on as well as calling into question respect, relationship, and results.

Tempo

Tempo is the speed with which you deliver your message. Most people speak at a rate of between 150 to 200 words per minute, but the brain can process or hear messages at the rate of 600 to 800 words per minute. Even though a message may be delivered with great speed that is not what you want to do with an important message.

When we must deliver a message that might be hard to hear, like feedback about poor performance, we tend to deliver the message as fast as we can. We rush or hurry a conversation we don't want to hold. Being on the receiving end of such a message is like trying to drink from a fire hose. If your conversation is important, slow your delivery to let the listener hear your message. You can always ask questions to ensure their understanding.

Slowing down your tempo or pace helps you to come across as deliberately thoughtful and helps you give emphasis to important ideas and issues.

Volume

Obviously, you want to be heard, but raising your voice is often interpreted as yelling, which turns people off. The louder you become, the more emotion is conveyed. The more emotion that is conveyed, the less meaning is understood. Softening your voice will gain others' attention and is useful for emphasis of words or ideas. Speaking softer is louder.

Pauses

Real power can be found in a pause. Pauses are useful to emphasize an idea. Pausing or putting some silence in the expression of an idea allows people to process or think about the idea in the spaces you provide while speaking. Pauses allow people to hear what you're really saying. Pausing forces people to listen and think about what you are saying. Deliberately doing something different allows you to emphasize what you want people to focus on. Recognizing how you express yourself today will determine how people will listen to you tomorrow.

LET'S PLAY SOME CATCH

After being out of town all week, I interrupted my three boys during their early Saturday morning cartoon fest. I said to them, "Hey guys, turn the TV off. Let's go out in the yard and play a little baseball—throw the ball, catch some fly balls, have some fun. Whattaya say, shall we do it?!" Of course, I was bouncing around the room with a high degree of energy, trying to get them up and moving. I was being rather loud and emphatic in my delivery.

My nine-year-old stood up and—timidly looking at the floor—said, "Dad, Dad, please stop yelling at us. We didn't do anything wrong!"

I walked over to him, put my hand on his shoulder, and I paused and then very quietly said, almost whispering, "I'm sorry, Matthew (pause). I just wanted to know if you wanted to play some catch (pause) in the yard."

He brightened and said, "That'd be great, Dad! Come on guys, let's do it!"

Sometimes less is more.

Managing Your Words

Although it is estimated that only 7 percent of any communication encompasses the words we use, word choice is still extremely important. Because the words we use can convey the positive intent of our message, we want to use words that do not create defensiveness.

Over the years, many individuals I have coached have asked for assistance with various conversational challenges. One individual recently called and asked, "What would you say to your boss who is a lousy manager?"

"I wouldn't say *that* to her," I replied.

"Well, she recently changed the priority of my work projects. I completed the project of priority, and then she blasted me for not completing a project that she had moved down the list of priorities. It's like she has amnesia or something!" she protested.

I offered a number of alternatives until finally I heard her say, "That's perfect! Say that again. Let me write that down!"

You have to find your voice and own your words. What do I mean by that? Craft what you want to say and say it out loud, hear it, and feel it. If it doesn't feel right, then redraft it and say it out loud again. The reason for saying it aloud is so you can resonate with it. If it doesn't resonate, trust yourself, abandon your script, and work it again. Then, when you hold the conversation, speak from your heart, from your pure intention.

When holding difficult conversations, you want to focus on the individual, not the words or what you think you are "supposed" to say. Your script is not the conversation. *You* are the conversation, so let "you" come out. Focus on the message, not the words—when you need the words, they'll be there.

We believe positive intent creates positive results. Why is that? Because when you come from the heart and from "We" rather than "Me," people get it. What you say will work because the energy in you and in your words will resonate with their heart.

Linking Attention Checks to Interaction Styles

Earlier we talked about using an Attention Check to successfully begin any conversation. Linking your Attention Check to a person's interaction style will really help you to connect with a person of a particular style—it will resonate with how they think.

Let's review the needs and then look at an Attention Check that would increase the engagement of that particular style. Some examples are shown in Table 7.2. To make this application, assume that a project is behind schedule and that the customer's deadline must be met.

TABLE 7.2   Linking Attention Checks to Interaction Styles

NEEDS	ATTENTION CHECK
Initiators like action, results, control, and completion.	"I'd like to talk about finishing this project on time. Can we talk?"
Builders like collaboration, appreciation, recognition, and ideas.	"I'd like to hear some of your ideas for mobilizing the troops to finish the project on time. Can we talk?"
Connectors like cooperation, collaboration, harmony, stability, and approval for their work.	"I'd like to talk about getting everyone together and using their strengths to complete the project on time. Can we talk?"
Discoverers like accuracy, data, organization, and thoroughness. They also like to demonstrate their expertise.	"I'd like your analysis of where this project has fallen behind. I'd like to know how you would finish the project on time. Can we talk about that?"

It isn't essential that you know someone's interaction style to offer such an Attention Check. What is important is that you begin the conversation simply, effectively, and respectfully. Take a moment to craft what you'll say and say it. A good beginning makes for a good ending.

Remember that your assumptions and intent will influence the tenor of the conversation. Suspending your negative thinking helps you get out of your own way so that you can identify a beginning that focuses on "We" rather than "Me." Focusing attention and creating engagement is the first step in creating powerful expressions.

Expressing Respectfully

Aside from avoiding emotionally charged words, a number of verbal skills will improve the intent of your expression. Let's review some of the skills that will improve the power of your expression.

Use "I-Statements"

Using "I-Statements" is an effective way of demonstrating ownership of an idea and openness to being challenged. Using "I-Statements" lessens the impact of the word "you" with which we frequently begin a sentence. Notice the difference in these two sentences:

"You don't know what you're doing!"
or
"I wonder if you know what you are doing."

Notice that the first sentence comes across as a definitive statement of judgment or accusation. Beginning a sentence with "you" seems to have that effect. The second statement says, "This is how I'm thinking, but I may be wrong." Remember that the purpose of expression is to create more expression from others. "Putdowns" turn people off and shut them down.

Beginning your expression with "I" makes your statements more powerful. If you listen to others, people often express their thoughts by using "we" or "you" rather than the "I." For example, you might see a peer who looks somewhat perplexed so you ask him, "What's going on?" He responds with, "Well, what if *you* have a problem with someone *you* work with who isn't following your directions?"

If I heard that, I would look at the person and say, "Who is 'you'? Me or you?" Listen to how much more powerful the preceding statement is if you use "I": "Well, I have a problem with someone I work with who isn't following my directions."

Using "you" or "we" keeps people at a distance and helps to avoid personal ownership and accountability, whereas "I" forms a powerful connection between yourself and the person you are talking to. If you can't own your message, you won't be able to connect with others.

Here is a short list of "I-Statements" that will improve openness and create more powerful connections through your expressions:

"I wonder . . ."
"I believe . . ."
"I'm thinking . . ."
"I'm guessing . . ."
"I'm assuming . . ."
"I know . . ."

I have often had people comment that these statements contain varying degrees of assertiveness or certainty. For example, notice the difference between "I wonder," "I believe," "I think," and "I know." Because the degrees of certainty expressed in these phrases differ, you must be the judge of how forceful and definitive you want to be. As long as your choice of words is deliberate and it works for you, then go with it.

Avoid "Is" Statements

"Is" statements turn your opinions and interpretations into statements of fact. Consider these examples:

"That is a dumb idea!"
"The bottom line is, 'I am right!'"
"You are wrong!"
"The reality here is. . . ."

Any form of the verb "to be"—is, am, are, was, were, or have or has been—make *opinion* sound like *fact*. When we present our thinking "as if" it is a fact or the truth, it often is interpreted to be the only truth. This approach is an instant recipe for defensiveness and resistance. Your expression of opinion or fact may not be the other person's opinion or view of the facts. Be careful in using "is" to express your interpretations.

Avoid Using "Absolutes"

Absolutes are those kinds of words or phrases that people want to inherently challenge because the "absolute" is rarely true. Such statements might be:

*"That will **never** work!"*
*"You are **always** late with everything!"*
*"Can you **ever** get it right?"*
*"You are **forever** asking too many questions!"*

Someone once said, "These are all 'fightin' words." We laughed, but it is usually the case. None of us are "always" anything. We hear absolutes and we immediately come up with examples to the contrary in defense of our behavior. Avoid absolutes to avoid defensiveness.

Stop the "Yeah, but..."

David Bohm's notion of shared meaning in dialogue occurs when people feel safe enough to candidly express their views. Qualifying what individuals attempt to add to the "shared pool of meaning" with a "but" is like saying, "Nice try, but you're wrong!" In fact, we have been telling workshop participants for years that "but" is really an acronym for "behold the underlying truth." "But" negates everything that has preceded it in the sentence. For example, notice how this sounds:

"I really like your idea, but. . . ."

Instead of "but," use any of the following words or phrases:

yes, and
and
and yet
in addition to . . .
to build on that . . .
I also think that . . .

Putting any of these words or phrases in a sentence would sound like this,

*"That is an important consideration, **and** doing something to fix our budget concerns would also help."*

We call this phrase a "building phrase" because we are trying to build or add more meaning to our reservoir of understanding.

Some people have indicated that using *and* phrases feels like you are agreeing with the other person's perspective. Building is about inviting everyone to share their perspective so more meaning is shared and more learning occurs. Using *but* is like hitting the mute button on someone's brain. They hear you *but* them, and usually they're done—they don't hear anything else you say.

Be Clear and Specific

Many times the reason people violate our expectations is because of our own lack of specificity. Being clear and specific in how we state a request will determine whether our expectations are met.

CHECK OUT THE FLOWER BEDS

Sam was a supervisor of maintenance at a city in South Florida. One morning he told one of his workers to go over to City Hall and "Check out the flower beds." The employee complied and returned two hours later.

Sam asked, "How's everything?"

"Just fine!" the employee responded.

Later that day, Sam went over to City Hall to meet with an executive. He chanced to walk by the flower beds and was shocked at what he saw. The beds were full of weeds, the sprinklers were on and one was broken, so a column of water was shooting 30 feet in the air, and there was trash on the lawn and in the bushes from a concert that was held over the weekend. Sam was furious. At the end of the day, Sam confronted his employee when he returned from doing another job.

"I thought I asked you to 'check out' the flower beds at the City Hall today. I went over there and things were a mess. What did you do?" Sam asked.

"Hey, you asked me to 'check them out,' and I checked them out. I just walked around and made sure everything was 'checked out,'" he answered.

"For two hours?" Sam demanded.

"Yep! If you wanted me to weed the beds, you should have told me to weed the beds."

"Unbelievable!" Sam retorted as he withdrew to keep from losing it.

In our minds, we are usually clear, but when we are vague or unspecific, others are left to interpret our requests or directions through the filter of their mental models. When that happens, we are at the mercy of others' interpretations. Clarity is the hallmark of results.

Express Confidence

Sometimes individuals express their opinions and ideas with hesitancy and indecisiveness. Worse yet, many offer their ideas by being self-effacing, and it happens so frequently that I have wondered whether individuals employ this tactic to gain attention. It almost feels as if they are trying to gain your respect and focus your attention on their ideas by belittling or disparaging themselves or their ideas as they offer them. It might sound like this:

> *"Well, you know, I'm not real sure about this.*
> *And, I don't know if this will work. It's probably not*
> *a very good idea. But I hope you'll listen."*

Not only does this phrasing feel manipulative, it also causes people to shut down and tune out. Remember the purpose of expression is to create more of the same. You need to present your ideas with confidence, conviction, and respect.

Managing Your Movements

If we speak at 150 words per minute and think at a rate of 800 words per minute, how does the rest of what we are thinking come out?[30] Body movement! Remember that 55 percent of your expression is conveyed through your nonverbal behavior or what is frequently called "body language." People's bodily movements convey a message to which most of us are oblivious. Learning to observe *nonverbal behavior* will tell you a lot about how your expression is being received.

Usually the verbal, vocal, and visual aspects of communication align themselves. For example, if you are upset, your choice of words might tend toward blame or accusation. Your tone might communicate frustration or anger. And your gestures will be expressive of your feelings. Understanding the meaning behind a number of nonverbal behaviors will help you understand what is being communicated aside from the content of a message.

Let's look at the meaning that the use of eyes, gestures, proximity, and posture convey. We'll provide some explanation of these nonverbal behaviors in the context of the different interaction styles: Initiator, Builder, Connector, and Discoverer.

Eye Contact

Generally, eye contact means someone is open and interested in what you have to say. On the other hand, when people look away, it leaves you wondering if they are interested or attending to what you have to say. Not looking at someone with whom you are speaking is usually taken as a sign of disrespect or disinterest. When you don't look at others you are withholding part of yourself and are disconnecting from them and what they are saying. Generally, it is difficult to feel a connection with people who won't look at you.

Initiators usually give direct, sustained eye contact. They don't have to look away as they think of what they will say. In fact, Initiators judge whether you are listening to them by whether you are looking at them. If you're the type of person who doesn't like to give long, sustained eye contact, they might interpret that behavior to mean that you are not listening to them.

Builders can also make frequent direct eye contact, but they are more comfortable looking intermittently.

Connectors have a difficult time making eye contact. They may take a quick glance, but they usually look all around or even at the floor. Don't think for a minute that they aren't listening to you if they don't look at you. They are the best listeners of the bunch.

Discoverers look to the sides when they are thinking. It takes them a few moments to consider what you may be asking them before they respond. They also give intermittent eye contact, but give direct, sustained eye contact if they are challenged and believe they are right.

Gestures

The gestures people use tell us a lot about what's going on with them. For example, many people use their hands when talking. Likewise, hands placed on a table in front of the person say, "I agree," whereas hands held to the side of the body, behind the back, or in a person's pockets communicate reluctance to engage or even holding something back.

A firm handshake conveys conviction and confidence. Most people respond positively to a firm handshake. Shaking hands palm-to-palm in an upright position establishes immediate trust, while a weak handshake where the palms are not touching because only the fingers are grasped usually communicates weakness, disinterest, or distrust.

People who put the hand to the side of their face or on their chin are thinking. Likewise, placing the hand over the bottom lip while both lips are tightly pursed indicates that the individual has something to say that they are holding back.

Individuals who drop their head into their hands are bored stiff. Individuals who place the hands behind their head and lean back are expressing their superiority. And individuals who stand with their hands on their hips are taking "the superman" stance to express overt confidence and superiority.

Individuals who fidget with their fingers, tap their feet, or crunch up their toes are releasing nervous energy and are usually uncomfortable.

Initiators often use their hands to make a point. They may use a chopping gesture with an open hand in front of themselves as they speak. Or, they may whip out their index finger and start tapping you on the chest or pointing at you.

Builders make many gestures while speaking. In fact, they may draw things with their hands in front of them as they speak. Sometimes, their gestures make you wonder if they could speak without using their hands.

Connectors use few gestures. They are casual, not overly expressive or demonstrative. They use minimal hand gestures. Their bodies are relaxed and calm. You will usually feel comfortable in their presence.

Discoverers are stiff and controlled. They usually speak with their hands and arms at their sides. They may become animated if you disagree with them, but their animation is portrayed in a cynical or sarcastic tone of voice rather than expressive gestures.

Proximity

Proximity is about space. All people have a personal space that they don't like other people to invade, particularly if they don't know you well. As a general rule, if you move toward others and they move away, you should likewise move away. They are creating space for themselves, so let them have it.

Initiators have no space limitations. That's why they might get right up in your face.

Builders like more space than Initiators, but they may touch you when talking to you. It is hard for them to follow the "No Touch" rule in today's business environment. They may touch you on the forearm, the side of your upper arm, or on back of your shoulder.

Connectors like lots of space unless they know you. I had a Connector in a class once whom I asked to come up to the front of the room and help me. She about crawled under the table while saying, "No, no, no, not me!"

Discoverers also like their space, at least an arm's length, maybe more.

When noticing proximity, just watch what people do. Some people are uncomfortable if you face them frontally. If they move away, you should then move away, or point your torso diagonally away from them. Facing some people directly is too confrontational. You'll notice what is comfortable for them, so simply maintain that spacing. Their body will tell you what to do.

Posture

Posture deals with how individuals carry themselves. Posture can indicate like or dislike. Leaning forward usually communicates comfort or interest in what others are saying. Leaning away usually means they are uncomfortable with you or the conversation.

Initiators usually lean forward, face people frontally, and sit with a formal posture.

Builders lean forward, face forward, and are more casual and comfortable in how they hold themselves.

Connectors usually lean away, hold a casual posture and are informal and slow moving.

Discoverers usually lean away, are stiff, and sit in a formal posture.

Vocally and visually the people you speak with are sending you messages other than just their words. Recognizing some of their messages will help you to manage your conversations more effectively. If you are in doubt about specific behavior, "check out" their behavior by asking questions to understand their meaning. Think of the impact of saying to someone you care deeply about, "How come when I bring up this topic, you roll your eyes?" Or, "I have noticed that when I bring up our finances, you change the subject. What are you thinking?" So, when in doubt, check it out!

Get REAL: Notice the physical movements that you and others use. If you are in doubt about what those movements mean, ask questions. For example, if someone doesn't make eye contact when you are speaking, you might ask them, "Are you uncomfortable with something I said?" You might pay particular attention to your own movements. If you have a hard time holding still while delivering an important message, practice holding still while delivering the message. You must notice movements to manage them.

Making Your Expression Pervasive, Not Persuasive

Expression has never been about persuading or convincing anyone to do anything. It's not about *winning an argument* or trying to convince someone that you are right and they are wrong. The intent of expression is to demonstrate the logic of your thinking while having people recognize that your ideas are compelling, credible, or valid. This approach causes people to want to explore and understand your thinking. Let's learn how you can create more interest in your message.

Beginning with Data

We defined *data* as *observable or verifiable facts or information*. In fact, the more people that observe the facts the better. A shared understanding of the obvious doesn't create defensiveness in anyone. Clearly identifying and stating the facts will greatly improve your expression.

Warning: If you can't find the facts, run! Why? Facts are not subject to dispute. We defined *interpretation* as *the meaning we assign to the facts*—synonymous with any inference, judgment, opinion, conclusion, assessment, or assumption drawn from the facts. When creating a powerful expression, we begin with data followed by our interpretation of the data.

Warning: Your assumptions are not the facts. Thinking a thought doesn't make it a fact.

Why Share Facts First?

Sharing the facts first is the basis for talking about anything, particularly in potentially difficult conversations. Sharing the facts before an opinion or judgment bolsters the strength of your idea. Here are some reasons to share the facts first.

- *Facts are objective observations.*
  Sharing facts is the safest way to begin a potentially tough conversation. Why? Because facts or events become the basis for the conversation you want to hold.
- *Facts don't create defensiveness.*
  Beginning with facts doesn't create defensiveness in your listener. The trouble begins when you share *your interpretations* of the facts. Consequently, beginning with interpretations and following with facts eliminates the objectivity of the listener. If someone said to you, "You really blew it yesterday by not finishing the report like you said you would!" As soon as they finish with their judgment of your behavior, you will immediately begin defending yourself—even if in your head. You'll never hear the facts or data that they share. You want your listener to hear the facts first.
- *Facts establish a logical connection.*
  Beginning with facts and then sharing your interpretations and assumptions allows your listener to see the logical connection between what you observed and your thinking. You are verbalizing your **Process of Perception**.

For example, someone said to you, "You haven't spoken to me for two days (data). I wondered if you were mad at me (interpretation)."

Notice, as illustrated in Figure 7.3, that facts logically give rise to your interpretation. Just as your interpretation leads to action, so your actions or behaviors lead to results. You want your listener

177

FIGURE 7.3 Facts Establish a Logical Connection

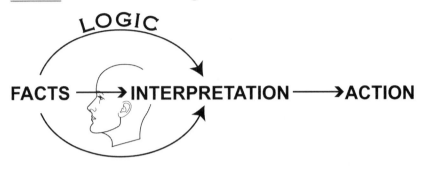

to connect with and understand your thinking. Don't worry about whether your thinking is wrong. Your listener will still understand the basis of your interpretation and may make any needed corrections or additions to your perspective by adding his or her perspective.

The challenge in sharing data and interpretation is in the quality of your interpretation.

How Do We Create Disrespectful Interpretations?

The challenge in sharing our interpretations is that our head is full of them, and they are usually negative. For example, you would never want to say:

> *"You agreed to finish my report by this morning.*
> *I haven't received it yet. I'm thinking that you*
> *just told me what I wanted to hear."*

This statement is the same as calling the person a "lying dog" to his face. Say that and the games will begin.

How Do We Come Up With This Thinking?

Years ago, social psychologists developed what is called **attribution theory**—how people assign meaning to the behavior of others based on certain personality and motivational factors. *In the absence of data, we make it up in the worst possible way*: we jump to judgment and assume the worst about people and their motives. Your mental "leap" in this instance usually leads to some type of labeling of the individual or that person's behavior.

Considering the foregoing example of the person who didn't provide the report, I might have thought, "That guy is a lazy liar!" Notice that this statement is a judgment about his person and his motivation. This phenomenon is called a *fundamental attribution error* because we attribute meaning to him and his behavior in error.[31]

So what? The challenge is that we make these *snap* judgments without even challenging the accuracy of our thinking. We observe an individual's behavior, and we make the judgment without understanding the motives behind his or her actions. As we already identified, we judge ourselves based on our intent, but we judge others based on their behavior and assign a negative meaning to their actions.

WHO'S BEEN SLEEPING IN MY BED?

Kim was a successful executive for a national hospital chain. She spent three weeks traveling across the country visiting 10 cities and was dog-tired when she returned home at about 4:00 p.m.

As she entered the house, she was greeted by her husband, Carl, and their two teenage boys who were busy making dinner. After a few hugs, Kim dragged herself into their bedroom, dropped her briefcase by the door, and slung her suitcase on the bed. Then she saw it. In the corner of the room was a multicolored silk blouse that wasn't hers.

Kim exploded. "Who's been sleeping in my bed?!"

"What are you talking about?" Carl asked, rushing into the room.

"You know darn well what I'm talking about. Who left this in our room?" Kim attacked while holding the silk blouse in her clenched fist.

179

"Gosh, honey, I don't know whose it is or how it got into our room," Carl offered.

"Carl, you tell me what's going on right now!" Kim demanded.

"Dad should be so lucky!" chuckled her two sons who were now standing in the doorway with their dad.

"Men!" Kim screamed. "And after all I do for you three!"

Kim dashed out of the bedroom, out of the house, and down the street. She hadn't gone a block, and she remembered the afternoon she left on her trip, her friend, Emily, had come by with some of her old blouses. Kim hadn't taken any of them except the silk blouse that she had wadded up and thrown in the corner on her way out the door to the airport.

How many of us are just like Kim? Things happen and without even thinking, we blast off, never taking a minute to think through the data and our interpretations. Let's take a look at creating more respectful interpretations.

Creating Respectful Interpretations

No matter how much true negative data you possess about people, if you share a negative or accusatory interpretation about them, their behavior, or performance, they will become defensive. It is difficult to proceed without rebuilding respect and the relationship.

To create a respectful interpretation that you can share with someone, you need to create an interpretation that gives the individual the "benefit of the doubt" by asking yourself the "Understanding Question."

To ask yourself the "Understanding Question," simply add positive descriptors or adjectives to a question that helps you create a more positive interpretation of the situation. For example,

> *"What would prevent Bill, who is **trustworthy**, **committed**, **loyal**, and **honest**, from finishing my report by this morning?"*

Possible answers:

- "Someone changed his priorities, so he couldn't get it done."
- "He underestimated a previous commitment that took longer than he thought it would."
- "He didn't record the deadline in his planner, so he forgot."

Use one of the answers you come up with to create a respectful interpretation:

> *"Bill, you agreed to finish my report by*
> *this morning, and I noticed I haven't received it* (data).
> *I'm thinking that something came up*
> *that changed your priorities* (interpretation)."

This interpretation doesn't create defensiveness, and using it allows the individual to maintain his or her rationality and respond to your thinking.

What if the interpretation you just made up isn't really what you are thinking? It probably should have been what you were thinking if you were giving the person the benefit of the doubt. In essence, sharing your "nasty" thoughts will not create a dialogue. You need to engage and get everyone to put as much meaning in the pool as possible to see what emerges.

Blaming people for their choices will entrench them more solidly in their position. Your focus should be on improving behavior in the future, not beating people up for the past.

What if the conversation between Kim and Carl had gone something like this?

KIM: "Carl, I noticed there is a colorful silk blouse on our bed. I'm wondering where it is from. Do you know anything about that?"

CARL: "No, dear. When I came home the afternoon you left, that blouse was in the corner. I thought it was yours."

KIM: "No, it's not mine."

CARL: "I didn't think so. It looked a little old, and besides, it doesn't look like something you would wear. At least, I haven't seen you wear it before. Did one of your friends leave it?"

KIM: "Oh, I forgot that Emily came by the day I left for the airport. She gave it to me, but I forgot to put it away."

Instead of throwing a fit, Kim might have remembered sooner if she had tried understanding rather than jumping to judgment and assuming the worst about Carl's extracurricular activities.

Putting Data and Interpretation Together

The next step in creating more powerful expressions is to combine data and interpretation. In order to do so you need to use the language of data and interpretation clearly.

The Language of Data

Notice the verbs that signal observable data.

I noticed . . .
I observed . . .
I saw . . .
I discovered . . .
I heard . . .
I feel . . .

These verbs describe observation or verifiable data. Be careful with the sentence stem, "I feel. . . ." If you are going to share data with "I feel," it would have to be a factual description of what you feel. For example, "I feel hot," or "I feel nauseous," are factual statements. Whereas, "I feel like you don't care about my work" is an interpretation even though the "feel" seems to describe something factual. Many people use "feel" to describe what they think. Be careful to make this distinction.

The Language of Interpretation

Here are some stems that signal an individual's thought process:

I wonder . . .
I think . . .
I assume . . .
I realize . . .
I believe . . .
I know . . .

These verbs signal that thinking is involved and is the logical consequence of the data shared previously. Once you have effectively shared the data and your interpretation of that data, you are ready to create engagement from your listener.

Increasing Contribution

The final step in creating a powerful expression is to end the "data-interpretation" sequence with a question. When you share an expression of data and your interpretation of that data, you want to invite people to respond, challenge, or assess your view. In short, you want them to **confirm** or **disconfirm** your thinking or add their own perspective. You do this by following your interpretation with a question.[32] For example, if we go back to our report example and end it with a question, it would sound like this:

> *"Bill, you agreed to complete my report by this morning, and I noticed I haven't received it. I'm thinking something came up that changed your priorities. Is that true?"*

The type of questions that seek confirmation can be answered by either "yes" or "no." Such questions would include "Is that the case?" "Is that true?" or "Am I seeing this correctly?"

Let's say that Bill answers that your interpretation is inaccurate; you would want to follow with an open-ended question like, "What happened?" The reason that we may use questions that confirm or disconfirm our thinking is an attempt on our part to make it easier to engage at the outset of a conversation if we perceive that the person is hesitant to engage.

On the other hand, some argue that using "confirmation" type questions decreases the likelihood that you will receive an honest answer—that asking an open-ended question forces the person to truly share their views rather than just telling you what they think you want to hear.

Whatever type of question you use is at your discretion—just ask questions at the end of the sequence that invite others to share their views, such as, "How do you see this issue?" "What am I missing?" or "What is your perspective?" Your desire should be to increase engagement and learning so that individuals' perspectives will improve problem solving, decision making, implementation accountability, and results. Balance your expressing with asking.

In Summary

The power of our expression is improved by understanding how our intent is expressed through our energy, our thinking, our feelings, the music of our message, our movement, and our words. Being more aware of how these elements help to create REAL conversation should help you to take specific steps to improve how you express yourself. Finally, understanding how to become more pervasive by using data, interpretation, and ending with a question will ensure that your message is heard and people engage you in return.

Get REAL: Apply these principles to a difficult conversation that you need to hold. Be sure to end your expressions with questions to increase the contribution of your listener.

Gentle Reminders

- The intent of your expression is reflected in your feelings and everything you say and do.
- "We" creates inclusion and contribution.
- You are the music of your message.
- Feelings are remembered more than your words.
- Be more pervasive, not persuasive—use data.
- "Put downs" lead to "shut downs."
- Express your intention—be deliberate.

You can find more information about this topic at www.overcomingfaketalk.com/gentlereminders.

CHAPTER 8

How Is the Answer in the Question?

The Discovery Principle—
Ask to Reveal

O n one of my first trips down the Grand Canyon, one guide took me into an old abandoned mine. He took me far back into the tunnel, turned off the flashlight, and then ran off through the dark. I had never been in total darkness before. It was so black that I couldn't even see my hand in front of my face. I slowly turned around and started feeling my way along the tunnel walls while tripping over the rubble on the cave floor. As I tried to find my way out, I kept searching the blackness for a pinpoint of light that would lead me to the cave's entrance and the safety of the sunlight.

Figuratively, we are all groping along in the dark, but we don't know we're in the dark because we're in the dark. Asking questions is the way that we move out of the dark and into the light. Asking the right questions helps us to move in the direction that will help us find the answers we seek.

What Are the "Right" Questions?

The "right" questions deliver the answers you are seeking. If you know what answers you are seeking, then you'll ask the questions that will take you where you want to go. Sometimes the question is the answer. Notice this approach requires that you know what you want to know, only then will you find the answer. Consequently, the answers we seek provide opportunities for discovery, learning, and understanding.

Why Don't We Ask Questions?

Consider the following example of a manager's typical response in dealing with a perceived problem.

YOU DON'T DELIVER!

Ann is a CAD/CAM designer at an engineering firm. Teri has recently been promoted to manage Ann's area. Early one morning, Teri marched in and confronted Ann.

"I heard through the grapevine that you haven't finished the outline for the required specs in the defense contract. I thought we agreed this task would take priority. I am disappointed and frustrated with you and your work! Pick it up! And no 'buts'!"

Teri turned and left as abruptly as she had entered.

Not one question was asked! Had Teri asked a few questions, maybe she would have remembered that she switched Ann's work priority to another project three weeks ago. Maybe she would have remembered that she forced Ann to attend a designer's conference that Ann told her was a waste of time because she was up-to-speed on the software being introduced at the conference. Maybe Teri would have remembered that today was Ann's first day back from a week's vacation that had been scheduled six months ago. Ann had done everything that Teri had asked, and then she had to suffer Teri's demeaning tirade.

Here are five reasons we hear from leaders for not asking questions.

- I don't ask questions because I assume I know the answers, so I act on my assumptions.
- I don't want to ask questions because I may appear weak or uncertain about my decisions or expertise.
- I don't ask questions because I don't want to find out that what I want is impossible or won't work given the circumstances.
- I don't ask questions because I don't want to give the impression that I am open to other points of view, other ideas, or suggestions.
- I just have so much on my plate that I am more interested in getting things done than listening to what everyone thinks. That stuff takes too much time.

All of these responses show how our thinking drives our behavior—and reveal that these individuals aren't interested in learning! You can ill afford not to engage in discovery given the increasing speed of working in today's environment.

What Should Discovery Create?

Engaging in discovery by asking questions lifts the conversation, creates respect, increases engagement, fosters openness, inspires reflection, and deepens understanding.

Lifting the Conversation

Noticing whether a conversation is going below or above the line enables you to change the direction and tenor of a conversation. The questions you ask help you to control the direction of a conversation. Above-the-line questions are *positive* questions that inspire discovery, learning, and change. They assume positive intent and value for the individual.

Below-the-line questions are *negative* questions that people often use to criticize, blame, accuse, or advise. Such questions lead people to become defensive, shut up, and then clam up and refuse to engage. Negative questions are born of the negative assumptions and intent held by the questioner and projected onto the listener. Sometimes it is as if the negative questioner is defending him- or herself. *Below-the-line* questions will either lead to "fight" or "flight" behavior, which derails your ability to create learning and reach resolution.

Be safe. Everyone wants to feel comfortable and secure in talking with others, particularly in discussing projects, procedures, or behaviors that might not be delivering the desired results. You want to ask questions that are safe for your listeners to answer. Review the difference in Table 8.1, which shows the *Defending Negative Questions* that are about criticism and the *Discovering Positive Questions* that are more about learning.

Get REAL: Pay attention to the types of questions you ask. Are they questions that cause people to think and then lift the conversation above the line, or do your questions take the conversation below the line and result in diminished respect and results?

Many negative questions are disguised "tells." For example, the question in Table 8.1, "Don't you think you should . . . ?" is really a "You should do this!" statement disguised as a question. Likewise,

TABLE **8.1** **Negative versus Positive Questions**

DEFENDING NEGATIVE QUESTIONS	DISCOVERING POSITIVE QUESTIONS
"Didn't you realize that's not what I wanted?"	"What results did you hope to create?"
"Didn't you finish that yet?"	"What's working or not working?"
"Don't you think you should . . . ?"	"What did you do?"
"Why did you do that?"	"What did you want to do?"
"Can you even do this?"	"Are you comfortable doing this?"
"When, if ever, will you be finished?"	"When do you expect this to be done?"
"Don't you know that . . . ?"	"Why is that so important?"

rhetorical questions, where the answer is obvious, are really negative questions intent on criticizing or punishing.

I almost missed the opportunity to lift a conversation above the line with my young daughter. I share it with you only to make the point that often when we leave work, we take our game face off and revert to behaviors that are less than effective.

BRIANNA'S HAIR

I got up early one morning and stumbled into the bathroom to brush my teeth. In the waste basket was a long, beautiful chunk of blond hair.

"Brianna!" I yelled to my seven-year old daughter. Her head popped up in the valley between where my spouse lay and I had been lying.

"Yes, Dad," she answered while rubbing her eyes, through the missing chunk of hair that was once her long bangs.

"Did you cut your hair?!" I demanded. (Duh, like that wasn't obvious.)

Her head immediately disappeared in the comforter and as I tried to catch her, she crawled under the comforter to the foot of the bed and vanished underneath the bed frame. I bounded after her and found her lying face-down in the carpet with her hands over her ears. I took a breath and sat down on the floor by the side of the bed.

"Brianna, can we talk?" I asked softly.

"No!" she snapped.

"Did I make you feel bad?" I asked.

"Yes, you did!" She let me know.

"I am sorry. I just wanted to know what happened," I affirmed.

"I don't like my hair!" she protested.

"I love the golden hair of my sweet girl," I offered.

Slowly, she crawled out from underneath the bed and into my lap.

"I don't like my hair!" she protested again.

"Why not?" I asked.

"Because when I wash it, it turns into a rat's nest. Then when Mom brushes it out, it hurts my head," she responded.

"So you cut it off, so it wouldn't hurt you anymore?" I asked.

"Yes, Daddy," she answered as she cuddled in my lap.

We then talked about how to remedy the situation and agreed on a plan of action.

It takes practice to notice when you are going below the line and ask questions that lift the conversations above the line. Controlling the direction of any conversation increases discovery and the prospect of improved results. Any time you find your conversation descending into the depths, ask positive questions that facilitate learning and discovery.

Creating Respect

Aside from lifting a conversation in a different direction, asking questions is the easiest way to create respect. Asking questions says, "I care enough to ask and listen to what you have to offer." Asking reverences the individual.

Years ago, we taught dialogue skills at an automotive manufacturing plant. We then left the plant for several months and later returned to see how things were going. A number of us wandered around and checked in with our former students. We asked, "How are things going?" Here is what we heard: "My boss asked me what I thought about something. When I finished telling him, he said, 'Next time, I'll ask an expert!'" Someone else shared, "My supervisor asked me what I thought, and as I was telling her, she walked off and left me talking to myself!"

These managers understood *the principle* of asking questions or soliciting the opinions of their people to create respect, but their behavior did more to create disrespect than anything else. With asking and no listening, you get no respect! If you don't want to know, don't ask!

Be Patient. Patience is required to create respect. The more questions you ask, the more respect will increase and the more you will learn, but it takes patience. Asking superficial questions is one

FIGURE 8.1   **Layered Understanding**

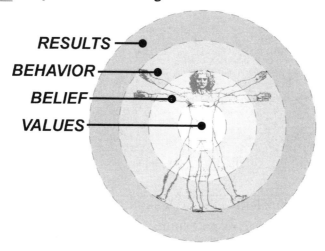

reason that problems are not effectively solved after a challenge is encountered.

Figure 8.1 provides a graphic of *The Vitruvian Man*. Notice in it that the different rings of the target suggest that different levels are possible to explore by asking questions. Unfortunately, most questioners don't push past results and behavior.

Note that the edge of the target overlaid on the man is labeled *Results* because *Results* are the natural consequences of behavior. The *Behavior* circle of the target encompasses the man's hands—what he might do or didn't do. The *Belief* ring of the target encompasses his head, representative of his beliefs about his choice of options or his rationale for doing what he did. Finally, the inner circle represents the *Values* or what is most important to the individual. Values are the basis for an individual's beliefs, behaviors, and results.

When expectations are violated or results aren't achieved, we often end up asking questions that only explore *Results* and *Behavior,* rather than also exploring beliefs and values.

Here are some **Results**-based questions that are typically asked:

- "What happened?"
- "What were the results?"

Next, if you listen for **Behavior**-type questions, you might hear:

- "What did you do?"
- "How did you create these results?"

To solve problems effectively (and avoid achieving the same results), you need to explore and address people's beliefs and values. Values find expression in beliefs that drive behavior, which in turn creates our results.

Here are some great **Beliefs**-revealing questions:

- "What did you want?"
- "What assumptions did you make?"

Once you explore a person's thinking or the rationale behind their behavior, you are ready to explore values. **Values** are revealed by asking the following questions:

- "Why was that so important?"
- "What was most important to consider?"

Patiently exploring all aspects of the target will help to address a challenge from the individual's perspective. Taking the time to ask questions and listen to answers really says, "I care and am concerned about you and your performance."

Get REAL: Notice how often you talk about an individual's beliefs and values when they don't meet your expectations. Take the time to get past results and behavior to explore what is really going on with them at a deeper level.

Increasing Engagement

One main reason we ask questions is to improve engagement, which increases contribution and collaboration. We can't make people answer our questions when they don't want to or don't feel safe to do so, but we can increase the odds that they will engage. Asking questions invites people to add their meaning—their perspective—to the *"pool of shared meaning,"* which increases the chances that we will be more effective as we work together.

Be Curious. A sincere spirit of curiosity and learning will pervade the questions you ask. People will resonate with the fact that you really are interested in what they have to offer. Being persistently curious will increase the likelihood that they will engage.

SEEING GREEN

One day at lunch, a workshop participant approached me and asked, "Would you be interested in understanding what the problem is around here?"

With curiosity I said, "Absolutely!"

"Follow me to the window," he said. I followed him, of course.

Standing at the plate glass window in the cafeteria, he said, "Look at the sky." I did. Then he asked me, "What color is the sky?"

"Blue," I responded. He replied, "No, it's not—it's green."

"Green?" I asked.

"Yes, it's green," he repeated. I was a little perplexed.

He asked me again, "What color is the sky?"

Again I answered, "Blue."

He adamantly insisted, "No, it's not. It's green."

Then I asked him, "Well, why is it green?"

His face lit up and he exclaimed loudly, "That's what people don't do around here!"

Still puzzled, I asked him what he meant. He eagerly answered, "Well, it's green to me, because I'm color blind, even though it looks blue to you. But when people see things differently around here, no one ever takes the time to ask why, or even to inquire any further as to why the other person sees things differently. Once people see something a certain way, that's the way they continue to see it. That's what's wrong around here."

Thank heaven I kept asking.

Being curious allows you to gain valuable information. Once your listener perceives you are really interested in his or her perspective, they will usually open up and engage more fully.

Get REAL: Start to notice when you assume you know the answers for challenges or solutions that are currently challenging you. Rather than just going with what you think, take time to ask others what they think—see if you can learn something that you didn't know. It may surprise you how much you don't know.

Fostering Openness

Asking questions will also help to increase openness or candor. Openness is increased as you display honesty and sincerity as you explore others' understanding or as you seek their perspective. Being open or candid with an individual also will give that person permission to reflect that same openness back to you. Your degree of interest and sincerity toward the other person is enhanced by giving a him or her your full attention, making eye contact, continuing to ask pertinent questions, and listening to what that person is saying.

Be Sincere. No matter what types of questions you use, sincerity in asking questions will carry the conversation 95 percent of the time. People resonate to the energy you exude. They know when you really want to know what they think, and so they resonate with and respond to you.

ELEPHANT ON MY CHEST

Jill was a professional business and life coach who helped executives to create balance in their personal and professional lives. She had been working with Robert for only a few weeks and hadn't really come to know him well. However, when she entered Robert's office one day, she could feel a dense, heavy stress occupied his space. They began by exchanging a few pleasantries and then Jill began: "I'm feeling a lot of stress today, Robert. What's going on?"

Looking down, Robert said, "I'm not doing well. I almost canceled our meeting."

"What does not doing well look like?" Jill asked.

"Well, I'm not a very good husband. I'm never there for my kids. I have a major report—a 100-pager—to write for a major client. I'm supposed to be overseeing the development and launch of the new company website. I also have to travel weekly and make day-visits to our other regions. I'm working on my MBA at night at the university. I have to give a presentation at a conference next week that I'm not prepared for. And, to make matters worse, I went off on a couple of my people today who aren't performing up to par!"

"How does it feel to be you right now?" Jill asked.

"Like an elephant is sitting on my chest! I can't move! I can't breathe! I feel like I'm being crushed, consumed, buried, and overwhelmed," Robert quietly answered.

Somewhat moved, Jill asked, "Are you willing to look at everything you just mentioned and make some serious changes?"

"Yes!" Robert responded. And so they began.

What led to Robert's willingness to be so open about how he saw himself? Maybe it was the desperation of his situation and his crying need for help. The safety Robert felt, the patience Jill displayed, the curiosity of her demeanor, and her sincerity in wanting to understand and assist Robert in his situation, led to the openness Robert displayed in candidly sharing his frustrations and feelings about his current challenges.

Inspiring Reflection

Good questions inspire self-reflection. The individual asking such questions has to think about what he or she wants to know—to learn something. Then, when that person asks the question and listens, he or she will learn something else. Likewise, the responder has to think to answer, and when the responder thinks and hears his or her own answer, he or she may learn something else. Asking good questions provides many opportunities for learning. People who don't ask questions don't want to learn. Learning can be casual, but to make it deliberate, you must look for opportunities to ask.

Questions that require reflection are self-revelatory. Such questions may reveal assumptions, opinions, and feelings that often go unnoticed or undiscovered. Answering questions that reveal us to ourselves serves to help us surface the thinking that drives the behavior that delivers undesirable results. Once we become aware of what is creating our results, we can make a different choice. Asking good questions helps us to see ourselves and our choices more objectively. Asking self-revealing questions of others also allows them to discover themselves.

ASK HIM IF HE'S DONE

As an attorney, I had the opportunity to ask the type of questions that would help individuals to reflect on what was really important to them. I often wondered why these people couldn't see what was right in front of them, but then most of us are so caught up in just living our lives that we often miss what should be obvious.

Jean had been in an abusive marriage for more than 15 years. In an attempt to save the marriage, she had persuaded her husband, Derek, to attend marriage counseling with her. Derek attended off and on, and then not at all. Jean kept attending the counseling to improve her relationship skills. Derek, on the other hand, became more emotional and even physically abusive. Jean probably called my law office no less than five to seven times a day to ask for advice. Finally, I told her that I wanted her to ask Derek a question.

"What question is that?" she queried.

"Ask him if he's done," I proposed.

"What?" Jean asked.

"Yes. Simply ask him, 'Are you done?'" I pleaded.

"But why?" she demanded.

"Does he act like he wants this to work? Is he going to counseling? Is he making an effort? Is he getting better or worse? Is this the type of relationship that makes you happy? Is this really working for you?" I fired back.

"Okay, I'll ask him," she agreed.

She called back five minutes later crying. "He said he was done with me two years ago," she reported. "And the questions you asked me made me realize that I have been living on false hope," she added.

"Good for you. Come in tomorrow, and we'll talk about your options."

Why did this situation go on so long? Because he didn't have the courage to speak up, and she really wasn't clear about what was happening and what she wanted. It took someone else asking her some simple questions that she hadn't asked herself. We could probably also surmise that Jean's hope obscured her objectivity and awareness of the reality of the situation. The questions I asked and she answered for herself allowed this wonderful human being to make a different choice. Asking questions allows us to connect our head with our heart and to change our results.

Be Thought-Provoking. Asking questions engages the brain and causes it to focus on a different line of reasoning. Asking thought-provoking questions is simply learning to ask questions that require people to think and self-reflect. Such questions demand that individuals step out of the normal process of their lives or their performance and view their thinking, actions, or results from a more objective perspective.

Thought-provoking questions require self-reflection, and they are not always easy to answer. Such questions are not always easy to ask if you haven't taken the time to think about the answers you are looking for. Also, people may struggle to answer your questions. If your questions take them by surprise, give them time to think through or process a response. Both of you will learn something.

WHY DO YOU ASK SO MANY QUESTIONS?

I once sat in a strategy meeting where the global distribution of a product was being discussed. Lisa was a marketing director in this manufacturing company. During the meeting, the VP of marketing proposed that they use a distribution company that also distributed products for their major competitor.

At the VP's proposal, Lisa exclaimed, "Do we really want to do that?"

"Oh, please! What kind of a question is that? Why do you ask so many questions? There is nothing wrong with what I'm proposing!" the marketing executive retorted.

"Why did you ask the question? Do you have a concern, Lisa?" asked the CEO.

"I don't know why I asked the question, but I do wonder if we really want to use the same distributor as our competitor. I worry that the distributor will not represent us adequately," Lisa offered.

After the meeting, Lisa approached me and shared, "That was an interesting question, 'Why do I ask so many questions?' In thinking about it, I realized in high school that I had a teacher who always made a comment when I answered his questions. He used to say, 'Now, that was a stupid thing to say!' I learned to ask myself as many questions as I could think of to avoid doing or saying something stupid before I opened my mouth. I guess that's why I ask so many questions now. I don't want us to do something we'll regret."

Sometimes answering thought-provoking questions takes time, and even then they might not be able to answer. I really believe that the answers that we are looking for are inside all of us. If you will just keep asking, the answer will eventually appear.

Be Observant. Being observant of our and others' behaviors will help to identify the questions we are trying to answer. I learned a wonderful maxim from one of my mentors. He said, *"Every behavior a person enacts is in response to some question they are trying to answer."* You want to be observant of your behavior to identify the questions you are asking.

Our thinking is a "question-answer" process. We ask questions within our minds for which we are searching an answer.

FIGURE 8.2 Question-Answer Process

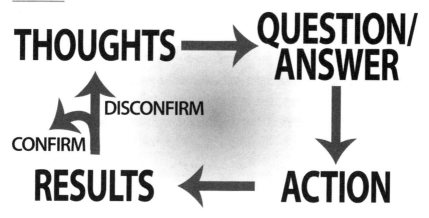

The search for answers causes us to act. Our actions in turn yield a result that either confirms or disconfirms our thinking. If our thinking is confirmed, we then move on to exploring other thoughts and developing questions in response to validating our thinking. However if our thinking is disconfirmed, then we seek an answer to a different question as the process repeats itself. The process would look something like the illustration in Figure 8.2.

The power in this process comes from the notion that changing your questions will change your results. If you don't like your results, change your questions. Questions stimulate action. By asking thought-provoking questions you increase the possibility of not only increasing learning and discovery, but also improving your results. Noticing your behavior will also help you to identify the question you are trying to answer.

10-MINUTE PHOTOS

Ann went to the drugstore early in the morning to make 100 copies of a photo she wanted to include in the annual company holiday card. As she walked into the store, she interrupted a team meeting in which the store manager was yelling and criticizing his employees: "This store is a mess; you're all a mess; and you better clean this place up, now!"

They scattered as Ann tiptoed around the meeting and headed to the camera bar at the back of the store.

After placing her thumb drive in the automatic photo reproduction unit, she began to follow the prompts so she could print her photos. After 10 minutes, the machine froze and she couldn't get it to work. The same angry store manager came around the corner, so Ann asked for his help. "It does this all the time! Either that or you're just not following the prompts. You know, this thing isn't idiot-proof!" He ripped her thumb drive out of the unit and handed it back to her. "You'll have to start over!" he demanded as he stormed off.

Ann put in her thumb drive and started over. She got to the same place in the program and the machine froze again. Then, she noticed a small, older gentleman stocking the shelves behind her.

"Could you help me with this?" she pleaded.

"I'm sorry. The boss wants me to stock these shelves and clean up my area," he answered.

"Please, I know you can help me! Is there something I'm not doing that is freezing the machine?" she asked.

He stopped, and, looking both ways, he scurried to her side.

"Sometimes the touch screen gets oil from your fingers on it. If you take this Windex and clean the screen, then it should work." He responded while cleaning the screen. Then he quickly went back to restocking.

She touched the screen, and it worked. She printed her pictures and was gone in 10 minutes. She thanked him as she left the store.

Notice her thinking was "I know this guy can help me." She took action, and she asked for his assistance. Her action created the desired results. Want to change your results? Change your questions, change your action, and change your results.

Get REAL: Here is a list of some thought-provoking questions you might add to a list of your own. Memorize them to have at your disposal when you need them. Try applying them to a challenge you are currently facing and see if you can gain a different perspective.

- "What do you want?"
- "What will that get you?"
- "What has become clearer to you since yesterday?"
- "What messages is your environment sending you?"
- "What is your greatest frustration? Why?"
- "If you could do anything to change something, what would you do?"
- "What conversation have you been avoiding? With whom? Why?"
- "What part of your work is most satisfying? Least satisfying?"
- "What threatens you the most?"
- "What relationship needs to be improved?"
- "How could you work more efficiently?"
- "How do you hold you back?"
- "What is current reality?"
- "What might be a different perspective of the same reality?"
- "Why do you want to stay stuck?"

Deepening Understanding

Among the many benefits to asking questions, this last reason for asking questions is paramount. There is just so much we don't know that we assume we do know. The challenge in deepening our understanding is learning to ask questions that take us to a deeper level of understanding. When individuals feel secure enough to answer our questions, they reveal themselves—their thinking, feelings, hopes, dreams, and aspirations. Our questions open the door to understanding ourselves and others.

Be Deliberate. When we talk about being deliberate, we are talking about intentionally using a specific skill to deepen our understanding. We call this skill, "Springboarding from the Answer." "Springboarding" is about using an individual's answer as the basis for the next question you ask. For example, suppose someone responded to a question by answering, "I don't like doing that!"

You, in turn, would ask, "What exactly don't you like?" Notice you are diving deeper on "what" they "don't like." Here's how this skill might be used in a conversation.

I'M NOT GOING TO SCHOOL!

One Monday morning, my spouse came into our bedroom and said, "You'd better have a talk with Zach. He says he's not going to school today."

First thing that goes through my head sounds like this, "Oh yeah? We'll see about that! As long as you live under my roof, we go to school. You'll do it! Or there'll be consequences!"

I knocked on his door, "Zach?"

"Go away! I'm not going!"

I entered the room and there he was sitting in the fetal position in bed with a blanket over him. He heard me enter.

"I'm not going! Do you think you can make me?" he protested.

"Did I say I would make you?"

No response. I sat down next to him and asked, "What's going on?"

"I don't want to talk about it!" he proclaimed. **(Springs to . . .)**

"What don't you want to talk about?" I asked.

"How I hate the people there!" he answered. **(Springs to . . .)**

"What do you hate about the people?" I asked.

"They laughed at me!" he retorted. **(Springs to . . .)**

"Who laughed at you, Zach?" I responded.

"The idiot kids in my class!" he protested. "They're all idiots!" He threw back the comforter so he could look at me.

"What happened?" I asked.

"I got asked to read in class. I tried my best, but I had trouble with the words, and the class laughed at me. Then I started to cry, and they laughed some more."

By suspending my judgment and criticism, being safe, patient, curious, sincere, thought-provoking, and deliberate, I deepened my understanding in this situation.

You'll also notice another skill I used in this conversation. I answered a "question with a question." Zach accused me of forcing him to go to school. In order to assist him to examine his thinking and my behavior, I asked, "Did I say I would make you?" This question allowed him to notice his thinking and what I was or wasn't doing and to create safety in the process.

Benjamin Franklin once said, "We don't know what we know until we see or hear what we know." *Springboarding* enables us to deepen our understanding and assists the other person to hear what they know. Being deliberate about using this skill will greatly help you to ask the "right" question to discover the answers you really want to know. The quality of the questions you ask is reflected in the quality of the answers you receive.

What Types of Questions Should You Ask?

Whatever question provides the answer you seek will work! However, five different types of questions will increase your chances of improving your discovery power: questioning, requesting, reflecting, guessing, and summarizing. When asking any of these questions, remember that sincerity will carry the day and that a person's body language will tell you what type of question to ask. When a person is physically uncomfortable, specific questions can help you to create the security he or she seeks.

Question to Know

Question to know is asking open-ended questions—questions that can't be answered with "yes" or "no." This skill is often referred to as "probing," but *questioning to know* is more about discovering, learning, exploring, and understanding—**NOT** about inquisition, interrogation, or manipulation. Use *questioning to know* when the nonverbal behavior of the person with whom you are speaking tells you that person feels safe in answering any question you might ask. *Questioning* encompasses the journalistic questions of **who, when, where, why, what,** and **how** (**why, what,** and **how** questions are the most powerful). These questions are used to gather more information, explore detail, and to understand others' experience, opinions, or thinking. For example,

- "What did you think?"
- "Why did you think that?"
- "How did you arrive at the conclusion?"

Each type of question we explore has a warning or a *caveat*. Here's the caveat:

Caveat: *Questioning* controls both the speed and direction of the conversation. Slow down in asking your questions. Allow the person to respond before asking another question.

Avoid Confrontational "Why" Questions. When you ask "why," be careful about how you inflect or intonate the "why" at the start of a question. "Why" sometimes comes across as an "order" or a "demand" and is often viewed as a precursor to blame. "Why" is sometimes seen as an invitation to offer an excuse. When possible, transform "why" questions into "what" questions. Listen for the distinction by reading these aloud.

- **"Why" question:** "Why did you do that?"
- **"What" question:** "What did you want to achieve?"

If you read them in your normal tone, you'll notice that the "what" question is softer or more neutral. "Question to know" questions are driven by curiosity and are effective in the absence of negative emotional reaction or discomfort.

Request to Gain Access

Requesting isn't always a question, but making a request and then pausing begs a response. When requesting, you are asking for access to their thinking, experiences, and perspective. *Requesting* is a discovery skill that is best used when someone starts to display some discomfort or a lack of safety. For example, people may not make eye contact, or may put their hands behind their back or in their pockets. Their tempo may display "starts and stops" or hesitancy. Their tone may display a lack of confidence or uncertainty. Such behaviors tell you, "I don't feel secure." Take the cue, and use requesting to create engagement.

Requesting may begin with a verb. Some requests would include:

- "Tell me what you think about this."
- "Help me understand your concerns."

Requesting may also be a personal expression for assistance or interest in what the individual has to offer. Here are some examples:

- "Could you help me with this?"
- "I'd really like to know what you think."

Caveat: *Requests* are broad statements of invitation for the person to engage. Therefore, requests may lead to broad and unfocused responses. If someone starts speaking, don't cut the person off right away. Let him or her go, and then ask a more focused question when appropriate.

Both "Questioning to Know" and "Requesting to Gain Access" are great inquiry skills to lift conversation above the line in creating upward spirals and increasing discovery.

Reflect to Connect

Use this skill to reduce a defensive or "hot" or emotional reaction. When people are emotional, you often can't get past the emotion to the meaning behind it—emotion is the mask of meaning.

William James noted, "A mirror isn't stained by what it sees." Reflecting is providing a *verbal mirror* or an *observation* as feedback to the recipient. It allows the recipient to discover his or her emotion or behavior from another's viewpoint. Making a reflecting statement acts as an *acknowledgment* or *affirmation* of emotions or actions. It is a way of saying, "I see you and accept what you're feeling." Such an affirmation creates a sense of acceptance and lessens the emotional state.

You may reflect either **emotion** or **action**. For example,

"I can see you're upset." (Emotion)

or

"The last four mornings I've said, 'Hello,' in the lobby and you haven't said anything to me." (Action)

The brain of the listener who hears such a statement relays the message, "Hey, this person is on our side." The effect of the reflection causes the emotional reaction to subside and signals that it's safe to talk about whatever the person is feeling and thinking.

Think about what happens to a person who is extremely angry, and you say, "Well, if you'd calm down for a minute, we could talk about this." And you wonder why the person goes ballistic! You just rejected his or her emotions—or the individual person. Then, that person's brain sends a good dose of chemicals to the body to prepare it for "fight" or "flight" as well as the message, "Get ready to rumble!"

When Do You Reflect? In "fight" mode when a person is angry or upset, he or she may yell, blame, or belittle others, or engage in any of those behaviors we talked about earlier that are aggressive and are below the line. In "flight" mode, you'll have to reflect the other person's action or behavior because an outward display of emotion will be nonexistent.

What If the Person Is Angry and Insists on Talking? Play brain-dead! Playing brain-dead is about making the interaction about you not them. Simply say something like, "I'm so frustrated right now that I can't think to hold this conversation. Please excuse me." Notice you made holding the conversation about you not them. Make the statement and leave. You don't want to say or do something you will regret later. It does help to raise your own emotional intensity when saying it, but do not blame the other person for the inability to hold the conversation.

    Caveat: When reflecting, you need to be sensitive to a couple of issues. First, never say to a person, "I know how you feel," because you don't! Second, in using this skill, you must be sincere. You have to want to know what's going on behind the emotion. If you use this skill solely as a means of manipulating a person's emotions, it may work once, but not twice. Third, reflect once, never more than twice. If you reflect and the other person's emotion doesn't subside, that person has had an adrenaline dump, and you are going to have to give him or her some time. Finally, do not engage at the other person's level of intensity. If you fight fire with fire, all you have in the end is ashes.

Guess to Confess

Guessing is the asking skill to use when people do not feel secure or safe to tell you what they really think. In fact, they may be totally shut down. You ask them a question, and they look down or away and say nothing.

    Guessing is a "closed-ended" question because it can be answered with a "yes" or "no." Guessing is really about sharing your interpretation as a question by raising your tone at the end of the statement, such as, "I'm thinking I've done something to offend you?"

    Figuratively, guessing is like offering your interpretation as a confession and asking your listener to confirm or deny the accuracy of your question. In this sense, "guessing" questions are about seeking confirmation of your thinking. The purpose of guessing is to create sufficient security that the person will feel comfortable enough to answer your open-ended questions.

Here are some guessing questions:

- "Did I offend you in the meeting?"
- "I'm guessing that you are mad at me for standing you up last night?"

Caveat: The only drawback in guessing, particularly incorrectly, is that you may bring up other issues of concern. For example, you might ask, "Are you upset with me because I didn't support you in the meeting yesterday?" They might respond, "No, but now that you mention it, yes!" Because this situation rarely happens, always do what works best for you!

Summarize to Clarify

Summarizing is rephrasing in your own words what you think you heard. Summarizing can be done at any time after you have used the other discovery skills during a conversation when important information has been shared. You want to summarize to check for clarity, or when you want to demonstrate to your listener that you are making a deliberate and concerted effort to understand them.

Here are some examples of summarizing questions.

- "So what I am hearing is . . . ?"
- "What you think is that . . . ?"

Or you can offer a summary and end with a "guessing" question that seeks confirmation as we learned in a previous chapter. Questions that seek confirmation include the following:

- "Is that the case?"
- "Is that accurate?"

Caveat: Summarizing is not parroting (repeating the person's exact words back to them). Simply restate the essence of your understanding in your own words. Don't worry if your summary isn't entirely accurate. Simply ask more questions until you understand.

What Skill to Use When?

Reduce the emotion and uncover the meaning. When people display "hot" or negative emotion, you must defuse their defensiveness first. You will want to reflect first and then move to requesting, guessing, questioning, or summarizing. Putting reflecting and guessing together makes a great one-two punch in discovering the meaning behind their emotion. For example,

"I can see you're upset." (Reflect) *"I'm guessing I've offended you?"* (Guess). Reflecting emotion and guessing at meaning allows the individual to see what you are seeing and to understand the logic of your thinking. Then, the listener only has to respond by answering "yes" or "no." If the person answers "no," then guess again, or make a request, *"I'd really like to know what's going on."*

Once the individual is more comfortable, you may ask any of the "what" or "why" questions. Finally, whenever you want to clarify what you have understood, summarize your understanding. Here is the only principle you need to remember: ***In the presence of "hot" or negative emotion or feelings, reflect first before asking other questions.***

Using the asking skills decreases the emotion present in conversation (see Figure 8.3). As long as you reflect the emotion or action first, you may follow that skill with any form of discovery.

FIGURE 8.3   The Security-Emotion Continuum

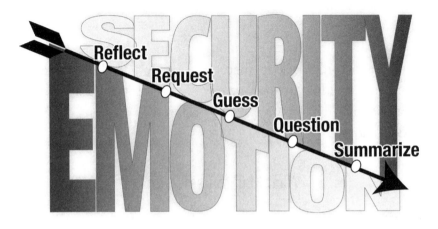

As the emotion decreases, the security increases. The greater the security, the more openness, engagement, and discovery you experience.

Questions and Interaction Styles

We are often asked whether some of these questions work better than others with certain interaction styles. In deciding which questions may be best, we emphasize that when security is at risk, choosing the type of question to increase the security and comfort is what is most important. Different types of questions might be helpful with different styles, as shown in Figure 8.4.

Initiators

Initiators want control and results. They are action-oriented, fast-paced, and decisive. They want answers, and they want people to perform. They may come across as short and abrupt. Many times their behavior is interpreted as anger. They are frustrated by those who take up their time or who offer too much detail.

FIGURE 8.4   Question Types by Style

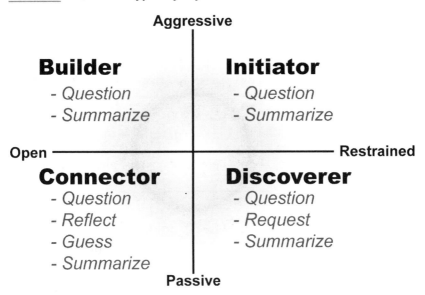

Question

- Ask them direct questions to identify expectations and priorities. Ask "what" questions and avoid "how" questions. They don't mind responding to "what," but they expect you to figure out the "how" in completing tasks.
- Ask them questions about the bottom line, what they value, their concerns, and challenges.
- Ask questions that let them be in control of the outcome and provide details. For example, you might ask, "*Would you rather do ___(option)___ because of ___(detail)___, or would you rather do ___(option)___ because of ___(detail)___?*" Providing options and supporting detail allows them to be in control and to make the best decision possible.

Summarize

- Summarize what you have heard to clarify their expectations of what needs to be done.

Builders

You will not have a problem getting builders to answer your questions. In fact, you may have difficulty getting all the questions you have answered. They seek appreciation and recognition and love to interact and collaborate with others often without time constraints.

Question
- Ask direct questions about their needs, goals, ideas, and vision.

Summarize
- Summarize to clarify your understanding. Their conversations often take twists and turns in topic. They also tend to process or think out loud, so it may be difficult to understand what they want or need. Summarize to clarify your understanding of what they are requesting.

Reflect and Guess
- Builders are the most emotional of all the styles. When they become angry, you will want to reflect their emotion and guess at meaning to reconnect with them.

Connectors

Connectors like collaboration, cooperation, and approval for the work they do. Of all the styles, these individuals are often the most quiet and reserved—they don't readily volunteer their ideas or opinions unless they feel safe.

Question
- Ask many questions to understand their views, needs, and the work they're doing.
- Use "why" questions to surface their opinions.

Reflect and Guess
- When conflict arises, you will probably not see many verbal or visual cues that signal their disagreement. Reflect their withdrawal or silence and guess at the meaning behind their behavior.

Summarize
- Summarize their ideas as a way of helping to clarify their thinking and demonstrate your desire to understand them.

Discoverers

Discoverers want data and detail in making recommendations for solving problems and overcoming challenges. They also want respect for their expertise and knowledge.

Question
- Ask questions that solicit their analysis, concerns, or recommendations.
- State your opinion as an expression that ends with a question. For example, you might say, "I think we should do this. What do you think?"
- Discoverers liked to be asked to demonstrate their expertise. For example, you might ask: "What do you think?" or "What am I missing?" or "Is there another way to see this?"

Request
- If the Discoverer seems to be reticent to engage, use a request to increase discovery.
- If you ask a question or make a request and the Discoverer does not answer immediately, don't ask another question. Pause and wait! Discoverers often take longer to think through an issue before they respond. Give them time to think. They want to give you the right answer.

Summarize

- Summarize their thinking and yours to ensure that you are both on the same page.
- Summarize to clarify the steps in a process or procedure and what is to be done.

In Summary

Discovery is about asking questions to learn. People who don't ask don't learn. The questions we ask help us to lift the conversation, create respect, increase engagement, foster openness, inspire reflection, and deepen our understanding. The types of questions we ask also help us to create the security required to increase the quality and quantity of discovery. Understanding what types of questions to ask individuals with different interaction styles will also improve the quality of your conversations.

But asking questions has a flip side. All the questions we ask of ourselves and others will never serve us unless we listen to the answers. Asking and listening are the keys to all we'd ever hope our conversations would create. That's where we're going next!

Get REAL: Internalize the different types of questions to use and apply them to different people in different situations. You might also want to identify the interaction style of those you work with and then use the different types of questions with individuals of differing styles.

Gentle Reminders

- Don't assume, ask questions.
- The easiest way to create respect is to ask questions.
- Sincerity and persistence increase engagement.
- Asking questions causes people to think differently.
- The quality of their answers is reflected in the quality of your questions.

- Emotion is the mask of meaning. Reflect the emotion to reveal the meaning.
- Your behavior is the result of a question you are trying to answer.

You can find more information about this topic at www.overcomingfaketalk.com/gentlereminders.

CHAPTER 9

Why
Ego Off?

The Connection Principle— Listen and Attend to Connect

When I first started running the rapids, I learned how important it was for the passengers to listen. On the first day of any trip, we usually ran House Rock Rapid. This rapid occurs as the river makes an abrupt right turn. Once in the rapid, the boat crashes through a foam wave that totally buries the passengers and hits them with the force of a cold-water freight train.

I told everyone to hold on tight. I also instructed them that if they were washed off the boat they should calmly wait until they surfaced and assume a sitting position in the water with their feet pointing downstream.

Having an uneasy feeling about two passengers, a surgeon and his son, I asked them to move to the center of the boat with the son sitting in front of the father. They refused. A few seconds later, we crashed through the first wave. When we emerged from the foam, the doctor was gone. Then, rather than follow my directions for navigating the rest of the rapid without the boat, the doctor, with flailing arms and hands, reached up and grabbed the prop of the motor. And that was the end of their vacation.

Why Listening and Attending?

We make the distinction between listening and attending because we listen with our ears, and we attend with the rest of us—our eyes, our heart, our body, and our thinking. Attending is listening with "all of us." Listening and attending creates authenticity and connection in conversation. It is not something you can fake. People know whether they have your full attention by what you do and how they feel; you must learn to be "people present."

Why Don't We Listen?

Ego! In our conversations we are often more preoccupied with *what is important to us* rather than the person sitting in front of us. We also struggle keeping our judgments in check, which leads us to not listen past what we think we know. In this instance, we listen more for validation of what we believe we know, not to discover what we don't know. Finally, when emotion or defensiveness shows up, we usually avoid the conversation, not knowing how to manage the moment and listen past the emotion. We become our own worst enemy.

Our listening and attending challenges stem from a lack of discipline to focus on others, the ability to get past our judgments, and the skill to recognize the emotional messages others send us. Because we may not recognize that we are unaware of our listening behavior, we need to deliberately and intentionally learn and practice certain skills to become better listeners.

All powerful listeners practice four skills: They focus their listening, they listen nonjudgmentally, they listen for details, and they listen empathetically. We'll review each skill to improve your ability to understand and connect with the thinking and feelings of others.

Focused Listening

Focused listening requires that we be disciplined and *fully engaged* in *hearing* what someone is saying and *attending* to that person's unsaid messages. My first experience with unfocused listening occurred in my first performance review. It went something like this.

THIRD TIME'S A CHARM!

My first performance review suffered from my manager's inability to manage his preoccupations and give me his full attention. As we started the appraisal, the phone rang. He snuck a peek at the caller ID, sheepishly looked at me, and said, "I've got to take this."

While speaking on the phone, he glanced at me and said, "Yeah, I don't know. About, hmmm, 15 minutes, I guess."

He replaced the receiver and picked up the conversation where he left off. About 10 minutes later, the phone rang a second time. He repeated the previous antics: snuck a peek at the caller ID, apologized, took the call, glanced at his watch, and indicated he'd be available in a few minutes.

Finally, we reengaged and in about five minutes, the whole scenario occurred again. After the third interruption, he quickly ended my review.

I was incredulous. As I left our meeting, I thought how disrespectful, rude, and undisciplined he was. To this day, I can't remember what was said in our meeting, but I can still remember how I felt—unsupported, unimportant, and worthless to him.

As time passes, people may not remember the details of a conversation, but they'll recall how they felt in your presence. Listening to others requires that we give our full attention.

Listening and attending requires that we *discipline ourselves* to be *fully present*. Being present may require both physical and mental focus. Consequently, if you are distracted, preoccupied, or emotionally spent, you will have difficulty giving yourself and paying full attention to a person and what that person is saying.

To discipline your ability to listen and attend, practice these tactics:

- **Be Attentive.** Give the person eye contact. Don't let your eyes wander. Stop your hand-wringing and drumming the tabletop with your fingers. Be grounded and present with the person to whom you are listening.
- **Manage Your Time to Be Present.** Don't tell people that you can listen to their concerns or answer their questions if you are reviewing your notes for a presentation you have to give in 10 minutes. Explain your situation, and set another time when you can be fully present and focused on what they have to say.
- **Excuse Yourself.** If you're preoccupied and can't silence your "headspeak," excuse yourself. You can't "fake it 'til you make it."
- **Take the Time and Plan.** Listening and attending to individuals' concerns, issues, and challenges takes time. You might ask them how much time they need for the conversation and plan accordingly. Be sure that if the conversation is important you don't cut it short. You'll short-change yourself and the individual.

Get REAL: If you want to assess your ability to focus, try this simple exercise: Sit in a comfortable chair, close your eyes, and count backwards in your mind from 100 while moving forward through the alphabet simultaneously.

For example, you would say 100a, 99b, 98c, etc., until you reach the end of the alphabet—without losing track of the number and the letter in order. This is a good measure of your ability to focus in the present. Practice this simple exercise every day, and your ability to focus will increase over time. As you exercise your focus muscle, the strength of your listening discipline will increase.

Listening Nonjudgmentally

We all make observations of our daily experiences and make interpretations of what those experiences mean. Our interpretations usually take the form of judgments, which are limited by our view of reality. That should inspire us to hold our judgments in abeyance and be more open to others' perspectives. Unless we're aware of what we are thinking, our thoughts and ensuing behavior may escape our awareness. So we resist or reject those realities that are outside the realm of our experience or that run counter to our personal version of reality.

Such a limitation leads us to form negative judgments of individuals and their ideas. Because we usually listen to others to validate what we think we know or what we think others should know, we listen from a judgment perspective—we listen to see if we agree or disagree with the individual. From this perspective, we are constantly making evaluations of what the person is saying. If we agree, then all is roses. When we disagree, the fireworks usually begin. Our evaluations and disagreement usually lead us to offer criticism, provide advice, or mount a defense of our thoughts or actions. You can tell when people are in judgment because they finish people's sentences, cut them off, talk over them, interrupt them constantly, or ignore them altogether. Unfortunately, many of us engage in these behaviors unconsciously.

Being nonjudgmental is difficult because of the ongoing "headspeak" that is constantly talking and analyzing, editorializing, or evaluating what others have to say. How often have you noticed thinking the following phrases when you were supposed to be listening?

- "What's your point?"
- "This is going nowhere!"
- "You should let someone else decide!"
- "You just don't get it!"

- "You're wrong and I'm right."
- "I don't trust you!"
- "I don't like you!"
- "Who cares?"
- "This is taking too long—boring!"
- "That will never work!"

These statements are not only negative judgments that show up as evaluation, advice, or defense, they also are expressed by your nonverbal behavior, your tone of voice, and the energy that you convey to the other person. They pick up on all these messages that you are sending them. And you wonder why no one wants to listen to you?

To make listening more challenging, listening to your thoughts causes you to miss elements of the message—the content or the delivery—that is being conveyed. To listen and attend more effectively, you must recognize that your negative judgments create negative emotional reactions and behavior. Here's how it might show up.

READY TO RUMBLE

Many matrix organizations have employees who live and work in one geographic location, but report to a leader in another location. Wes was the senior VP of human resources at the corporate headquarters. All the people in HR report to corporate even though they work in a region. Jack is a general manager who heads up one region.

Jack wanted to give salary increases to the human resource personnel in his region. As soon as Wes got wind of this, he called Jack.

"Jack, we need to talk about the proposed salary increases for my people working in your region," Wes requested.

"We don't need to talk about a thing! I know what I am doing. Besides these people work for me! I pay them with my budget. I don't care whether they report to you or not. I can do what I want, so stay out of my business!" yelled Jack.

"Jack, all I said was, 'I think we need to talk about your proposed salary recommendations,'" Wes offered.

"Look, I know what's going on. Tell me one thing I don't know about these people!" demanded Jack.

"Well, you might want to know that one of the individuals has only worked here for about eight months, and we usually don't give a salary increase until a person has been here at least a year," Wes replied.

"OK, that's one thing! So tell me something else I don't know!" Jack demanded.

"The other person that you want to give a raise to, I gave a raise to two months ago," Wes responded. *"All I said was, 'We need to talk,' nothing more."*

Notice that Jack made a negative evaluation that Wes was trying to tell him what to do, override his authority, and undermine his leadership. Jack was also very defensive and had some advice about what Wes ought to do. All Wes wanted to do was collaborate to make the best decision for the company. But Jack's negative judgment ruled how he responded. People avoid working with the "Jacks" of the world because dealing with them takes time and energy that is more easily focused elsewhere.

To listen nonjudgmentally, practice these tactics:

- ***Listen for Examples.*** When listening to others, you will notice that they will share their negative evaluations without providing supporting data. When they do, ask questions that will surface supporting examples. For example, if someone said, "You don't support me!" you might ask, "If I was more supportive, what would that look like?" or "Can you give me an example?"

- ***Ask for Permission to Offer Advice.*** If you are listening and are tempted to offer advice, ask for permission to offer your advice. Don't be surprised if permission is "denied."

- ***Be an Observer, Not a Reactor.*** When people mount a defense, don't react to it. Ask questions to understand what the

source of the reaction is. Likewise, if you notice yourself reacting, stop it. You just make a reactor out of the other person.

Get REAL: Start by noticing any "hot" emotions you experience and then identify the thinking behind your feelings. Or,
notice someone who is in reactive mode and ask them questions to identify their negative judgment. Remember: you can't
change your thinking unless you first notice what your thoughts
are.

Listening and Attending for Specifics

One easy way to stay focused and avoid being judgmental is to
focus on the specifics of the conversation—including data or facts.
Using data makes your conversations more pervasive, credible, and
valid to your listeners. If you listen for the specifics of facts, your
attention will be on the content of the conversation and not the
negative judgments and nonverbal behavior of the speaker. Beyond
listening for facts, you can make visual and virtual observations.

Focusing Attention—Observing the Details

Many of us haven't learned to listen or attend for anything past the
words or content of a message. We want to not only listen to what
is said in a conversation, but also everything that is unsaid—the
emotions and the nonverbal behavior that are displayed. Listening
and attending to the observable dynamics will create a connection
with the other individual and deepen your understanding. Your
challenge is to listen to the words or the content of a conversation
and to attend to the other messages that the speaker is sending.

Making Visual Observations. The easiest way to fully experience a
speaker's message is to be in their presence. When listening to
someone, observe the visual messages conveyed through these
behaviors:

Posture
Proximity
Eye movement
Eye contact
Tone
Tempo or pace
Volume
Hand gestures
Lips
Blinking
Pupil dilation
Emotion
Pauses
Swallowing

Many of these visual observations show up in people who communicate with different styles. For example, people blink when they are listening because blinking is the result of mental processing. When people stop blinking, they have gone to another planet. Or you may know that volume goes up when people become upset or don't feel like they are being heard. Or you should know that tempo increases when people just want the conversation to be over with, so they pick up the pace to finish the race. Also, swallowing occurs when people are nervous and don't want to speak up. They figuratively *swallow what they want to say* so that it won't come out. Practice attending to others' delivery in order to understand what else they are telling you.

Making Virtual Observations. Much conversation today occurs not in face-to-face interactions but by phone, e-mail, and teleconference. When you communicate by e-mail, only 7 percent of the message is available to the recipient—you leave 93 percent of the interpretation of your message to the reader. If the conversation is important or concerns a sensitive issue, don't communicate by e-mail. They will usually interpret your message in the worst possible way and attribute a negative motive to you.

When making virtual observations, you need to attend to *what is being said* and to *what is not being said*. When communicating by phone, pay attention to the following dynamics:

Pauses
Sighs
Hesitation
Tone of voice
Tempo (level of commitment to goals or actions)
Inflection
Word choice
Energy or emotion
Your impressions
Your feelings (level of commitment to goals or actions)
Willingness or ease in answering questions

Most of these behaviors are auditory; however, you also need to attend to the feelings, ideas, and impressions that seem to come out of nowhere. Because people's thoughts are conveyed energetically, we pick up on them. Simply pay attention to thoughts or ideas that present themselves, and check them out by asking questions.

What If I Don't Know What Any of These Observations Mean? Ask! Asking about meaning communicates, "I noticed and I want to understand." To clearly understand the message behind the observation, simply share your observation with a guessing question. For example, you might ask:

"I'm hearing some tension in your voice." (Observation)
"I'm thinking that maybe what I am asking you to do may not be possible?" (Guessing question)

Attending visually and virtually and checking out your observations will greatly improve your understanding and forge connections with your speaker. Here are some suggestions for being able to listen and attend for specifics.

- **Look to Learn.** Start noticing all the visual and virtual observations available to you. Most people rarely stop to observe these verbal and visual cues.
- *Clarify Meaning.* If people are behaving in ways that you don't understand, ask them what their behavior means or guess at the meaning and ask them to confirm.
- **Ask Questions and Listen.** You won't help your cause by doing all the talking. Let the person speak and listen to them. Don't add your perspective, cut them off, or finish their sentences. You may ask questions for clarification, but then go back to listening and attending to the messages that are offered.

Get REAL: Pick a situation in which you can engage in visual or virtual observation and ask questions to identify the meaning of what you are observing.

Listening Empathetically

Listening empathetically is about being more emotionally intelligent, understanding why we become defensive and what you can do to defuse an emotional reaction. Do you work with people who become emotional easily? Do you know why some people are always defensive in conversation? Would you like to learn to defuse defensiveness and lift your conversations above the line? If so, learn to listen empathetically.

Emotion Signals Meaning

All human beings have feelings. In conversation, the emotions we display on the outside reflect what is going on inside. E-motion, or "energy in motion," is the outward expression of hidden meaning. When people display "hot" or negative emotion, these feelings signal there is more to understand. Our emotions are always telling us something, because they reflect our thinking. A thought precedes every emotion that we observe or display. Our emotions are the tip of the proverbial iceberg.

When people become emotional, we may not know what to do, so we avoid emotional interactions altogether or become emotional ourselves. Neither strategy contributes to the success of conversations. The first step in managing emotion is to be aware of how emotion is created.

Perception Triggers Emotion

Our emotions are the product of our Process of Perception. As listeners we interpret everything that others do or say. We often interpret others' actions negatively even if they didn't intend to be offensive, which explains why offense is taken where none is given. In any case, a person's emotion says more about that person than it does about you because the other person created it.

Defensive behavior occurs because the person perceives that he or she is being attacked. Consequently, the perceived attack creates "attack-back" behavior; and once we become embroiled in or "hijacked" by our or others' emotion, all rationality flies out the window. The emotion then becomes the energy that fuels our reactions—what we say and do. The challenge is to defuse the emotion and to discover the meaning behind it.

Negative Emotion Reflects Violated Values

"Hot" or negative emotional responses signal the perceived violation of our values. Conversely, a positive emotional response signals a value affirmed. So it makes sense that a negative emotion is a cue to understanding others' values or ego needs.

For example, suppose an individual believes he is doing a good job at work. Then his manager provides feedback that he is performing poorly. This individual perceives a form of loss, whether fictional or factual, because of the incongruity of what he thought and the feedback he has received about his performance. In essence, the feedback challenges his perception of himself. Unfortunately, some individuals equate individual worth based on their performance.

The emotional responses we see in others and feel ourselves are the end result of a string of interpretations that strike at our personal values. Once we recognize a negative emotional response, we can defuse the emotion and discover the meaning behind it.

WHO ARE YOU TO GIVE ME FEEDBACK?

Jane is a facilitator who works for a management consulting firm. She was asked by her boss, Rob, to take a new trainer, Keri, and observe her teaching a program.

After the program, Rob asked Keri how the training went. Keri told Rob that Jane had dismissed some questions that had been asked. Keri also told Rob that Jane had become quite aggressive with some individuals who were working on their laptops rather than paying attention. Rob asked Keri if she had given this feedback to Jane. Keri said that she had not. Rob asked Keri to give Jane the feedback as soon as possible.

Rob called Jane into his office and told her that Keri had some feedback to give her from the session. He then indicated that he would like to speak with her afterward.

Jane went ballistic. "I shouldn't have to take feedback from some trainee! You should have the guts to give it to me yourself!"

Rob responded, "I want you to talk to Keri first because she was at the training, then we'll talk about what happened."

Jane stormed out of his office.

Sometimes we just react to our circumstances, and at other times our emotions seem to come from out of nowhere. In either case, we need to defuse the emotion so we can understand the meaning behind the emotion.

Using the EASE Model: Unmasking the Meaning

When I first started examining why people become defensive or emotional in conversation, a class participant made this brilliant statement: "The way we treat each other either allows our personality to stay at rest or not." The notion of "rest," or EASE, suggests a conversation that is held in a respectful environment where individuals create shared meaning by openly sharing different ideas and perspectives and asking rigorous questions to identify assumptions and increase understanding.

EASE, then, is an acronym that describes all the components that are present in any emotional reaction: Ego, Aim or Intention, Stories, and Emotion.

The EASE Model illustrates the dynamics behind the mask of emotion. The challenge in conversation is to defuse the *mask of emotion* and discover the meaning behind it.

Exploring EASE from the Outside In

We will begin with *emotion* because it is visible on the outside—it's what a person displays. Then we'll move inward, layer by layer, to discover the meaning behind the emotion. These layers are illustrated in Figure 9.1.

Emotion is the mask of everything that we think, want, and value. Emotion would encompass any feeling that is displayed, the tone of voice (rising pitch, sarcasm, or intonation), volume (yelling), or specific body language (reddening face, rolling eyes, or exasperated sighs). Emotional displays range from intense and dramatic to subtle and guarded.

Stories involve the beliefs we hold about the way the world works, what is true or false, right or wrong, just or unjust. Our stories may be our explanation of events or the excuses we offer for our results.

FIGURE **9.1**   **EASE from the Outside In**

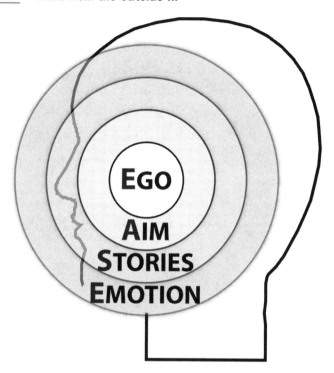

Aim is about intention. To identify aim or intention, we listen for a statement of purpose—what is wanted or desired. Aim or wants are usually embedded in the stories that people tell. Everything that a person shares is usually an expression of something they wanted and didn't get. Otherwise the issue wouldn't have been mentioned.

Ego is about how we esteem ourselves. Everyone is invested in esteeming themselves positively. Consequently, we all have certain "ego needs" or personal values that drive our behavior. When our ego is threatened or challenged, we usually respond defensively or emotionally. Consequently, the EASE Model not only describes emotion present in conversation, but also the components that go undiscovered or are "masked" by the emotional reaction.

Understanding Ego from the Inside Out

Ego drives Emotion, Stories, and Aim. A violation of "ego needs" or personal values gives life to the model. Our perception of our violated values leads to our defensiveness.

In search of personal values, psychologists have identified more than 1,400 ego needs. Our own research has identified five primary ego needs that surface at work and at home:

- Capability
- Respectability
- Likeability
- Acceptability
- Security

Let's seek to understand these five ego needs.

Capability is about **performance**. Issues about performance arise at work as we are given feedback from bosses, coworkers, and subordinates about results and productivity. When our performance is called into question, it is easy to become defensive.

Respectability is about respect and **reverence** for the individual—their person, ideas, and feelings. People want to be treated in a way that affirms their worth as human beings. Many employee surveys make it clear that people do not always feel respected.

Likeability speaks to the quality of the **relationships** and the value people experience in those relationships. We all want to be cared for, valued, or even loved by those with whom we have a trusting, respectful relationship.

Acceptability is concerned with **externals** or the **image** we portray to others. Our image is reflected in our dress, grooming, physical condition, body odor, or general appearance. For most adults this aspect is not so much a factor in the workplace. But if you own a few teenagers, acceptability is huge. Consider accept-ability to be the "way cool" factor.

Security deals with the need to feel **safe**. We want to be safe physically, financially, and emotionally. Many people fear the con-sequences for being open or honest; "What if I get fired?" Many people have had previous experiences that have taught them that honesty doesn't pay—it costs. So, they keep their mouths shut to ensure their security.

Recognizing these "ego needs" is the beginning of understand-ing and addressing individual values.

How Do You Defuse Defensiveness?

In an emotional emergency, part of our brain goes into *martial law mode.* In this mode, all rationality and learning cease, and individ-uals defend themselves by throwing up shields of excuse, justifica-tion, blame, attack, or denial to escape the perceived attack. Their reaction then causes you to counterattack—ending any sense of rationality in the conversation.

The easiest way to defuse a negative emotion reaction is to ask opened-ended questions. This approach disengages the amyg-dala and reengages the neocortex, the logical-rational part of the brain. This physiological shift quells the emotion and recreates EASE or calm in the conversation.

Creating or Staying at EASE

The EASE Model is used by asking certain questions and work-ing from the outside in. It begins with acknowledging a person's Emotion or behavior and then asking questions to surface a per-son's Stories, Aim, and Ego. An illustration is shown in Figure 9.2. Using the EASE Model requires that you learn to listen for Emotion, Stories, Aim, and Ego as you listen and attend from the outside in.

FIGURE 9.2 Creating EASE with Questions

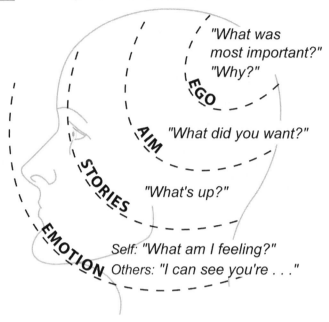

"What was most important?"
"Why?"
EGO

"What did you want?"
AIM

"What's up?"
STORIES

Self: "What am I feeling?"
Others: "I can see you're . . ."
EMOTION

Applying the EASE Model

Let's revisit the previous story to apply the EASE Model. Jane was upset because Rob wouldn't give her feedback about her presentation. Notice how the conversation might have turned out differently if the EASE Model had been applied.

> ROB: "*I can see you're upset.* (Reflected emotion) *What's up?*" (Asking to understand stories)
>
> JANE: "*I shouldn't have to take feedback from some trainee! To be honest, I don't think she liked what I did. She asked a ton of questions that I answered, but she had a 'comeback' or justification for everything I told her. You know these young people. They want to show you that they know it all.*" (Story)"
>
> ROB: "*What do you want?*" (Asking for Aim)
>
> JANE: "*If you have feedback from her, I would rather you give it to me. I won't negate it unless it is untrue.*" (Her Aim)

ROB: *"Why is that so important to you?"* (Asking for Ego needs)

JANE: *"You know my work and I know that you will listen to me and consider my viewpoints. This doesn't put my job in jeopardy, does it?"* (Capability, respectability, and security)

Notice that Jane wants to be recognized for her **capability**— her work. She also wants Rob to listen to her because her history with Keri has led her to believe that Keri is not open and does not listen. That comment by Jane goes to **respect** as a value. Lastly, she is concerned about the **security** of her job. If Rob can recognize these issues, he can then address them one by one. Not addressing them may leave Jane feeling incapable, disrespected, and insecure.

Using the EASE Model will help you to defuse and understand a person's emotion, and identify what a person values.

Get REAL: Observe emotional interactions and listen for the various components of EASE in the interaction. Once you feel comfortable, reflect the emotion of the individual and then ask questions to uncover his or her Stories, Aim, and Ego needs.

What If You're to Blame?

If you use the EASE Model and learn that something you said or did created an emotional backlash, you can then use your ABCs: Apologize, Build Ego, and Clarify Intent.

Apologize—Get Over It and Get On With It! Why is it so hard to apologize? Ego. We have a difficult time in acknowledging or owning our behavior because we judge ourselves based on our intent rather than our behavior. We have a difficult time in owning up to anything that is perceived as negative. But like it or not, we need to admit when we say or do something that is offensive. Apologizing allows us to put the past behind and move forward. Also, an apology commits you to changing your behavior.

When you apologize, own it. I once heard an executive say to an employee, "I'm sorry **YOU** didn't understand me." I almost laughed out loud because he was saying, "I'm sorry, but you're still at fault." He could have just as easily said, "I'm sorry I wasn't clear."

When apologizing simply say, "I'm sorry," or "I apologize for . . . ." Don't add anything else to it, be done, and move on.

Build Ego—Reinforce the Truth. When what you say or do cuts a person's ego in some personal value close to the heart, you need to say something that repairs the damage and reaffirms the value that you violated.

However, *you cannot repair a damaged ego without stating the truth*. You must be truthful and sincere. Being insincere and manipulative will only do more harm. So, reaffirm the value that has been put in doubt.

What do you say? First you have to identify the value has been called into question. The following list contains values and an example of what you might hear in the expression of those values.

Capability (performance or expertise)
"What do you mean I did it wrong?"

Respectability (reverence for the individual)
"I don't deserve to be spoken to like that!"

Likeability (relationship, care, or value)
"And I thought we were friends!"

Acceptability (image or appearance)
"What's wrong with this dress for the office party?"

Security (physical, financial, and emotional safety)
"So do you think I'll still have a job in six months?"

Once you have identified the bruised ego, you are ready to rebuild it:

Capability (performance or expertise)
"What do you mean I did it wrong?"
- Build: "I know that you can make the changes that will satisfy the customer."

Respectability (reverence for the individual)
"I don't deserve to be spoken to like that!"
- Build: "You're right. You deserve better."

Likeability (relationship, care, or value)
"And I thought we were friends!"
- Build: "I would not knowingly do anything to jeopardize our friendship."

Acceptability (image or appearance)
"What's wrong with this dress for the office party?"
- Build: "This event requires more formal attire. Besides, you look fantastic in 'formal' attire."

Security (physical, financial, and emotional safety)
"So do you think I'll still have a job in six months?"
- Build: "You are one of only two who possess the expertise we need."

Each *build* should be preceded by an *apology*, then the *build*. Again, you can't build what isn't true. If a build doesn't exist, you need to apologize and move directly to clarifying intent.

Clarify Intent—State Your Purpose. Any time you need to hold a potentially difficult conversation, safety is a risk. That's why we do the *Intention Check*—to be clear on our intent in order to share it. You can identify and focus your intent by asking yourself:

- "What do I want?"
- "What do I want to accomplish with this conversation?"

Once you are clear on your intent, you are ready to share it. For example, suppose you have to speak to someone on your team who needs to take a bath—daily. Everyone has complained to you about how distracting this person's body odor is. No one has the courage to bring it up, so you take the challenge. Let's call this person Ed.

> YOU: *"Ed, can we talk for a minute?"*
> ED: *"So now what did I do wrong?!"*

Notice that Ed has attributed negative intent to you before the conversation has begun. He has gone below the line, and you must now lift the conversation above the line without creating more defensiveness.

> YOU: *"I'm sorry I wasn't clear about what I wanted to talk about.*
> (Apologize)
> *I want to talk about how you might improve*
> *the influence you have with our team.*
> *Can we talk about that?"* (Clarify Intent)

You can't build his ego around image because anything positive about his acceptability or current image issue would not be true. If you can't build the ego, apologize and clarify intent.

Here are five suggestions for listening empathetically.

1. *Practice!* Take the time to listen for each of the components of the EASE Model: Emotion, Stories, Aim, and Ego. Once you get used to hearing them succinctly, you will know how they fit together.

2. *Identify Violated Values.* The intent for using EASE is to defuse defensiveness and identify values. After you ask them, "What do you want?" don't forget to ask, *Why?* Values flow from *Why* questions.

3. *Apologize.* An apology allows both parties to move forward out of the past and into the future. You must be sincere!

4. *Build Ego.* Because you want to affirm the value of the individual, whatever you say to affirm his or her values must be true.

5. *Clarify Intent.* Recognizing and stating where you want to go will get you there.

Get REAL: Look for opportunities to sincerely apologize. Notice how it shifts the energy of the conversation. Prepare an ABC script that you can use in a situation where you know that the person will become defensive.

Listening and Attending with Style

Everyone wants to be listened and attended to, but even more important everyone wants to be understood. Nothing is more frustrating or causes more defensiveness than being "blown off" or ignored when you have important things to say.

The following styles are listed in descending order from those with the greatest listening skills to those who are more challenged. Let's review them one by one.

Connectors

Connectors are *people- and ask-oriented*. They are the best listeners of all the styles. They love to listen and attend. They are patient and present when listening. They like to make a personal connection before getting down to business. In fact, they may become defensive if you don't show an interest in them first or take a moment to share something personal about yourself.

They will respond to any mention of feelings, important information, or detail. They like to be asked questions that allow them to share their needs and how you can support them. To connect with them you will want to reflect the warmth they reflect to you.

Connectors listen for feelings, support, and direction.

Discoverers

Discoverers are *ask- and task-oriented*. They love to demonstrate their expertise and knowledge and are focused on being analytical, logical, and precise as they figure things out. They will ask questions to try to learn what they believe they need to know. They listen carefully to the responses to their questions and ask more questions.

They are not interested in personal information or an expression of feelings. Going down that path will shut them down. They are not particularly warm, but are more matter-of-fact and deliberate in solving problems and analyzing situations.

Discoverers listen for facts, figures, and logical analysis.

Builders

Builders are *people- and tell-oriented*. They love to talk about their ideas, the big picture, their vision for accomplishing tasks, and their feelings. They want you to listen and accept their ideas. Listening and attending to them will tax your time and patience. Once they begin talking, it's difficult to get a word in edgewise.

They are also good at motivating and inspiring others, and they are appreciative of those who support them. They have difficulty in listening to facts, details, figures, and predetermined solutions. They also have difficulty with those who are more impersonal and who don't agree with their ideas or decisions. They are easily the most emotional of all the styles.

They listen for agreement, recognition for accomplishment, and validation for their ideas.

Initiators

Initiators are **task- and tell-oriented**. They have difficulty listening and attending to others because of their penchant for action and results—completed "yesterday." They love to be in control of any situation they are responsible for.

They like to be approached directly to discuss business issues. They are uncomfortable with personal expression of feelings or emotion. In fact, if someone was emoting, they may not even recognize it, and they certainly wouldn't stop to explore the meaning behind the emotion if they did recognize it.

They listen for facts or details that support their decisions or will help to deliver results or ensure success. If you disagree with them, you had better have data that supports your point of view. They value their time and like it when people communicate precisely and concisely.

They listen for options for solutions and results-focused action.

Listening and attending to connect with these particular styles depends on your ability to recognize their style and adapt your style to "match" theirs.

In Summary

We *Ego Off* by effectively listening and attending to others. Listening and attending require that you get out of your own way to forge connections. You need to be focused and present in the conversations you hold. Likewise, your negative judgments prevent you from listening and attending to others because you are preoccupied with your own thoughts. Being able to identify the specific details and facts as well as visual and virtual observations in conversation will assist you to understand and assess not only your own perspectives, but also those of others. Finally, defusing defensiveness and unmasking the meaning behind the emotion will increase your understanding of yourself and others.

Get REAL: You might choose any number of skills to practice from this section. Because we lack the ability to defuse defensiveness in others and ourselves, being able to identify the different elements in a reactive situation is the first step to restoring rationality to an emotional conversation. Once you are able to identify the various components in the situation, use the EASE model's questions to defuse the emotion and discover the meaning behind the emotion.

Gentle Reminders

- The more you think, the less you listen.
- The more you talk, the less you listen.
- Listening and attending require active, deliberate participation.
- A person's emotion says more about that person than about you.
- Defensive or negative emotion signals a violated value.
- Listening and attending requires presence.

You can find more information about this topic at www.overcomingfaketalk.com/gentlereminders.

CHAPTER 10

Progression: How Do You Move Forward?

What I loved about running the Colorado River in the Grand Canyon for 13 years was that nothing was ever the same. When the water level was high, the rapids changed. When the water level was low, the rapids changed. If I messed up running a rapid one week, I knew I would have a chance to get it right the next.

The water, the weather, the people, the flora and fauna—everything changed, and each day had something new to offer—glimpses into self and life lessons that are enduring.

I remember sitting on a small bluff overlooking the river by the light of a full moon. Everyone had gone to sleep and all was quiet except for the hushed roar of the rapids echoing farther down the canyon. In the moonlight, the river appeared as a river of molten silver, cutting a path through the darkened landscape, giving life wherever it wandered. I would have missed that night vision if I had not taken the time for personal introspection and solitude.

Likewise, no two conversations are ever the same. But each offers insight into ourselves and others. We learn what we know, and we learn what we don't know by what we do.

We all have personal and professional challenges. Our ability to address our challenges resides in our ability to hold REAL conversations. We place so much emphasis on results; and yet, we can't achieve the results we desire without creating respect and improving relationships. Only you have the power to talk about what matters most and to create what you want.

Failing to achieve *results, respect,* and *relationship* signals *fake talk* or counterfeit conversations. Holding REAL conversations creates what you desire most. So don't just think and talk about conversations—jump in and swim in the current of every conversation that you hold. Doing is learning. Internalizing the principles and going where the conversation takes you will make all the difference.

To internalize the principles of REAL conversations, we offer five suggestions: be patient, be persistent, be prepared, be active, and be in practice. Let's explore them.

Be Patient

When learning to hold REAL conversations, be patient with yourself. Look at your thinking, assumptions, and judgments. When you arrive at interpretations too quickly, they are usually negative, and they drive your behavior. Being patient with yourself and with others can help you to examine your thinking before you act on it.

MISTAKEN INTERPRETATION

Steve had asked Anna, his company's desktop publisher, to create a new marketing brochure for the company website. She completed the assignment and sent it to Steve for his review.

When he saw the brochure, he was angry and frustrated because Anna had omitted the last section of the brochure that contained the sales call to action.

"Why can't people just follow directions?" he fumed.

Steve sent an e-mail to Anna and reattached his original draft of the brochure. He asked her to remove what she had added and include what was in the original document.

A few minutes later, Steve received the following e-mail: "See what happens when you don't scroll all the way to the bottom of the page? I didn't see the rest of what you had written, so I added some text to complete the document. I'll totally replace what I wrote. Yours is way better!"

Steve was relieved that he had been patient and hadn't picked up the phone to make an idiot out of himself by emotionally expressing his accusations of Anna's performance.

We're all guilty of failing to give one another *the benefit of the doubt* and jumping down people's throats the first time they violate our expectations. We just can't believe everything we think, so we need to slow down and patiently assess the accuracy of our thinking and feelings.

Our patience also must be extended to others. We've already established that it takes two to tango. Some people simply can't dance and others won't until they know it is safe. You can't force people to engage, but you can increase the odds that they eventually will engage. Remember: a person's emotion and behavior say more about that person than it does about you. Others' thinking, not yours, creates their results. Unfortunately, when people become emotional, we tend to take it personally and respond in kind.

Realize that you'll have setbacks. In fact, your conversations may get worse before they get better, but don't get caught up in the *Law of Extremes*: "I'm very good" or "I'm terrible." When a conversation doesn't go as well as you had hoped, be patient and keep trying—be persistent.

Be Persistent

Being persistent is about moving forward and doing what you need to do.

EATING A BICYCLE

When I was in college, I had a roommate who was determined to get into the Guinness World Records *book for eating a bicycle. Every night when we returned from studying in the library, we would all sit in front of the TV and watch* M.A.S.H. *He would take a file and grind himself a teaspoon of bicycle. Then he would place his bicycle "grounds" in his hot cereal the next morning.*

During the eight months that I lived with him, he ate the front tire, the rim, all the spokes, one of the forks, and part of the handlebars. I moved out before he finished.

His inane behavior does make an important point: **You can eat a bicycle one teaspoon at a time**. You can improve your conversations by continuing to work on one skill at a time, and over time, you will improve. What is important is that you persistently and consistently do something. This story may be a stupid one, but you'll never forget it.

It is easier to be persistent if you select a specific time and place to practice and a particular skill to work on. You might identify a certain situation or person with whom you need to communicate in a particular way. What is important is that you're doing something.

Be Prepared

Prepare by clarifying your assumptions and suspending them if need be. Identify your intent for the conversation. Focus the attention of your listener, and share data and a respectful interpretation. Internalizing the framework and phases of *initiate, discover, connect,* and *build* will help you to hold an effective conversation while enabling you to know exactly where you are in the conversation and where you want to go.

YOU LIED!

Amy was hired as a nurse straight out of college. When she was hired, the manager promised her that she would work Thursday, Friday, and Saturday for two weeks a month, alternating weekends. Since she was hired, Amy has worked every weekend for eight weeks straight. She is exhausted and frustrated. She needs to hold a REAL conversation about the broken commitment.

Obviously Amy needs to think through this conversation. It may be foolish to share what she is really thinking: "I think you lied to me to get me to accept the job, and I feel betrayed and manipulated." She would be more successful by using one of the following interpretations:

"I'm thinking that you aren't aware
of what my schedule has been these last two months."

or

"I'm wondering if I've been scheduled every weekend
because of some crisis that is overriding the
commitment that was made to me when I was hired."

The questions following these interpretations start the dialogue and lead to *shared understanding* and *firm commitments* going forward. After all, the reason for holding such a conversation is to *initiate change*. Positive change can only occur if the issue is surfaced, explored, and resolved.

What If You Need to Hold a Conversation on the Fly?

If you have the model internalized, you're prepared. If not, be clear about your intention and what you want. Ask questions—tons of them. Then, be clear when you state what you want. Remember, if you don't know where you are headed, you'll never know when you have arrived. And if you don't ask, the answer is always, "No!"

MY MOTHER'S FLOWERS

Peggy finished doing some consulting work in the area where her mother had lived. Although her mother had recently passed away and her home had been sold, Peggy was struck by the thought of how nice it would be if she had some of her mother's flowers. Her mother had been a wonderful gardener.

249

She was petrified and did not know what she would say, but she drove to her mother's old house and knocked on the door. A man answered.

"Are you the people who bought the house from Mrs. Jarvis?" Peggy asked.

"Yes," he answered.

"Well, she was my mother. She used to have all kinds of flowers. I wondered if I could have a few?" she queried.

"There are no flowers here, only weeds," he replied.

"Could I at least look?" she asked.

"Go ahead. Take whatever," he said, closing the door abruptly.

Peggy walked around to the back of the house, where she found an old, rusted shovel leaning against a massive oak tree. Shocked, she recognized it as her father's shovel that he had placed there sometime before he died—nine years previously. She marveled at the gift of providence.

The backyard was a mass of dead, dried weeds. She cleared them away, and there, coming out of the early spring ground, were the flowers. Peggy dug and scooped all she could find. She took them home and planted them in her own backyard.

Now every summer when Peggy goes into her yard, she enjoys the wondrous red, yellow, blue, pink, and purple of her mother's flowers. And sometimes she sees her mother standing in the midst of all their glory.

When we begin our conversations, we must admit that we never know where they will lead or what we will discover. REAL conversations will change you—and others. You will learn and discover new things that you never knew or that you never thought possible. Respect and results will improve, and your relationships will be strengthened as you work more effectively with and for others.

Be Active

Part of being prepared means being actively engaged and recognizing how your thinking and behavior creates your results. We often hold ourselves captive by not taking responsibility to speak up and make a difference. We engage in what we call the *Delusion-Collusion Cycle*.

This cycle occurs when we think we are "talking the talk" and "walking the walk," but we aren't—we are deluded. We don't accurately see our behavior and its consequences. Certainly, we may be well-intended, but we don't stop to challenge our assumptions and the justifications for our behavior from an objective perspective.

The *Delusion-Collusion Cycle* is in play every time you observe people saying and doing things that aren't in the best interest of an organization, your team, or your relationships, and you still choose to say nothing. By saying nothing, you enable the behavior you despise. And you get more of the same. This "observe-but-don't-tell" cycle can have a huge impact on results on a number of fronts.

TOO CASUAL FOR CASUAL DRESS?

One organization we worked with had adopted a casual dress policy. After several months of receiving positive feedback on the new policy, two executives dressed a little too casually for the liking of the other executives.

These two typically wore old Pendleton wool shirts and tan Dockers that looked like they had been dried while tied in a knot. The other executives asked us to give feedback to the offending parties. We suggested the executives provide the feedback to their colleagues. After all, the organization espoused the values of teamwork and individual development. With such values, we assumed that the executives could step up and tell one another in the spirit of respect and personal development that the choice of attire could be improved.

Rather than hold the conversation, the offended executives sent out a memo that changed the dress policy for executives, requiring them to wear dress slacks and a tie. Everyone conformed, but at what cost?

Everyone who wasn't a senior executive started talking and wondering why this distinction was made. Some hypothesized that the leaders were trying to distinguish themselves from everyone else—which killed the idea of being "one team." Others thought the change in dress was an expression of superiority. Still others scrutinized and worried that it was only appropriate to visit the executive floor if one were dressed in slacks and a tie. The rumor mill started churning.

One person taking the responsibility to hold a REAL conversation would have saved this company much emotional energy and speculation about what was going on with the dress code. The unintended consequences of no one taking responsibility resulted in lost effort, continued negative assumptions, endless speculation, lower morale, and mounting frustrations. One conversation could have focused individual energy and increased productivity rather than allowing individuals to second-guess a needless change. It was easy to understand how more important issues might never reach the discussion table.

None of us sees ourselves the way that we are seen. In a sense, we are all deluded or hampered in our view of reality and our place in it. When we see the delusion and refuse to address it out of our fear of perceived consequences, then we perpetuate the behavior and the very consequences that we desire to avoid.

When you keep your mouth shut at work, in relationships, with friends, with the neighbors, and even with those to whom you are the closest, *you are part of the problem*!

If others engage in behavior that creates negative consequences of any kind, you need to say something. You can't assume that others "get it" or understand how their behavior impacts others, even if it's obvious to you.

Get REAL: Try asking yourself these questions to identify if you are caught in a *Delusion-Collusion Cycle*:

- "How much money is lost by people for whom I am responsible?"
- "How much frustration or tension exists in my relationships that I don't speak about?"
- "How has my silence contributed to my current results?"

Doing a little self-reflection on the quality of your results may serve as the impetus to change your thinking and your behavior and create different results.

Here's an example of someone who took responsibility and pro-actively spoke up and improved a frustrating situation.

BACK OFF!

Todd, an obnoxious real estate salesperson, turned in a customer's file to a new underwriter, Tina. Once the file is completed and approved, then the real estate closing can take place, which results in a commission check being cut to Todd.

About 30 minutes after Todd turned the file into Tina, he called her.

"Are you done yet?" he asked.

"No! I'll call you when I've finished," she promised.

Todd waited about 15 minutes and called her again.

"Have you finished my file yet?" he demanded.

"No! I said I'd call you when I'm done!" she retorted.

This continues for at least half the day. Frustrated, Tina asked some of the other underwriters if they have had the same challenge with Todd.

"Yeah, I guess that's his way of hurrying you up," answered one.

"Has anyone ever told him to just back off?" Tina asked.

"No. That wouldn't be polite or wouldn't be considered 'good' customer service," another countered.

Todd called again and berated Tina.

"Look, Todd! Your 50 calls today have kept me from working on your file. Every time I have to answer your phone call, you keep me from finishing the file. So, cool it! I'll call you when I'm done!"

Todd got the message.

To Tina's credit, she didn't get caught in the *Delusion-Collusion Cycle*, and she displayed personal responsibility by calling Todd on his unproductive behavior. Todd's strategy for increasing Tina's productivity was to nag and badger her to death. The very behavior he enacted was hindering the work he wanted her to do. If Tina hadn't stopped him, he would have created the thing he hated—an unproductive underwriter.

Be in Practice

Deliberately seek or create opportunities every day to practice REAL conversation skills. Every interaction is a chance to practice and improve. Here are nine suggestions.

1. *Be clear about your intent.* Being clear about what you want is even more important than memorizing the REAL conversation framework: when you know what you want, you will work toward that goal more instinctively.
2. *Be authentic.* Authenticity comes from the intent of your heart, and it is what resonates with people. The authenticity behind your words really matters.
3. *Be with yourself and your thoughts.* We become so hurried that we often don't take time for ourselves. Self-reflection is wonderful practice. Take time every day to be clear about your intent in various situations. Reflect on your conversations—what worked and what didn't work. Then, make plans and set goals to improve.
4. *Identify other great communicators.* Look for people who inspire you, make you think, and cause you to feel that you really matter. Watch what they do and say and incorporate whatever you can learn from them.
5. *Use cueing to remind you.* Cueing is using a visual reminder to reinforce use of a particular skill. Years ago, I had a friend who painted a small yellow dot on the end of his pens and all his notepads to remind himself of a behavior he wanted to adopt. He even put Post-it notes on his mirror, on his steering wheel, and on the case for his glasses to remind him of

his commitment to himself. Improve your practice by giving yourself a visual reminder about a particular behavior with a particular person in a specific situation.

6. *Teach and practice with others*. Teach the principles to your spouse, your companion, your family, your team, your boss, your peers, or your friends. Find someone to teach and then practice the skills together. You will lift yourself and those around you.

7. *Look to your emotions*. Remember that your emotions say more about you than any person or situation that you face. Your emotion can help you identify the thinking that is driving your results. Make conscious choices about what you want and change your thinking if necessary. When you have an emotional response, explore the thought behind the emotion. You might avoid saying or doing something you would regret later.

8. *Discover the meaning*. Every emotional or defensive reaction has a meaning. Acknowledge a person's emotions and then ask questions to reveal the meaning hidden behind the emotion.

9. *Be aware of your own and others' reactions*. We began this journey by emphasizing *awareness*. You need to be an observer and a participant in conversation, not a reactor. Participating in the conversation and observing it at the same time will help you to manage your conversations more objectively and effectively.

So, Now What?

It's up to you. Will you recognize and suspend your judgment and thinking more? Will you have the courage to speak up and express your thoughts, feelings, and experience? Will you ask more questions to broaden perspective and increase understanding of others and their ideas? Finally, will you listen to others—to what is said and what goes unsaid? Paradoxically, holding REAL conversations requires vulnerability to engage others—not really knowing where the conversation will go, but being pleasantly surprised when you arrive.

REAL conversations are conversations that you hold every day with yourself and everyone else. These conversations take patience, persistence, preparation, proactivity, and practice. May you have the courage to discover and learn, and to change your conversations. Please take on the challenge, get REAL, go with the flow, and enjoy the ride. Best of luck!

Here are some self-reflective questions to start you on your journey:

Awareness
"Of what do I need to be consciously conscious in conversation?"
"What do I do that creates less-than-desirable results?"

Knowledge
"What do I know and how does it manifest in what I say?"
"What part of the REAL conversation process do I need to work on?"

Reflection
"What reflective messages am I projecting?"
"What reflective messages am I missing?"

Perception
"What thinking or assumptions do I need to suspend?"
"How does my thinking create my results?"

Preparation
"What types of conversations usually go awry?"
"How might I improve those conversations?"

Expression

"How might I improve my expression to match my intention?"

"How does my intention influence my expression?"

Discovery

"When and where do I need to ask more questions?"

"What questions do I avoid asking? Why?

Connection

"With whom do I need to connect? Why?"

"To whom do I need to listen more deeply?"

APPENDIX

APPENDIX

Understanding Different Styles

Purpose: To understand how people of different styles like to communicate and interact.

Instructions: Read through the following list and circle the behaviors that describe how **you** like to communicate, or how you would like others to communicate with you.

"Personally, I prefer to . . .

INITIATOR
1. . . . communicate by being precise, concise, and to-the-point.
2. . . . focus on results.
3. . . . be offered solutions and alternatives for action.
4. . . . remain professional, never personal.
5. . . . avoid distractions and stay on task.
6. . . . receive factual information in support of a solution.
7. . . . have people understand exactly what they need to do.

BUILDER
1. . . . understand the big picture before being given supporting details.
2. . . . be acknowledged for my strengths and successes.
3. . . . communicate my vision, goal, or ideas with passion and optimism.
4. . . . take time to demonstrate personal interest in others.
5. . . . provide advice/suggestions to improve projects, problems, or people.
6. . . . be asked about my ideas for solutions.
7. . . . enroll others to my way of thinking.

CONNECTOR
1. . . . work with, support, and be involved with other people or teams.
2. . . . have people make a personal connection before getting down to task.
3. . . . avoid conflict and stress.
4. . . . be invited or asked to share my ideas and opinions.
5. . . . be given time when making decisions, not be pressured.
6. . . . minimize risks by covering steps in detail for assignments.
7. . . . take time to understand the benefits and rationale for change.

DISCOVERER
1. . . . provide the verifiable, tangible, or supporting facts or evidence for a problem.
2. . . . be given time to think before answering questions.
3. . . . hear the supporting facts before the main points.
4. . . . not be rushed into making decisions.
5. . . . be analytical and logical.
6. . . . remain focused on relevant information, not opinions or feelings.
7. . . . be provided clear structure and parameters to task completion.

Check Yourself Out!

Record the total number of items you circled in each category:

_____ Initiator _____ Builder _____ Connector _____ Discoverer

Putting It All Together!

Prepare for a difficult conversation by working backwards through the quadrants. Begin in the "Build" quadrant.

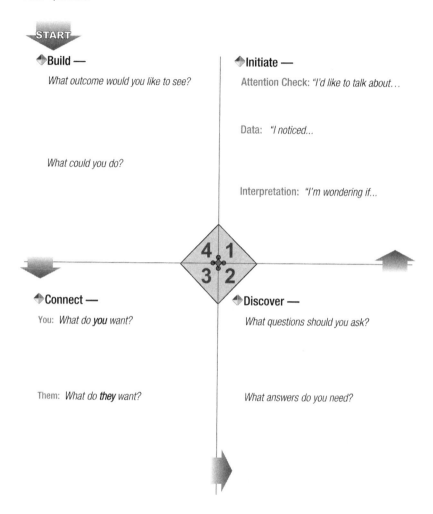

START

◆Build —

What outcome would you like to see?

What could you do?

◆Initiate —

Attention Check: *"I'd like to talk about…*

Data: *"I noticed…*

Interpretation: *"I'm wondering if…*

◆Connect —

You: *What do you want?*

Them: *What do they want?*

◆Discover —

What questions should you ask?

What answers do you need?

NOTES

Chapter 2: Why Can't You See What's Happening?

1. Albert Mehrabian, *Silent Messages* (Belmont, CA: Wadsworth, 1971).

Chapter 3: What Are REAL Conversations?

2. Chris Argyris, *Knowledge for Action* (San Francisco: Jossey-Bass Publishers 1993), 51.
3. David Bohm, *On Dialogue* (London: Routledge Classics, 1996).

Chapter 4: Do You Ruin Everything by Being You?

4. Eric Wargo, "How Many Seconds to a First Impression?" *Association for Psychological Science Observer* 19.7 (July 2006): 1. http://www.psychologicalscience.org/index.php/publications/observer/2006/july-06/how-many-seconds-to-a-first-impression.html (accessed October 17, 2012).
5. Daniel Coleman, *Social Intelligence: The New Science of Human Relationships* (New York: Random House, Inc., 2006), 4.
6. Ibid, 5.

Chapter 5: How Do You Get Out of Your Stinking Thinking?

7. The term *mental models* was coined by Kenneth Cruik, a Scottish psychologist; the concept first appeared in his 1943 book, *The Nature of Explanation*. The term has received renewed popularity through Peter Senge's book, *The Fifth Discipline: The Art and Practice of the Learning Organization* (New York: Doubleday, 1990).
8. Marcia Reynolds, *Outsmart Your Brain* (Phoenix: Covisioning, 2004), 22.
9. Daniel Kahneman, "A Perspective of Judgment and Choice; Mapping Bounded Rationality," *American Psychologist* 58.9 (September 2003): 701.
10. Daniel Coleman, *Emotional Intelligence* (New York: Bantam Books, 1995), 14–21.
11. Larry R. Squires and Eric R. Kandel, *Memory: From Mind to Molecules* (New York: Macmillan, 2001), 168.
12. Reynolds, 25.
13. David G. Myers, "The Powers and Perils of Intuition," *Scientific American Mind.* 16.3 (June/July 2007): 26.
14. Sterling G. Ellsworth, *How I Got This Way and What to Do About It* (Provo, UT: Maasai Publishing, 2002), 128–130.
15. Robert K. Merton, *Social Theory and Social Structure* (New York: Free Press, 1968), 477.
16. Stephen R. Covey, *The Seven Habits of Highly Effective People* (New York: Simon & Schuster, 1990), 71.
17. The Arbinger Institute, *Leadership and Self-Deception* (San Francisco: Berrett-Koehler Publishers, 2000), 91–96.
18. Rosa M. Garcia Hernandez, "Where Does What We See Go?—Visual Information Processing," Weblog post (July 14, 2008), http://rosavisionenglish.blogspot.com/2008_7_01_archive.html.

Chapter 6: Can You Talk About What Really Matters?

19. Chris Argyris and Donald A Schön, *Theory in Practice: Increasing Professional Effectiveness* (San Francisco: Jossey-Bass Publishers, 1974). Chris Argyris and Donald Schön introduced the concept of "Undiscussables." They encouraged

people to explore the contents of their left-hand column as a means of improving their learning in order to solve problems and make more effective decisions. The authors believe that exploring and sharing tough issues creates the learning that is the key to solving the challenges that confront us.

20. Chris Argyris, *Knowledge for Action* (San Francisco: Jossey-Bass Publishers, 1993), 51.

21. Wilson Harrell, "Entrepreneurial Terror," *Inc. Magazine* (February 1987, http://www.inc.com/magazine/19870201/4032.html.

22. Towers Watson (global professional services company), "2009/2010 Communication ROI Study Report: Capitalizing on Effective Communication," http://towerswatson.com/research/670.

23. Ibid, 5.

24. Marie Snider, "Change Your Thoughts to Change Your Life," *Fort Frances News Online* (March 17, 2010), http://www.fftimes.com/node/231889.

Chapter 7: Do You Open Your Mouth and Remove All Doubt?

25. Philip Babcock Gove, ed., *Webster's Third New International Dictionary* (Springfield, MA: Merriam-Webster, 1986), 498.

26. David R. Hawkins, M.D., PhD, *Power Force: The Hidden Determinants of Human Behavior* (Carlsbad, CA: Hay House, Inc., 2002), 68–69.

27. Bradley Nelson, *The Emotion Code* (Mesquite, NV: Wellness Unmasked Publishing, 2007), 46.

28. http://wiki.answers.com/Q/what_is_the_meaning_of_abracadabra_in_aramaic.

29. Adapted with permission from Action Design, *Organizational Learning in Action* (1995).

30. Michael Coleman, *Collection Management Handbook: The Art of Getting Paid* (Hoboken, NJ: John Wiley & Sons, 2004), 44.

31. Lee Ross, "The Intuitive Psychologist and His Shortcomings: Distortions in the Attribution Process," *Advances in Experimental Social Psychology* (New York: Academic Press, 1977), 173–220.

32. Chris Argyris, Robert Putnam, and Diana McLain-Smith, *Action Science* (San Francisco: Jossey-Bass Publishers, 1985), 34. Chris Argyris, along with his colleagues Phillip McArthur, Robert Putnam, and Diana McLain-Smith, developed "Advocacy" and "Inquiry" as the means of generating valid information and testing knowledge to create more effective action. The terms *Expressing* and *Asking* are "Advocacy" and "Inquiry," simplified for easier retention. You always want to balance expressing with asking.

INDEX

ABOUT THE AUTHOR

John R. Stoker has been immersed in organizational development and change for more than 20 years. He is the founder and
president of Light Storm Consulting, Inc., and DialogueWORKS,
Inc. In these roles John has worked extensively with a number of
companies, helping them increase their capacity to enhance effectiveness and improve results.

John's work focuses on increasing the capacity and effectiveness
of individuals as professionals and leaders. He helps professionals
talk about what really matters by teaching them how to hold those
difficult conversations that people tend to avoid. He has experience in the fields of leadership, change management, dialogue,
critical thinking, conflict resolution, and emotional intelligence.
Companies throughout the United States and in several foreign
countries have called on John for training and coaching; his list
of clients includes Honeywell, Cox Communications, Comcast
Cable, Banner Health, Wheaton Franciscan Medical Group, Pres-
byterian Healthcare Services, Lockheed Martin, Turner Broad-
casting, Eastman-Kodak, Regeneron Pharmaceuticals, AT&T,
OG&E, Alcon Labs, and AutoTrader.com.

In the past, John worked as a practicing criminal defense attorney and spent summers as a Grand Canyon whitewater guide. He
taught for 13 years as an adjunct faculty member at a leading university. John and his wife, Stephanie, spend their free time with
their five engaging children.

About DialogueWORKS

DialogueWORKS is a training and organizational development firm. The organization emphasizes that REAL conversation is the key to increasing individual capability and capacity to achieve results. Founded in 1998, the company is headquartered in the shadows of the Rocky Mountains and has affiliates throughout North America, Europe, India, and Asia.

Performance of people is central to personal, professional, and organizational effectiveness! DialogueWORKS helps organizations put people back into the business of the business. The company's training focuses on time-tested models and principles that improve individual performance and effectiveness by creating a culture based on respect, trust, candor, collaboration, learning, and accountability to achieve results.

DialogueWORKS proprietary training products, assessment tools, and design expertise produce results in the following areas:

- Strategic alignment
- Organizational culture
- Performance accountability and improvement
- Conflict resolution
- Leadership development
- Contribution and collaboration
- Change management
- REAL conversation

The company mission is simple and direct: To get people talking about what matters most!

For more information about products and services, please contact us at info@dialogueworks.com or call us at 801-491-5010.